ROMAN BARTOSCH
JULIA HOYDIS (Eds.)

Teaching the Posthuman

Universitätsverlag
WINTER
Heidelberg

Bibliografische Information der Deutschen Nationalbibliothek

Die Deutsche Nationalbibliothek verzeichnet diese Publikation in der Deutschen Nationalbibliografie; detaillierte bibliografische Daten sind im Internet über *http://dnb.d-nb.de* abrufbar.

Herausgeber:

Prof. Dr. Gabriele Linke
PD Dr. Holger Rossow
Prof. Dr. Merle Tönnies

ISBN 978-3-8253-6991-0
ISSN 0344-8266

Imprimé en Allemagne · Printed in Germany
Druck: Memminger MedienCentrum, 87700 Memmingen

Gedruckt auf umweltfreundlichem, chlorfrei gebleichtem und alterungsbeständigem Papier

Den Verlag erreichen Sie im Internet unter:
www.winter-verlag.de

ANGLISTIK UND ENGLISCHUNTERRICHT

Herausgegeben von
Gabriele Linke
Holger Rossow
Merle Tönnies

Band 89

Contents

Roman Bartosch
Julia Hoydis

Teaching Otherwise? Towards Posthuman(ist) Pedagogic Practice

The present collection, dealing with English as a discipline and school subject, takes stock of the theoretical developments in philosophy, literary and cultural studies, and the environmental humanities more generally, discussed as posthumanism. It thus scrutinises the current "ambition of contemporary critical thought to grasp phenomena that resist the labels of the human and humanism" (Vermeulen 2014, 121). There is good reason in framing this enterprise (also) as an educational question, not only because some of the work informed by environmental or ecological criticism, climate change research, or human-animal studies aligns with developments in curricular and pedagogical theory and practice (Education for Sustainability, for instance). Moreover, the role and implications of humanism have a direct bearing on conceptions of education that still to a large extent draw on eighteenth- and nineteenth-century idea(l)s of subject formation, critical distancing, and affective discipline. At the same time, however, transferring post-humanism into the practical fields of school or university education comes with a number of challenges. This is partly because post-humanism constitutes no single field of inquiry but is built on different, sometimes even contradictory, traditions and positions. Though, nearing the end of the second decade of the third millennium, posthumanist scholarship has come of age, it presents a highly heterogeneous critical ground consisting of, as John Weaver suggests, "almost as many ideas and definitions of the posthuman as there are people writing about the subject" (Weaver 2010, 10). In the face of the multitude of different branches of posthumanism – which are outlined only briefly in the following –, and the fact that it is still considered by some as a specialised discourse dealing with cybernetics and biotechnology, Neil Badmington observes polemically: "Posthumanism, the story often goes, needs no theorizing. How could it? Only the most foolish or self-absorbed cultural critic would spend time speculating about something that is actually staring him or her in the face" (Badmington 2003, 10). How, then, can a concept be mediated in a teaching context which is, on the one hand, tied to a vast and interdisciplinary discursive field, far from easy to navigate even for scholarly experts, and, on the other, taken to refer quite simply to obvious contemporary realities (such as humans' increasingly symbiotic relationship with technology and the need to acknowledge nonhuman agency)?

In their summary of the debate, Snaza et al. conclude that "[w]hile the posthumanist literature is far from uniform, its central claim is that the human has been misconceived by nearly all thinkers in the Western tradition" who "consider the human to be unlike any other kind of being" (Snaza et al. 2014, 42). This decentring of the human, however, can take the form of ecological investigations of nonhuman agency and cultural ecology, or it can be geared towards a focus on technologies and prosthetic enhancement. While the latter perspective is often rubricated as 'trans-' rather than 'posthumanism,' it still plays into ontologies of the posthuman as presented by influential scholars such as N. Katherine Hayles (1999) or Peter Sloterdijk (2008). What is more, even for approaches to posthumanism of different vintage, the meaning of the prefix 'post' remains as a troubling paradox in need of clarification (Bartosch 2019). As Christopher Peterson remarks,

> the assertion that humanism can be decisively left behind ironically subscribes to a basic humanist assumption with regard to volition and agency, as if the 'end' of humanism might be subject to human control, as if we bear the capacity to erase the traces of humanism from either the present or an imagined future. (2011, 128)

Similarly, theorists like Badmington are weary of the phenomenon that, whilst posthumanism is finding its fee within the academy, some approaches are a little too quick to affirm its absolute break with humanism. Arguing that there are strands of posthumanism that run the inevitable risk of repeating humanism "*in a certain way*" (Badmington 2003, 15; original emphasis), the pitfalls of speaking of posthumanism are, of course, that "[t]he 'post-' is forever tied up with what it is 'post-ing'" (20). Lastly, 'the human' or 'humanism' too are far from being unambiguous points of reference, as both terms more often than not rely on an unexamined notion that the human could and should be taken as a meaningful "unit of analysis" (Ferrante and Sartori 2016, 180). This has important repercussions both for scholarly practice in the humanities and for educational theory and pedagogic institutions.

As scholars positioned in the current debate on the 'Anthropocene' have worked through the contradictory notion of 'the human' or 'humanity' as a unified whole endowed with specific forms of agency (Chakrabarty 2012; Woods 2014; Crist 2016) and presented a critique of the human exceptionalism and hubris underlying this concept of the *anthropos*, pedagogy, too, might benefit from related forms of scrutiny. Indeed, as Alessandro Ferrante and Daniele Sartori put it, education is widely considered "a human proprium" and is conceptualised irrespective of non-human, or more-than-human, actants and in the firm belief that educational processes rely on "a rational faculty that [only] human beings develop" (Ferrante and Sartori 2016, 178-9). The subsequent forms of "compulsory humanity" (McKay cited in Pedersen 2010, 237) have important epistemological and ethical or political repercussions, not only with regard to the very ontology of the human but with regard to pedagogic concepts of personhood and moral standing, for instance, and their significance for racism, speciesism, and ecological crises.

As cursory glances at only two recent examples – of ecocriticism and human-animal studies – show, the decentring of the human and human exceptionalism at the heart of posthumanism takes many forms. Before approaching posthumanist implications for teaching practice, it is therefore useful to briefly recap how it developed 'in theory.' Though the debates, fears and hopes surrounding scientific advancement can be traced back centuries and have also continuously sparked fictional imaginations, it is just over forty years ago that Ihab Hassan wrote a paper "Prometheus as Performer: Toward a Posthumanist Culture?" (1977). This text is nowadays seen as one of the founding documents of posthumanist theory, fixing its origins in literary and cultural studies and continental philosophy. There is an important emphasis in Hassan's understanding of posthumanism and/as performance which is crucial to different later stampings, namely that it is a dual process: the human (being) actively transforms nature just as it is being transformed by it. Hassan writes:

> At present, posthumanism may appear variously as a dubious neologism, the latest slogan, or simply another image of a man's recurrent self-hate. Yet posthumanism may also hint at a potential in our culture, hint at a tendency struggling to become more than a trend. [...] How, then, shall we understand posthumanism? [...] [T]he human form – including human desire and all its external representations – may be changing radically, and thus must be re-visioned. We need to understand that five hundred years of humanism may be coming to an end, as humanism transforms itself into something that we must helplessly call posthumanism. (Hassan 1977, 843)

Thus acknowledging our still no less "helpless" choice of title for the present essay collection, the potential Hassan alludes to here, the uniting effect of posthumanist culture to heal or redraw divisions and transcend limitations, as well as the focus on radical change and the revision of human(ist) categories, still underlies a majority of posthumanist theorizing today; meanwhile the term and its application have diversified greatly.

In the broadest possible sense, the term posthuman has been used since the 1980s to refer to the intersections between humans and technology. Reflecting the need to frame human nature in an age of biotechnology, it is commonly employed to designate a complex, and yet often rather loosely, entangled set of attempts to reframe conceptions of the relationship between human embodiment, identity, and technology, species distinctions between human/animal/machine, and ethically charged ontological distinctions between human/nonhuman/inhuman. With the 'post-' designating – as the prefix typically does in conceptions such as this one – an 'after' as well as an 'against' – posthumanism has long grown into a "shape shifting" term, liberally employed in fields as diverse as animal rights, ecocriticism, disability studies, social network theory, and the digital humanities (see Jordan 2015, 22). Challenging pervasive binaries such as natural/artificial, organic/machinic, mind/body, virtual/material, it draws on (intersections among) disciplines including biology, cybernetics, philosophy, political theory and literary studies (see Wolfe 2010; Snaza and Weaver 2015, 5) – or, to specify the various subfields, as Istvan Csicsery-Ronay does, it developed out of "deconstruction, cyborg feminism, research in Artificial Intelligence, Virtual Reality and Artificial Life, queer studies, evolutionary epistemology, nanotechnology, complexity theory, and sf"

(Csicsery-Ronay 1999, 313). A shared line of attack, to underline it once more, is directed against "the classical humanistic paradigm in which an ideal human Self/Subject stands at the center of creation and commands all that is not made in [...] ['His'] image" (ibid.).

Whereas 'antihumanism' is unequivocally critical of Western liberal humanism and the inherent paradigm of scientific progress and advancement, 'critical' or 'cultural posthumanism' is essentially a discourse of its deconstruction, but not a complete negation of it (see Callus, Herbrechter, and Rossini 2014, 108); it embraces post-humanism's emancipatory critical potential to break and redefine categorical and other boundaries. Theoretical impetus continues to come from feminist technoscience philosophy and critics such as N. Katherine Hayles, Karen Barad, Donna Haraway, J. Jack Halberstam and Ira Livingston. Early landmark studies, such as Hayles (1999) and Donna Haraway's "Cyborg Manifesto" ([1985] 1991), focus on the links between biology and information technology, perceiving of the hybrid fusion of human bodies with intelligent machines as a potentially liberating and inclusive way of transcending discriminatory humanist ideologies. Haraway's metaphorical feminist text prepared the stage for one of the classic figures of the posthuman imagination: the cyborg, "a hybrid of machine and organism" (Haraway 1991, 149), which evokes popular filmic images from the *Terminator*, *Robocop*, or *Matrix*. While Clynes and Kline (1960) are credited with first coining the term to describe technologically enhanced human beings equipped to survive in space, Haraway employs the cyborg as a symbolic figure of transgression. She includes it in her list of "odd boundary creature[s] – simians, cyborgs, and women – all of which have had a destabilizing place in the great Western evolutionary, technological, and biological narratives" (Haraway 1991, 2).

In tune with the new possibilities of a "species cosmopolitanism" as envisioned by Pramod K. Nayar (2014, 150), Haraway has since broadened her work from the cyborg metaphor to notions such as companion species (2003) and, even more radically, the "oddkin" (2016), giving priority to questions of co-habitation and inter-species relations over ontological differences. Other important broadenings of critical posthuman theorizing include the focus on black bodies and humanist histories (see e.g. Lillvis 2017). While concepts like Haraway's companion species seek to avoid the much fetishized cyborg and 'the posthuman' and, in addition, seek to get away from the overdeterministic focus on technology, Herbrechter and Callus (2003) have tried to challenge the relationship between posthumanism, theory and technology all together.

Aside from the concern with identity politics, debates of what technology does and can, and should or should not do, link cultural and critical posthumanism to the branch of popular thought it is radically turned against: the unapologetically progressive technophile trajectory of 'transhumanism.' By comparison, transhumanism is a much more unified movement and ideology, carried forward by globally leading figures such as Ray Kurzweil. Traced back to Julius Huxley's *New Bottles for New Wine* (1957), it emphasises the need to transcend human limitations with the help of science and technology (see Deretíc and Sorgner 2016, 14). As such, transhumanism, which hinges on problematic categories such as the 'normal' and the 'able,' has provoked exclusively negative perceptions of posthumanism and apocalyptic warnings. Francis Fukuyama's description of it being the "world's most dangerous idea" (see Miah 2008, 79) comes to mind. Conservative, dystopian accounts of the posthuman condition and future such as Fukuyama's capture the perceived risk of losing the essential traits of the human in urgent need of protection, which he, for lack of a better term calls the "Factor X" (Fukuyama 2002, 149).

Conceptual attempts have been made to build a bridge between the radical transhumanist and the critical posthumanist perspectives, for example Jaime Del Val and Stefan Sorgner's 'metahumanism' (2011). But be the prefix as it may, the consequences of technological advancement are grasped and judged differently in each branch of posthumanist thought. Concerning the histories of posthumanism, one can therefore agree with Andy Miah, who notes that it largely consists of "an ongoing undecidability over the value of transgressing boundaries, in some cases as they relate to biological change" (Miah 2008, 93).

As a philosophical concept, posthumanism interrogates the legacies of Western humanism; meanwhile posthumanist ethics comes with a criticism of the Western tradition of humanist thought that shares the premises of Levinas's understanding of ethics as 'first' philosophy, meaning that ethics, centrally a concern and responsibility for the other which determines action(s), must necessarily precede ontology (and the potentially harmful distinguishing categories it brings in its wake).

Common ground between different approaches from cultural, feminist and ecocritical studies can thus be found in the emphasis on moral narratives and political concerns dealing with the need to put entangled relations between genders, races and species, between human/animal/ non-human, before claims to primacy and identity. As Cecilia Åsberg puts it, "concerns for alterity and care for others is prior to selfhood" (Åsberg 2013, 8).

To further sum up the above, as a critical tool posthumanism appears as a wide lens rather than as a distinct perspective and it incorporates much of deconstructionist thought prevalent in the humanities since the latter half of the twentieth century. Postulating and signalling a move beyond established truth regimes and binary oppositions, the posthuman is an inherently political category, present, whether explicitly named or unnamed, in a number of critical discourses (feminism, postcolonial criticism, ecocriticism and animal studies) which challenge the ontological difference of the human and seek to acknowledge agency in nonhuman subjects. Despite its theoretical superstructure, it thus responds to and entails a "relatively straightforward imperative to think beyond humanism, anthropomorphism and anthropocentrism" (Callus, Herbrechter, and Rossini 2014, 112). It presents a critical discourse very much tied up with the future, with global survival and with living together – in and outside the 'teaching machine' (to borrow Spivak's term). And whilst we can debate its radicalness, its uses and abuses, and its definitions, it is hard to dispute its value of leading to questioning and that this questioning of "humanism – posthumanism itself – begins to build ways for being different in the future" (Badmington 2003, 23). Enter posthuman(ist) pedagogy.

As posthumanism opens new paradigms for reading contemporary as well as older texts, it has the potential to rearrange pedagogic practices in a number of ways, as the present collection shows. In literary studies, posthumanism is often perceived as the discourse that investigates the figure of the posthuman in fictional narratives and as "a perception-based identity project" (Jordan 2015, 33). While Mary Shelley's *Frankenstein* (1818) is commonly referred to as an early narrative dealing with the posthuman *avant la lettre*, recent studies have even looked at Shakespeare's works from this vantage point (see e.g. Herbrechter and Callus 2012). Stories of cyborgs, robots, animals, and automata help to draw attention to the differences between humans and non-humans and the grand old question of what it means to be human. As far as the endless debate about proposed changes in the human condition and their judgment and meaning goes, one can argue that it is indeed "the visual images and the stories that are being told with them that bring the point home" (Hauskeller, Philbeck and Carbonell 2015, 4). In fiction, we can encounter marginal characters and communities we know that exist, as well as those which yet do not (e.g. the clone children in Ishiguro's *Never Let Me Go*). Realist and speculative fictions, historical and contemporary alike, thus allow for the reflection of an agenda uniting critical/cultural posthumanists: seeking justice and a voice for marginal beings and communities. To borrow Miah's definition, they reflect posthumanism as "the theoretical consideration of the ongoing redefinition of an 'ethics of bodies that matter'" (Miah 2008, 94; see Zylinska 2005).

That this set of intersections outlined above warrants transdisciplinary collaboration is widely recognised by now, especially in order to enable reciprocal sensibility towards the blind spots of the respective approaches. As Nathan Snaza purports, "feminism, antiracist, and postcolonial studies on the one hand and posthumanism on the other must supplement each other":

> The former provide powerful critiques of the historical complexities of dehumanization without offering a theoretical account of how these realities derive from a structural problem with 'the human,' while the latter is too focused on the present moment to realize that the political importance of posthumanism's reconceptualization of 'the human' is most clear in relation to the history of dehumanization. (2013, 48)

A similar point could and should be made in educational debates. This is why we argue that educational theory, and subject-specific teaching in the field of literature and culture in particular, needs literature and literary studies: While educational research has its very own subfields of research, protocols, and contexts, approaches in literary and cultural studies helpfully historicise, contextualise, and theoretically undergird educational objectives and literary-pedagogical praxes in ways that point beyond the institutionalised procedures of teaching English. Two examples, one practical, the other methodological, can illustrate this co-dependence.

Let us begin with the practical implications of the theoretical debate on technology, especially digital computing and cybernetics. Summarising the developments of posthumanist thought over the last years and across disciplines as diverse as literary and cultural studies, science and technology studies, philosophy, and the sciences, Ivan Callus and Stefan Herbrechter ask, "[i]s there anything that connects these disparate modes and foci of inquiry?" (2012, 250). Their suggested answer is "technology" and "biomedia": "If there is anything monolithic in the posthuman it is here, in this technological imperative to which posthumanism appears subject" (250). Against this technophiliac outlook, they offer the idea of a "posthumanism without technology" (Callus and Herbrechter 2007), or a "critical posthumanism," as attempts to rethink human exceptionalism and essentialism in line with other work in the environmental humanities. In education, however, the rather uncritical endorsement of a narrative of digitalisation as a means of progress and a blessing merely and rather unreflectedly underlines the dominance of technology that a critical posthumanism calls into question. In lieu of critical investigations of modern, or posthuman, subjectivities, educational research on technological affordances remains, in the majority of cases, dedicated to optimistic outlines of future possibilities or polemics against those who do not embrace the brave new world of digital learning environments (Greenfield 2015).

That this should be the case is surprising not only because it has by now become clear that even initial ambassadors and pundits of digitalisation are increasingly critical and agitated as to the effects of digital media in educational contexts, and for societies and democracy more generally (O'Neil 2017; Turkle 2017; Lanier 2018). Educational experiences in the United States, moreover, hint at the limitations of concepts build on digitalised environments (see Robson 2014) – but educational debates in Europe seem unperturbed. Posthumanist analytical frameworks may provide theoretical and conceptual tools to address these paradoxical developments more precisely and more productively.

The second example pertains to the research strategies employed for investigating the abovementioned processes as well as concomitant educational concepts more generally. While traditionally, pedagogy used to be informed by anthropological and philosophical perspectives, and subscribed to hermeneutics or qualitative empiricism, it has, over the last decades, become more than difficult to get around quantitative and statistical methodologies. These measures have their undisputed merit, yet an exclusive reliance on 'data' and the consecutive construction of 'facts' have led to what John A. Weaver and Nathan Snaza call "methodocentrism" (2016): "the belief that particular, pre-formed methods can guarantee the validity of an intellectual investigation into the world by factoring out the vicissitudes of the observer's entanglement with the world" (2).

Posthumanist pedagogic inquiry therefore has pointed out not only the restrictive consequences of certain ways of quantitative empirical observation – "methods that are wholly inadequate to the more-than-human world" (2) – and the complexities of (human) relations and learning processes (cf. Künkler 2011; Ceder 2016). It has, moreover, pointed attention to a "shrinking of 'educational research' to mean randomized, large-scale quantitative studies of specific pedagogical and curricular interventions" that have rendered educational studies "tedious, instrumental, and boring" (Snaza and Weaver 2015, 7). With regard to the points raised above about digitalisation and transhumanisation, recent studies on the benefits of digital technologies in classrooms, with their implicit imperative for creative disruption and their 'the future is now' rhetoric surely underscore this characterisation (see, for instance, Holmes et al. 2018 and, critically, Bethke 2018). This is not to contest the use and usability of new technologies and media in general but asks us to consider closely the narrative and ideological framing of 'innovation' as well as the underlying interests of corporations (rather than educators), and the poverty of analytical perspectives that ask, as Snaza and Weaver put it, "what works?" only and never: "works for *what*?" (7). Following up on this latter question, posthumanism asks us to reconsider the normative and historical dimensions of educational objectives just as much as current practices of teaching as it creates "a few cracks and fissures" and adds "a little bit of posthumanist 'noise' into certain socio-political particularities of the education apparatus as they have emerged under modernity" (Pedersen 2015, 56).

With an eye on said apparatus Snaza et al. point to the fact that "[y]oung people enter primary schools and become instantly a part of the school as anthropological machine" (Snaza et al. 2014, 44): discipline, temporality and rhythms, hierarchies, and nutrition and medication are all part of the educational regime under scrutiny in an emergent posthumanist pedagogy. This is why John A. Weaver avers that "one cannot address the natures and meanings of posthumanism without acknowledging the primary places where humans are indoctrinated into anthropocentrism and where they intersect with nonhuman sentient beings and machine: educational institutions" (Weaver 2015, 183). In current debates in Europe and elsewhere, systemic critique of educational systems is endorsed mainly in the context of inclusion and diversity (Booth and Ainscow 2011; Macnamara 2014; Niccolini et al. 2018; Reich 2014; Zembylas 2018). Bringing together the demands of systemic change for inclusion and the posthumanist critique of rights and human essentialism through which "the political struggle becomes one of securing the borders of 'the human'" (Snaza 2013, 48) and, hence, of exclusions, would be a worthwhile undertaking indeed that would have to be built on various forays into posthumanism and literature pedagogy, as well as postcolonial, feminist and queer, and ecological research.

In order to provide first steps into this direction, this collection moves from this macro- to a microperspective of interdisciplinary dialogue between literary studies and pedagogies, as outlined above. It is the aim of the essays here to present literary readings and analyses that suggest teaching objectives or methodologies beyond the myopic focus on digital enhancement or the improvement of learning situations or the methodocentric fetishism of statistics. Instead, they present potential teaching materials, hermeneutic readings that identify topics and possible tasks, as well as empirical teaching projects in order to explore the breadth of posthumanist education. Because we believe that posthumanism ought to include topics such as technology, ecology, and the nonhuman world in equal measure, we have not tried to distinguish these fields but invited essays that combine these various perspectives Rather than arranging the contributions thematically, we have organised the volume according to the different stages of primary, secondary, and tertiary education in order to provide recommendations for teachers at all levels. Choice of material and design of tasks remains a teacher's obligation, of course, and we hope the essays collected here serve as inspiration rather than instruction, and that they invite dialogue rather than suggest definite answers.

We begin this dialogue with an investigation of the links between anthropocentrism and anthropomorphism: In her essay on animal stories for children, Berbeli Wanning asks in how far the representation of animals accommodates or thwarts posthumanist objectives. Considering the importance of children's literature and, therefore, animal stories for socialisation processes and the initiation of literacy, looking closely at the shared phenomenological worlds of fictional humans and animals is as important as being aware of many texts' ultimate endeavour to keep species apart. Educational practice thus needs to (re)consider its appreciation and evaluation of anthropomorphic tales. Young learners are at the centre of attention in the essay by Christian Ludwig and Elizabeth Shipley, too. They present a research project and teaching sequence that uses comics and creative approaches to fiction in early English education and with secondary-level pupils by asking young learners to imagine and actively construe posthuman characters. While it is clearly too much to expect – and not the main objective of language education – that children in primary school and lower-secondary settings reproduce all the intricacies of posthumanist thinking, the essay makes a strong point for an early engagement with rethinking what it means to be human.

Stefan Herbrechter also engages with educational practice and discusses a teaching project with pupils in lower secondary education that uses digital technology such as blogs to meet what he calls the "*double* imperative" of posthumanist education and the current demand for the inclusion of new media in English teaching contexts, namely to develop a nonanthropocentric approach to teaching that reconsiders humanist tenets as well as an openness to the affordances of digital technology for learning contexts. In their essay on the literary means of going beyond the strictly anthropocentric, Christian Schmitt-Kilb and Roman Bartosch discuss two novels by Eva Hornung and John Berger, respectively, and ask, with the latter of these writers, "why look at animals?" Their analysis shows in how far literary fiction uses its own means of creating ambivalence for imaginative human-animal communities that challenge rigid dividing lines between species and facilitate deliberately ambiguous moments of 'anamorphosis' expedient in literary education.

In the final section, Gigi Adair complicates the present discussion by bringing in postcolonial perspectives that underline the importance of indigenous perspectives in and of literature for a truly posthumanist stance. Her extensive survey of writing from Non-European contexts provides a rich resource and numerous teaching suggestions for advanced English classes. Likewise, Eckart Voigts and Alessandra Boller discuss literature on the higher secondary level but focus on biotechnology and its ethical dilemmas in their discussion of a novel by Kazuo Ishiguro and a play by Caryl Churchill. Using the example of cloning, they investigate the potential of literary fiction for understanding and discussing the question of what counts as a grievable life over and against allegedly fixed categories of the human and with a specific focus on the role of language as well as the representation of death and finitude. Julia Hoydis concludes this section with an essay that also traces the posthuman(ist) across genres, offering close readings of a play (*Charlotte Brontë's Villette Re-Imagined*), a TV-series (*Westworld*) and a novel (*Midnight Robber*). Broadening the discussion, she points to intersections in reading and teaching 'otherness' in literature and science studies and other critical contexts at university level, emphasizing a focus on history, identity politics, and technology.

While the present volume brackets the question of teaching 'posthumans' (i.e. the itself changing, ever-more technology-dependent nature of the pupil/student body we are confronted with), it takes its cue from the first few book-length studies engaging with posthumanism, curriculum studies, and educational philosophy (Weaver 2010; Snaza and Weaver 2015), as well as from the critical currency the posthuman has gained over the last two decades across a number of disciplines and in English literary and cultural studies: It is certainly no longer "struggling to become more than a trend" (Hassan 1977, 843, see above). As Callus, Herbrechter and Rossini observed in 2014: "Post-humanism is in the air. It has been so for some years, and the times and concerns that it names are now shaping English Studies in discernible ways, even when these themes are not designated by the term *post-humanism*" (2014, 103; original emphasis).

There is much more work to be done to tease out these themes and the many forms and guises posthumanism comes in, yet the examples discussed in the following chapters demonstrate how a "growing assemblage of texts that can be understood as 'posthumanist' has the potential to reconfigure education" (Snaza and Weaver 2015, 1). They all invite us to review and rethink pedagogic practice in light of the challenges of posthumanism and the posthuman world in which it finds itself. While we have tried to take ample account of the most relevant developments and perspectives, it goes without saying that no collection of essays can provide definite overviews, let alone answers (for helpful introductions, refer to Badminton 2000; Wolfe 2010; or Herbrechter 2013). But we think that readers will be able to use the ideas developed here for (critiques of) educational debates and for mapping potentially new grounds for teaching otherwise.

Works Cited

Åsberg, Cecilia (2013). "The Timely Ethics of Posthumanist Gender Studies." *Feministische Studien* 31.1, 7-12.

Badminton, Neil (ed.) (2000). *Posthumanism.* Basingstoke: Palgrave Macmillan.

--- (2003). "Theorizing Posthumanism." *Cultural Critique* 53, 10-27.

Bartosch, Roman (2019). "We Have Always Already Been Becoming Posthuman? Posthumanism in Theory and (Reading) Practice." *New Approaches to the 21st-century Anglophone Novel.* Eds. Sibylle Baumbach and Birgit Neumann. Basingstoke: Palgrave Macmillan (forthcoming).

Bethke, Hannah (2018). "Hundertzwanzig Seiten Verblödungslektüre." *Frankfurter Allgemeine Zeitung* 30 June. Web. 18 September 2018. <http://www.faz.net/aktuell/feuilleton/debatten/verbloedungslektuere-bosch-studie-personalisiertes-lernen-15666579.html>.

Booth, Tony, and Mel Ainscow (2011). *Index for Inclusion. Developing Learning and Participation in Schools.* CSIE. Web. 18 September 2018. https://www.eenet.org.uk/resources/docs/Index%20English.pdf.

Callus, Ivan, and Stefan Herbrechter (2007). "Critical Posthumanism, or, The Invention of a Posthumanism Without Technology." *Subject Matters* 3.2/4.1, 15-29.

--- (2012). "Introduction: Posthumanist Subjectivities, or, Coming After the Subject..." *Subjectivity* 5.3, 241-64.

Callus, Ivan, Stefan Herbrechter, and Manuela Rossini (2014). "Introduction: Dis/Locating Posthumanism in European Literary and Critical Traditions." *European Journal of English Studies* 18.2, 103-120.

Ceder, Simon (2016). "Cutting through Water: Towards a Posthuman Theory of Educational Relationality." PhD thesis. Lund University. Web. 18 September 2018. <http://portal.research.lu.se/ws/files/6008016/8411680.pdf>.

Chakrabarty, Dipesh (2012). "Postcolonial Studies and the Challenge of Climate Change." *New Literary History* 43.1, 1-18.

Clynes, Manfred, and Nathan S. Kline (1960). "Cyborgs and Space." *Astronautics* 26/27 Sept., 74-75.

Crist, Eileen (2016). "On the Poverty of Our Nomenclature." *Anthropocene or Capitalocene? Nature, History, and the Crisis of Capitalism*. Ed. Jason T. Moore. Oakland: Kairos, 14-33.

Csicsery-Ronay Jr., Istvan (1999). "Review: Till We Have Interfaces." *Science Fiction Studies* 26.2, 312-323.

Del Val, Jaime, and Stefan L. Sorgner (2011). "A Metahumanist Manifesto?" *The Agonist* 4, 1-4.

Deretíc, Irina, and Stefan Lorenz Sorgner (2016). "Introduction." *From Humanism to Meta-, Post- and Transhumanism?* Eds. Irina Deretíc and Stefan Lorenz Sorgner. Frankfurt a/M. et al.: Peter Lang, 13-20.

Ferrante, Alessandro, and Daniele Sartori (2016). "From Anthropocentrism to Post-Humanism in the Educational Debate." *Relations* 4.2, 175-94.

Fukuyama, Francis (2002). *Our Posthuman Future.* New York: Farrar, Straus and Giroux.

Greenfield, Susan A. (2015). *Mind Change. How Digital Technologies Are Leaving Their Mark on Our Brains.* London: Rider.

Haraway, Donna J. (1991). *Simians, Cyborgs, and Women. The Reinvention of Natur*e. London: Free Association Books.

--- (2003). *The Companion Species Manifesto: Dogs, People and Significant Otherness (Paradigm).* Chicago: Prickly Paradigm Press.

--- (2016). *Staying with the Trouble: Making Kin in the Chthulucene*. Durham, NC: Duke University Press.

Hassan, Ihab (1977). "Prometheus as Performer: Towards a Posthumanist Culture?" *Performance in Postmodern Culture*. Eds. Michel Benamou, Charles Caramello, and Cheryl Bernstein. Milwaukee: University of Wisconsin Press, 201-220.

Hauskeller, Michael, Curtis D. Carbonell, and Thomas D. Philbeck. (2015). "Posthumanism in Film and Television." *Palgrave Handbook of Posthumanism in Film and Television*. Eds. Michael Hauskeller et al. Basingstoke: Palgrave Macmillan, 1-10.

Hayles, N. Katherine (1999). *How We Became Posthuman: Virtual Bodies in Cybernetics, Literature, and Informatics*. Chicago: University of Chicago Press.

Herbrechter, Stefan (2013). *Posthumanism. A Critical Analysis.* London: Bloomsbury.

---, and Ivan Callus (2003). "What's Wrong with Posthumanism?" *Rhizomes* 7. Web. 18 September 2018. < http://www.rhizomes.net/issue7/callus.htm>.

---, and Ivan Callus, eds. (2012). *Posthumanist Shakespear*es. Basingstoke: Palgrave Macmillan.

Holmes, Wayne et al. (2018). "Personalisiertes Lernen mit digitalen Medien. Ein roter Faden." Stuttgart: Robert-Bosch-Stiftung. Web. 18 September 2018. <https://www.bosch-stiftung.de/sites/default/files/publications/pdf/2018-06/Studie_Personalisiertes_Lernen.pdf>.

Huxley, Julian (1957). *New Bottles for New Wine*. Chatto & Windus, London.

Jordan, Richard (2015). *Posthuman Drama: Identity and the Machine in Twenty-First-Century Playwriting*. PhD Thesis. University of Queensland. Open Access. Web. 10 August 2018. <https://doi.org/10.14264/uql.2015.1010>.

Künkler, Tobias (2011). *Lernen in Beziehung. Zum Verhältnis von Subjektivität und Relationalität in Lernprozessen.* Bielefeld: Transcript.

Lanier, Jaron (2018). *Ten Arguments for Deleting Your Social Media Accounts Right Now.* London: Bodley Head.

Lillvis, Kristen. *Posthuman Blackness and the Black Female Imagination*. Athens, GS: University of Georgia Press, 2017.

Macnamara, Looby (2014). *People and Permaculture. Caring and Designing for Ourselves, Each Other and the Planet.* East Meon: Permanent Publications.

Miah, Andy (2008). "A Critical History of Posthumanism." *Medical Enhancement and Posthumanity*. Eds. Bert Gordijn and Ruth Chadwick. Springer, 71-94.

Nayar, Pramod K. (2014). *Posthumanism*. Cambridge: Polity Press.

Niccolini, Alyssa D., Shiva Zarabadi, and Jessica Ringrose (2018). "Spinning Yarns: Affective Kinshipping as Posthuman Pedagogy." *Parallax* 24.3, 324-343.

O'Neil, Cathy (2017). *Weapons of Math Destruction. How Big Data Increases Inequality and Threatens Democracy.* New York/London: Penguin.

Pedersen, Helena (2010). "Is 'The Posthuman' Educable? On the Convergence of Educational Philosophy, Animal Studies, and Posthumanist Theory." *Discourse. Studies in the Cultural Politics of Education* 31.2, 237-50.

--- (2015). "Education Policy Making for Social Change." *Posthumanism and Educational Research*. Eds. Nathan Snaza and John A. Weaver. New York and London: Routledge, 56-75.

Peterson, Christopher (2011). "The Posthumanism to Come." *Angelaki. Journal of the Theoretical Humanities* 16.2, 127-41.

Reich, Kersten (2014). *Inklusive Didaktik. Bausteine für eine inklusive Schule.* Weinheim: Beltz.

Robson, Garry (2014). "'You are forced to be who you are': Embodiment and Social Media in Intercultural Experience." *Digital Diversities. Social Media and Intercultural Experience.* Eds. Garry Robson and Malgorzata Zachara. Newcastle upon Tyne: Cambridge Scholars, 12-34.

Sloterdijk, Peter (2008). *Regeln für den Menschenpark. Ein Antwortschreiben zu Heideggers Brief über den Humanismus.* Frankfurt am Main: Suhrkamp.

Snaza, Nathan (2013). "Bewildering Education." *Journal of Curriculum and Pedagogy* 10.1, 38-54.

Snaza, Nathan et al. (2014). "Toward a Posthumanist Education." *Journal of Curriculum Theorizing* 30.2, 39-55.

Snaza, Nathan and John A. Weaver (2015). "Education and the Posthumanist Turn." *Posthumanism and Educational Research*. Eds. Nathan Snaza and John A. Weaver. New York and London: Routledge, 1-14.

Turkle, Sherry (2017). *Alone Together: Why We Expect More from Technology and Less from Each Other*. New York: Basic Books.

Vermeulen, Pieter (2014). "Posthuman Affect." *European Journal of English Studies* 18.2, 121-34.

Weaver, John A. (2010). *Educating the Posthuman. Bioscience, Fiction, and Curriculum Studies.* Rotterdam: Sense.

--- (2015). "To What Future Do the Posthuman and Posthumanism (Re)Turn Us; Meanwhile How Do I Tame the Lingering Effects of Humanism?" *Posthumanism and Educational Research*. Eds. Nathan Snaza and John A. Weaver. New York and London: Routledge, 182-94.

---, and Nathan Snaza (2016). "Against Methodocentrism in Educational Research." *Educational Philosophy and Theory* 49.11, 1-11.

Wolfe, Cary (2010). *What Is Posthumanism?* Minneapolis, MN, and London: University of Minnesota Press.

Woods, Derek (2014). "Scale Critique for the Anthropocene." *The Minnesota Review* 83, 133-140.

Zembylas, Michalinos (2018). "The Entanglement of Decolonial and Posthuman Perspectives: Tensions and Implications for Curriculum and Pedagogy in Higher Education." *Parallax* 24.3, 254-267.

Zylinska, Joanna (2005). *The Ethics of Cultural Studies*. London and New York: Continuum.

Berbeli Wanning

Posthuman from the Beginning? How Animal Stories for Children Shape the Anthropocentric Worldview[1]

Introduction

There is no childhood without animal stories. Animal characters in children's literature have a great influence on the mind of young readers. This essay delineates why and how animal characters constitute and strengthen the child's anthropocentric understanding of the world. Beginning by conceptualizing the human-animal-relationship in the field of literary studies, it discusses the function of animal speech in fictional settings and introduces some prominent examples of British and German children's literature, focussing on picture books with mice as the protagonists. Finally, it demonstrates how children gain an anthropocentric focus by reading animal stories.

Every child knows stories in which humans and animals live together, embark on curious or daring adventures, and either have a close, friendly relationship or even depend on each other existentially. Literary interspecies encounters of this kind are not limited to fables and fairy tales. Rather, the motif of human-animal friendship permeates a diversity of media and narrative forms and genres intended for children. A childhood without this topic is, in fact, barely conceivable. Contrary to the common-sense assumption that this introduces children to the diverse world of animals, however, this essay argues that in fact, children's literature significantly contributes to the solidification, or even introduction, of an anthropocentric worldview precisely by seeming to *suspend* this perspective. In children's stories, humans and (speaking) animals encounter one another not only as friends but also as equals. And yet, because children know that, unlike their fictional counterparts, actual flesh-and-blood animals do not speak, they learn something they have not been aware of before: that the capacity for language is unique to humans and, conversely, that language is a marker of human uniqueness. The distinctiveness of the human capacity for language is thus something children become aware of precisely through and because of their literary encounters with speaking animals, and it is this reading experience that changes their view of reality. Now the children know that humans are in fact the only living beings that 'have' language. Now they know about one of the most frequently invoked characteristics of human uniqueness, and this knowledge then serves as a foundation and as a catalyst for further reflections about humans' exceptional status vis-à-vis the nonhuman world.

At a first glance, in many children's stories humans and animals belong to a shared world that does not make, or depend on, any specific distinctions between them, a world in which they encounter and communicate with one another on the same level and through a mutuality of emotions. They are compatible. Viewed from a more critical angle, however, it is in fact this portrayal of animals and human-animal relations that bolsters anthropocentric patterns of thought, which children develop precisely in those moments in which they identify themselves or empathize with animal characters. If in most of such stories all living beings, be they human, animal, or creatures of fable and fantasy, seem to form a harmonious community, a more critical look reveals a consistent anthropocentric conceptualization on the levels of both plot and (especially) character. In order for animal heroes to be able to address children in a literarily appropriate manner, they will not only have to represent but virtually *assume* human characteristics. In doing so, however, their animal being is highlighted all the more forcefully, because the human abilities (such as language) they assume are always perceived as extraordinary and not, as is the case with human characters, as natural. This corresponds with Max Horkheimer and Theodor W. Adorno's dictum that in European history conceptualizations of the human have always been delineated in contradistinction to the animal (Horkheimer and Adorno 1980, 219). Because the boundaries between genres seem to become blurred, with the human-like animal character thus acquiring supernatural traits, the dominance of the anthropocentric perspective in the children's worldview is solidified. However, as Horkheimer and Adorno (221) explain, the idea of such forms of human-animal metamorphosis is immediately comprehensible to children without requiring any further explanation. The central medium in this dialectical process is that of linguistic communication, which takes place on two levels: on the one hand, between the acting characters, all of whom employ human language, even though some of them are not naturally able to do so precisely because they are animals; on the other, between the reading child and the text. Because children are thus introduced to a world in which humans and animals participate on an equal footing and to which they themselves temporarily belong in their fantasy, over the course of and especially after their reading experience, they realize that the distinctions between human and nonhuman creatures exist even as they may be temporarily suspended within the boundaries of a fictional world. While the anthropocentric perspective is thus cognitively bolstered, the harmony that has been experienced on the literary level persists as a subtext that holds this perspective in suspense. The key to this is language.

As soon as a child is able to understand simple animal stories, it has already learned an important life lesson: that animals are unable to speak in a language that is clearly and easily intelligible to humans but nonetheless communicate both among themselves and with us (at least vertebrates do). Onomatopoetic language games such as "woof woof" or "meow" are a crucial part of the language acquisition process and sometimes temporarily replace the correct designation of the animals making these sounds. Children thus know that animals 'speak' differently than humans, but at the same time they are perfectly able to ignore this fact and to approve of animals who speak like humans in particular contexts. Literary animal figures as well as those in other media benefit from this ambiguity because the basic communicative ability of animals in the real world is complemented by their mastery of human language in the worlds of fiction. In fact, it is not only young readers who, contrary to their daily experience in the real world, accept literary animals' verbal utterances.

Animal Communication in Literature

Speaking animal characters have a very long tradition, the oldest and most popular of which is the fable. However, other genres such as novels, poetry, and drama are no less dependent on animals able to communicate in human language. Countless widely read examples from literary history provide ample proof of this. As a distinct form of communication, the interaction with speaking animals generates a kind of openness that induces us to take a benevolent stance towards the message they convey, and this is particularly true in the case of children. Thus, those who wish to appeal to and deeply move a young readership have to make animals speak. Within the bounds of their age-dependent interpretive capabilities, and due to the mild estrangement effect generated by their literary encounter with a speaking animal, children are able to grasp the extent to which the animals' messages essentially mirror human ideas. The paradox of children's literature, then, lies in the fact that the figure of the speaking animal has a high amount of credibility precisely because it is so unrealistic, which further bolsters the truthfulness and authenticity of its message in the children's imagination.

It is indeed far from unimportant who exactly conveys the message to the child. As communicative partners and literary actors, animals have very different opportunities compared to a human narrator. It is because nonhuman animals supposedly lack reflexive consciousness that, in the fictional world, the human ability for language and thought – the hallmark of human uniqueness – can be transposed onto realistic or fantastic animals or animal-like figures. Animals do not have to abandon any part of their 'nature' in order for this to work. In fact, they only benefit from the process. Because of this, the respective animal changes – or, more precisely: the human concept of the animal, which now differs strongly from the real(-world) creature and becomes readily available for processes of symbolisation. As the most distinctive sign of this anthropomorphisation, the ability to speak creates a different kind of animal – one that only exists in literature (or other, related media, such as movies or video games). This animal becomes an actor either in what is represented as its natural habitat or in a distinctly human environment, and it is accepted in this role in the story despite its unreality. As a result, an illusion of reality is created through which the boundary between nature and culture becomes blurred to a degree that, from the children's perspective, it is hardly recognizable at all.

The anthropomorphic speaking animal moves close to the young reader but at the same time remains a being of a different kind, thus actually reinforcing the anthropocentric worldview that it has seemingly suspended within the fictional framework of the story. Even though the speaking animals readers are faced with are often civilized and educated and thus thoroughly *cultural* beings, they also remind them of, and indeed embody, their own animality. This dialectics, which first disarranges and then repositions the categories of belonging that make up the 'chain of beings,' generates a kind of emotional force that accounts for the seemingly irreplaceable role of speaking animals for child readers. As actors in fur, scales or feathers, speaking animals evoke a wide range of emotions, from fear and disgust to attachment, consolation, and even love. Thus wrapped in emotion, the rational messages conveyed by the animals reach the children in a kind of holistic situation in which they get to know and experience themselves as genuinely *human* beings. This is what is claimed by the thesis that, contrary to all appearances, animal stories play a particularly significant role in creating and reinforcing an anthropocentric worldview in young readers.

Literary animal figures primarily convey their messages through human language, occasionally complemented with onomatopoetic elements that employ animal sounds in terms of a secondary semantics. Literary animals actively communicate, be it with other animal figures, with humans, or, sometimes, with inanimate or vegetal nature. According to the categories of anthropomorphism suggested by Sasha Matthewman, such stories can be characterized as "theriomorphic phantasies" – animal stories centred on humans – that are distinct from other types of animal stories such as fables (Matthewman 2011, 64).[2] Literary animals live with humans in a human world which continues to shine through even when we are presented with the ostensibly 'natural habitat' of an animal (for example, a mouse hole that is furnished with anthropogenic objects like table and bed). They speak and interact with animals and humans in a human context, they make plans and show emotions, and also reflect on them. And yet, the animals exhibit more or less strictly species-specific behaviours with regard to their respective habitats, their food, or other aspects (the fish lives in the water, the bird has a nest, and so on). What both theriomorphic and anthropomorphic fantasies have in common, however, is that they are centred on animals capable of directly communicating in human language and, thus, of immediately making themselves understood to child readers. This language may in fact be regarded as a specific form of code, because as the readers engage in its decoding – that is, during the process of literary comprehension – they are influenced by who it is that is speaking. The more 'sympathetic' the respective animal figure is to them, the easier they will accept its message, and so it is by no means irrelevant whether the speaking animal is a lion, a raven, a fox, a snake, or a mouse:

> Neither the physical size nor the species-specific, natural behaviours of the speaking animal pose an obstacle in this process. But the higher an animal's degree of familiarity, and the more the respective audience knows about an animal's character and image, the more immediate the effect of the statement or message is likely to be. (Dichtl 2008, 159; translation DO)

Studies have shown that children tend to identify with sympathetic figures and to distance themselves in the case of negative projections (Zitzelsperger 2012: 43). Speaking animals who appear as a regulatory force in fairy tales, for example, are likely to be perceived as sympathetic figures in this specific function. If these animal figures convey moral messages within the story's framework of fictional events, child readers are addressed on two different levels: on the ethical level, embodied by the animal figure, and on the level of the children's subjective experience as they try to understand the story in which the animal figure acts.

The Fascination with the Mouse

There are a number of literary animal species that are consistently endowed with positive connotations, with mice occupying the higher ranks of this popularity scale. They are small, often (seemingly) help- and harmless, but they are also clever, quick and agile, and derive their strength primarily from these (bodily) attributes. This perception of mouse characters from the similarly 'small' and 'subordinate' perspective of young readers already accounts for the rodent's status in children's literature as an identification figure *par excellence*. Numerous famous mouse characters testify to this: most obviously Walt Disney's Mickey Mouse, but other figures such as Bernard and Bianca, Speedy Gonzales, Stuart Little, or Basil – the "great mouse detective" – have also served to solidify the popular status of the mouse as a (multi-)media sympathy figure in, and even beyond, the world of children. As courageous heroes, most literary mice contrast strongly with the lived realities of the flight-oriented rodent: the former rarely come alone but are almost always accompanied by their 'natural' enemy, the cat. This constellation has given birth to a plethora of stories not only in the realm of traditional narrative and fairy tale but also in the world of modern media, as is the case with what is arguably the most popular example, Tom and Jerry.

The implicitly antagonistic structure of the mouse figure, which is rooted in the supposedly natural relationship with its feline predator, is characterized by a wide narrative variability. While in actuality mice are hunted not only by cats but also by raptors or foxes, in the cultural memory of a mediated natural world it is the proverbial pair of "cat and mouse" that has left the most enduring mark and remains most easily accessible.[3] This is the case, for example, in the humorous title of Ursel Scheffler's classic *Geschichten von der Maus für die Katz*, which also alludes to the motif of futility expressed by the idiomatic 'für die Katz' ('for the cat(s),' similar in meaning to the English 'for the birds'). Other variants of this antagonistic pattern, which sometimes manages without the cat, are the well-known duo of orange mouse and little blue elephant of the German public-broadcasting institution WDR or the valiant mouse in the two-volume picture book *Gruffalo*. For the reasons stated above, I will focus here on the example of the literary mouse figure in order to show how this creature, in its common representation as cute, endearing, and in need of protection, can teach children a literary way of dealing with terrible events, thus empowering them to cope with real, human horrors. At the same time, however, I will point out in which ways this potential links with an inherent anthropocentrism to be found in all stories I analyze.

City Mouse and Country Mouse

The counterpart to the mouse can also be a mouse. The most well-known pair of mice who despite their species identity diverge in many points is that of city mouse and country mouse. According to Matthewman's proposed categorization, this story is an anthropomorphic fantasy because, while the worlds of mice and humans touch (when the city mouse is chased by humans, for example), no communication takes place between them. The narrative core of this story can be traced back to a fable of Aesop that was later adapted by Horaz and Martin Luther: The humble country mouse, who leads a hard life full of privation but is satisfied nonetheless, visits the city mouse in her comfortable but, from a mouse perspective, also very dangerous home. Confronted with the threats posed by cats and humans, she quickly realizes that she would not want to trade her peaceful country life for a life in the city. The moral of the fable can be found in the motif of the 'poor rich,' whose wealth is accompanied by worries that the actual poor do not have to cope with. The story, in other words, deals with the question how to live one's life in order to find happiness, and both Aesop and Luther have a clear answer to this question: "*It is better to live in self-sufficient poverty than to be tormented by the worries of wealth*" (Gibbs 2002, 191; original emphasis). They do not talk about any easy life in wealth and abundance, and so city mouse and country mouse in fact represent opposing principles of life, with the seemingly humble, close-to-nature way of life of the latter contrasting positively with the apparent decadence of a life in carefree gluttony.

This essentially ideological motif that deeply anthropomorphizes the mouse figure has since occurred in various forms in children's literature. The mouse perspective here conceals the human perspective that informs it, which in this context is presented to the children in an inverted form. The 'good life' is a universal problem that also exists in and shapes the world of mice. A comprehensive anthropocentrism is indispensable here and only ceases to be relevant as a rhetorical figure if a connection between human and animal worlds can be established without it (cf. Schmidt 2013, 128). The fable, however, remains incapable of establishing this connection in any other than an anthropocentric way. In order to make use of the fable's techniques of representation and symbolisation in a pedagogical sense, this anthropocentrism only seemingly paradoxically realizes itself in animal form. Children, whether they live in the city or in the country, recognize their own reality of life in these representations, even though, in contrast to Aesop and Luther, it is no longer in keeping with the times to prefer and regard as appropriate only one particular lifestyle.

The pair of mice as a foil for the projection of different views and ways of life, however, still exists. The modern adaptation leaves open the decision for a particular lifestyle, and, in contrast to earlier versions, the city and the country mouse do not go their separate ways at the conclusion of the story but remain bound in friendship. Tolerance and coexistence in combination with the positioning of one's own identity have become the fable's core message. One example of this can be found in the adaptation of the fable by children's books illustrator Kathrin Schärer (2008). After their mutual visits, both mice are positively impressed by their new experiences, but both also feel vindicated that their respective choice of environment and lifestyle is indeed the most appropriate one for them: it is the sense of home that is most important. The advantages of city and country are captured in a few pictures in which the simplicity, quiet, and 'unspoilt' nature of the country are juxtaposed with the liveliness and luxury – and, as a humorous signal, with Mickey Mouse – of the city (cf. Jansen n.d.).

This successful modern adaption of a very old fable can be read in terms of an ideology of globalized childhood. In the accompanying text, which briefly discusses the fable's ancient origins and the history of its subsequent reception over the centuries, Schärer writes: "The most important thing is that every child can enjoy his or her own lifestyle while respecting that of the other. This is the synergy of identity and tolerance" (2008, last page; translation DO). In the sequential arrangement of the picture book, yet another motif is being adjusted: that of the relationship of the two mice, who have now become intimate friends and who, holding hands, sometimes watch the sunrise and sometimes the starlit sky. Both of these natural phenomena are constants in a world otherwise defined by perpetual change, and in this way both of them correspond with the role of friendship in the mesh of social relations: it transcends, or outlives, all antagonisms.

In the adaption of the fable by the famous Irish children's book author, Elizabeth Shaw (1920-1992), the lifestyles of city and country move closer towards each other. As in earlier versions, country mouse, living with her grandparents, receives an invitation to visit the city, which, however, is described in less than glamorous terms. There are some conveniences such as a fridge and running water, but the price for these is high, because, like the majority of her conspecifics, city mouse has to spend her days toiling in the factory. After having shared this alienated and alienating life with city mouse for a number of years, country mouse finally leaves the city, only to find her home thoroughly transformed: The domesticated nature of the country has become a tourist attraction for mice seeking to escape city life without having to relinquish (m)any of its comforts. Country mouse's grandparents have long adapted to these changes, shrewdly serving the newly developed economy by renting out rooms and selling hot dogs in the highly frequented but barely recognizable nature idyll. Country mouse is much displeased with these changes and misses the serenity of country life that now seems to be lost forever. During her years in the city, she had held on to this ideal of the country and now contemplates joining the hippie mice, who are apparently still living (according to) this ideal. But she remains unconvinced that a self-imposed isolation of a small group will make a difference with regard to the broader circumstances she now finds herself in, and so she decides for a more direct intervention. Upset by the way in which nature increasingly exists only in commercialized form, country mouse devotes herself to guerrilla gardening and eagerly scatters flower seeds along the road, imposes a speed limit for cars, and brandishes posters that challenge tourist mice arriving from the city to reconsider their way of life. However, the transformation of country life according to the principles of the city has not only destroyed the spaces but also the time of country life – the mice who visit from the city miss it, but it can be restored in the mise-en-scène, since country life and stress do not go together. As a kind of happy ending, country mouse's grandparents now run their former snack stand as a fancy country restaurant, a decelerated nature idyll 2.0, as it were. The final sentence reads: "After dinner, everyone could take to the garden behind grandma's restaurant, relax and enjoy nature" (Shaw 2005, n.p.; translation DO).

Both picture books use the fable of city and country mouse as a literary pattern of representation to encourage children to think about different ways of life that, as such, can only be chosen by humans. In doing so, the books are not so much concerned with the mouse as a cuddly toy but rather employ this anthropomorphized creature as a reflexive figure that, in the guise of a speaking animal, constitutes a distinct form of aesthetic communication and in this way keeps a certain distance to the narrated events. Thus, the distinction between nature and culture itself becomes an object of observation, and the animal story in its picture book adaptation, even though derived from the fable and its cultural tradition, a figure of knowledge. According to the definition of Benjamin Bühler and Stefan Rieger, animals as figures of knowledge are "agents of a form of knowledge that is generated through these figures" (2006, 12; translation DO). While the authors are concerned with 'real animals,' or, more precisely, with how they are perceived and represented by humans, the example of the media mouse shows that this phenomenon also applies to animals as cultural ciphers. The duo of city mouse and country mouse is endowed with a cultural potential that is also employed in a different context and which is thus transferable, as can be shown with the example discussed in the next section. This example can be similarly characterized as an anthropomorphic fantasy (according to Matthewman), even though its background differs significantly: The connection to the fable and thus to a longstanding literary tradition is dissolved in favour of a didactically motivated narrative that is particularly focused on helping war children as well as those living through the immediate aftermath of war cope with their own or familial trauma. In this context, it is helpful to remind ourselves of the above-mentioned regulative function of literary animals as sympathetic figures that can establish a specific relation with children and thus address them in two important ways: Children are empowered to comprehend and overcome painful and traumatic events on the level of subjective experience while they are also offered orientation on the level of ethics. Anthropocentrism, from this perspective, seems to be the price to pay.

The Journeys of Little Mouse

In 1951, a small and sparsely illustrated volume with the title *Kleine Maus auf Reisen* (*The Journeys of Little Mouse*) was published by Hermann Schaffstein publishing house in Cologne. It is the only children's book written by its author, the Eastern Westphalian local historian, Wilhelm Süvern, who is mostly known for his contributions on the history and vernacular of the region. Süvern's book, subtitled "An Animal Story," was approved in the same year by Lower Saxony's Ministry of Education and Cultural Affairs for use in schools and subsequently stocked by school libraries as reading material for classes.

In contrast to the story of city mouse and country mouse, however, Süvern's narrative is little-known today and almost non-existent as a subject of scholarly research. It thus makes sense to briefly summarize its content here. Arranged in eleven chapters, the text tells the story of a mouse named Lisettchen who, as the lone survivor of her family, embarks on an adventurous journey and finally finds a suitable mouse partner in Waldemar, with whom she settles down to raise a family of her own. What at first glance reads as a harmless and simple story, from a cultural ecological perspective, which attributes a subversive potential to literary engagements with the natural world, turns out to be a fairly controversial narrative for child readers, in particular because of its in part gruesome details and its mode of presentation. The story begins with an idea that must seem particularly frightening to young children: that of being completely on one's own. Given the book's year of publication (1951), this element of the story surely reminded many war children of their own experiences. Lisettchen finds herself in an abandoned basement filled with scents coming from a mouse-proof supply cabinet. Squatting on a pile of coal, she looks at the world through a basement window, waiting. Sometimes there is danger and excitement when the cat peers through the glass with fiery eyes, unable to enter through the small hole in the window. In the evening, Lisettchen lies in her bed crying. Due to the empathy function of the mouse figure, young readers are encouraged to inquire into the reasons for Lisettchen's grief and thus motivated to follow the developing plot. As Kaspar Spinner has argued, empathy plays the emotional role in the adoption of perspectives ("Perspektivübernahme"), which is a crucial part of the process of literary comprehension and closely connected to cognitive activity and analysis (cf. 2006, 6-16). Empathy – participating in the life of others – or, in the terminology of literary pedagogy, *Fremdverstehen* ("understanding of the other"), which is facilitated by the sympathetic figure of the speaking animal, allows for an experience of relief from one's own difficult circumstances (cf. Groeben 2004, 27).[4]

After this prelude, the story is told in flashbacks. It begins with happy days, with Lisettchen and her parents and her siblings Purzel, Bommeli, and Schlanka living in aforementioned basement, in which the supply cabinet still had a hole in it, allowing the mouse family to live in plenty. But then Lisettchen has to witness her brother drowning in a syrup trap, her father dying from poison, and her sister being killed by a mouse trap. These almost unbearable events are somewhat mitigated by the mother's narrative of mouse paradise:

> The mouse paradise, my child, is a marvellous country with neither dogs or cats nor evil humans with their traps and toxic baits. There, mice eat sweet cake and nice-smelling bacon every day, and they drink sugared cream and delicious milk. Young mice play Ring around the Rosie on

> green meadows, and at night they sleep in silken sheets. (Süvern 1951, 10; translation DO)

The mother immediately sets out to find this paradise, leaving Lisettchen and her sister Bommeli behind. But after several days the mother still has not returned, and so Bommeli decides to leave and go look for her. All alone, Lisettchen has to take her life into her own hands. She embarks on an adventurous journey without a clear purpose but full of dangers she is narrowly able to escape from. She finds shelter in a mouse hole that also happens to be the home of her uncle's family. Here she learns that her mother is dead and her sister missing:

> Child, your mother is dead! She came to us and told us about your hardship, and we would have gladly taken you in. But as she left to fetch you and your sister, the evil tomcat Maunz was already waiting beside the hole. He grabbed your mother and carried her away, as he has done with so many of us before. How sad this was for the little mouse! She sat in the corner very quietly and cried. The uncle did not know anything about Bommeli. She had not been here. (Süvern 1951, 19; translation DO)

Life with the family of Lisettchen's uncle seems to be paradise because their dwelling is located in a bakery. Of course, this idyll is not left undisturbed by the omnipresence of danger in the guise of the tomcat Maunz, which points to the antagonistic structure this mouse figure shares with other literary mice and serves to remind the children of the established friend-foe pattern. As is the case with the life of city mouse, the convenient way is not without risks. And how fragile this world really is, soon becomes starkly evident:

> One morning, men came into the flour chamber. They moved all the sacks from the wall, put pieces of broken glass in the mouse holes and fixed them with cement. All of the mice that were inside their holes had to die miserably. And this was also how uncle Döppken and his family died. (Süvern 1951, 20; translation DO)

It is only by chance that Lisettchen is absent at the time and thus able to avoid this terrible fate. However, she is unable to find another mouse hole and has to hide in a shopping bag, in which she is carried away without being discovered. In the chapter "A ride in the bus," we find the motifs of city life in a condensed form – the hustle, the wheels, the reek of petrol, and also the chase, as startled humans strike and kick at her.[5] Exhausted, Lisettchen escapes into an old woodshed:

> In a corner of the old shed was a mouse hole. In it lived a mouse mother with her son, Waldemar. The mother had been sick since the day before, because a little cat had played with her and badly wounded her with her paws and teeth. The mother had barely been able to drag herself back into the hole, but now she lay there, no longer able to move. [...] [Waldemar] stood sadly beside her bed. 'She is dead,' he spoke quietly. (Süvern 1951, 24f; translation DO)

This scene constitutes a turning point in the plot, because Lisettchen's misery is alleviated by her meeting with Waldemar and their decision to build a future together. Like her, Waldemar has experienced the pain of losing someone, as becomes evident from the drastic description of his mother's death struggle. The hope for a secure and harmonious life does not last long, however, and this new world of wishful thinking is equally haunted by catastrophe: Evil men, mouse hunters, attempt to capture Waldemar, who manages to escape but is severely wounded in the process:

> Dutiful Lisettchen did not leave his side. It was a long and dismal night, but at the break of dawn Waldemar had already recovered well enough to be able to drag himself away with Lisettchen's help and much effort. They found scanty shelter under some old junk. Lisettchen cared for her husband with touching love. (Süvern 1951, 29; translation DO)

Lisettchen's devotion paves the couple's way into mouse paradise. She returns with Waldemar to the coal cellar and finds her old home intact, already imagining herself as mother of a flock of mice. A dream brings fulfilment:

> The little mouse was so glad, so happy! During the first night she slept in her own bed again, she had a wonderful dream. But what did she dream of? She dreamed that she had finally arrived in mouse paradise with her beloved Waldemar. And that is indeed what happened, isn't it? (Süvern 1951, 32; translation DO)

Lisettchen, who, in contrast to city mouse and country mouse, does have an individual name, shows through her own life's journey that the traumatic confrontation with flight, persecution, and death can be overcome; that, in the end, the order that has been temporarily disturbed by violence and catastrophe will prevail and the promise of salvation fulfilled.

In principle, it is the structure of the fairy tale that is illustrated in this children's story. Despite all the objectionable elements of ideologisation, the story thus also incorporates an element of relief that children's literature can hardly dispense with if it seeks to address topics that might otherwise be too much especially for very young children. And yet, it is striking in how detailed and barely concealed a manner the story portrays scenes of violence. Unlike in other fairy tales, it is not the 'evil' characters that perish but the sympathetic figures, and all of them in unnatural ways: they are hunted, killed with gas, or tortured to death. As the story unfolds, there are no hints that might point towards a happy ending, with the minor exception, perhaps, of the mother's short narrative of mouse paradise. The young readers thus have to completely rely on their experience that nothing irreversibly destructive is going to happen to child literary protagonists even outside the framework of the fairy tale.

Literary Animals as Trauma Helpers

In the systematic interweaving of those lines generated through the pattern of city mouse-country mouse, the symbol of paradise, and the narrative of anthropogenic horrors, the attention is directed at the function of this story as children's literature. The speaking mouse as both projection surface and encoding principle conveys a message of consolation and affirms in an eschatological sense the ideology that, in the end, things will always take a turn for the better. The text can thus also be seen as a historical document that demonstrates how a children's story was employed to help a generation of war children who have lived through bombardments, hunger, and displacement cope with their traumas.

As a both sympathetic and vulnerable figure, the mouse harbours significant potential for readers to identify with while at the same time, as an animal, keeping a certain distance that produces an estrangement effect. Children's literature is also a distinct element of (literary) socialisation, which means that, on the one hand, it supports the emotional and social development of young readers and, on the other, mirrors or addresses their reality in a way that is uniquely tied to the realm of literature. This includes literary fiction's role in encouraging children to tap into the potentials, and experiment with the possibilities, of literary interpretation. Bettina Hurrelmann distinguishes between three important aspects that characterise the reading process of children: the thematisation of the children's (everyday) reality, their emotional involvement, and the possibility of media and cultural learning ("medial-kulturellen Lernens") (cf. 1998, 45-60). All of these aspects are realized in Süvern's story: For children in the 1950s, displacement, flight, and death still constituted a very tangible reality either in their own memories or because of the experiences of people close to them. As mentioned above, the emotional involvement is realized primarily through the presence of the literary animal as a sympathetic figure of identification and the children's receptiveness towards the message it conveys. Finally, because the story draws upon and retells several classic motifs that are a part of cultural memory and/or a longstanding literary tradition, it allows for media and cultural learning.

The rather drastic manner in which the story portrays the death of sympathetic figures is, of course, highly unusual for a children's story and has to be understood with regard to the specific historical context of its emergence. Unlike what is possible in fairy tales (cf. *The Wolf and the Seven Young Kids*), the dead do not return, and neither is there a form of punishment for those responsible for the calamity that has befallen them. The latter at first remains present in its unmitigated form, none of the characters being able to put it into words, and only gestures and behaviours (Lisettchen cries, Waldemar stands paralyzed) allow some insight into the characters' reaction to the tragic events. The mice are capable of human(-like) communication even as suffering has silenced their voices, and so the connection with the reading children remains unbroken or is perhaps even strengthened through the compassion evoked by the (mental) image of a crying little mouse. This image, in its repeated occurrence (for example, at the end of the frame story), indeed functions as something of a leitmotif. It is only through the narrative of mouse paradise, which is already promised at the beginning of the story and finally realizes itself as an illusion of reality ('Wirklichkeitsillusion'), that Süvern's story actually becomes bearable for children. To make sure that this message is understood, in the last sentence of the story the narrator directly addresses the reader. Here, the animal perspective comes to an end, and in consequence the hitherto blurred boundary between humans and animals is foregrounded all the more forcefully. Whether or not the mouse Lisettchen, whose perilous 'journey' is more akin to the experience of flight, can also be attributed a diagnostic value in a cultural animal studies sense (cf. Borgards 2015, 76) – one that might give us insight, for example, into the mental state of children traumatized by war – is a subject for further research. These and similar questions can only be pointed towards but not resolved here.

However, what becomes evident after the animal perspective – and thus the children's empathetic mode of reading – has ended is what Dietmar Schmidt refers to as "the secondary rhetoric of the anthropomorphic" (cf. 2013, 129; translation DO), that is, the moment in which humans (here: children) adopt their own, human perspective and the animal (here: the mouse) once again assumes the pet-like status of a cute little creature it also holds in real life. Accordingly, it is doubtful whether what we are confronted with here is a truly posthumanist perspective that effectively negates the rigid distinction between humans and animals and can thus also be read as a challenge to human exceptionalism. From such a perspective, it is not the human subject alone but also nonhuman animals who (can) appear as actors. We might argue that the part of the narrative that assumes an animal perspective is expressive of such a posthumanist stance, because here the human-animal boundary appears to be suspended, humans do not assume a position of superiority, and both humans and animals are attributed with agency. But given the ways in which the animal story ultimately serves to reinforce the anthropocentric worldview, the idea of a 'posthumanism from the beginning' must be rejected. In the example discussed here, anthropogenic violence and cruelties are negotiated in a child literary manner by way of an animal figure, and this figure's primary function consists in establishing a distance that serves to illuminate the dark side of unmistakably *human* life and agency. This anthropocentric worldview not only permeates all of the mouse stories discussed in this chapter, it is in fact what young children are effectively *introduced to* by reading such stories. Only through an engagement with, and analysis and interpretation of, these stories by rereading and comparing them a critique of the anthropocentric worldview that informs them becomes possible. Whether this can in fact help us overcome anthropocentrism in favour of a more posthumanist viewpoint, however, is anyone's guess. It is also the crucial obligation of a posthumanist teaching practice.

Notes

1 The essay is a slightly revised version of "Posthuman von Anfang an? Wie Tiergeschichten für Kinder das anthropozentrische Weltbild prägen," originally published in German in *Mensch – Maschine – Materie – Tier. Entwürfe posthumaner Interaktionen* (2016), edited by Christa Grewe-Volpp and Evi Zemanek. We thank the publishers for the kind permission to reprint the text. Thanks to Dominik Ohrem (DO) for the English translation.

2 Matthewman characterizes fables or other animal-centred (animal) stories in which animals communicate in human language as "anthropomorphic fantasies," because here animals and humans do not communicate with each other, even though their worlds may touch. Humans are sometimes privileged in such stories in that they are able to understand the communication between and among animals, but this is not always the case (cf. Matthewman 2011, 64f).

3 As the title of a novel by Günter Grass, for example, or in set expressions such as "cat-and-mouse game."

4 See Abraham and Kepser (2005, 11). For the sake of completeness, it should be stated that at the time of the story's publication the now often criticized instrumentalisation of literary texts for pedagogical purposes was a common practice and that the strengthening of empathy was understood in an overgeneralized sense as an aspect of "life assistance"/orientation ('Lebenshilfe').

5 As a reminder: In Matthewman's concept of "anthropomorphic fantasy," the worlds of humans and animals touch without, however, any direct linguistic communication taking place. The human-mouse confrontation portrayed here is a good example of this.

Works Cited

Abraham, Ulf, and Matthis Kepser (2005). *Literaturdidaktik Deutsch. Eine Einführung*. Berlin: Erich Schmidt.

Äsop (1979). "Die Stadt- und die Landmaus." *Tiermärchen aus aller Welt*. Ed. n.n. Gütersloh: Prisma, 188-89.

Aesop's Fables (2002). Translated with an Introduction and Notes by Laura Gibbs Oxford: Oxford University Press.

Borgards, Roland (2015). "Cultural Animal Studies." *Ecocriticism. Eine Einführung*. Eds. Gabriele Dürbeck and Urte Stobbe. Cologne: Böhlau, 68-80.

Bühler, Benjamin, and Stefan Rieger (2006). *Vom Übertier. Das Bestiarium des Wissens*. Frankfurt am Main: Suhrkamp.

Dichtl, Fritz (2008). *Sprechende Tiere in Literatur und visuellen Medien*. PhD thesis. Universität Augsburg. 19 Nov. 2018. <https://opus.bibliothek.uni-augsburg.de/opus4/frontdoor/deliver/index/docId/1192/file/Dichtl_Sprechende_Tiere.pdf>.

Groeben, Norbert (2004). "Einleitung: Funktionen des Lesens – Normen der Gesellschaft." *Lesesozialisation in der Mediengesellschaft. Ein Forschungsüberblick*. Eds. Nobert Groeben and Bettina Hurrelmann. Weinheim and Munich: Juventa, 11-35.

Horkheimer, Max, and Theodor W. Adorno (1980) [1947]. *Dialektik der Aufklärung*. Frankfurt am Main: Fischer.

Hurrelmann, Bettina (1998). "Kinderliteratur – Sozialisationsliteratur?" *Kinderliteratur im Unterricht*. Eds. Karin Richter and Bettina Hurrelmann. Munich: Juventa, 45–60.

Jansen, Gabriele (n.d). Review of Kathrin Schärer "Die Stadtmaus und die Landmaus." *Kinderbuch-Couch.de*, 19 Nov. 2018. <http://www.kinderbuch-couch.de/schaerer-kathrin-die-stadtmaus-und-die-landmaus.html>.

Matthewman, Sasha (2011). *Teaching Secondary English as if the Planet Matters*. London: Routledge.

Schärer, Kathrin (2008). *Die Stadtmaus und die Landmaus*. Düsseldorf: Sauerländer.

Scheffler, Ursel, and Barbara Moßmann (2014) [2003]. *Geschichten von der Maus für die Katz*. Freiburg: Kerle Verlag.

Schmidt, Dietmar (2013). "Mann und Maus." *Tier – Experiment – Literatur 1880-2010*. Eds. Roland Borgards and Nicolas Pethes. Würzburg: Königshausen and Neumann, 127-150.

Shaw, Elizabeth (2005). *Die Landmaus und die Stadtmaus*. Weinheim und Basel: Der Kinderbuchverlag.

Spinner, Kaspar H. (2006). "Literarisches Lernen." *Praxis Deutsch* 200, 6-16.

Süvern, Wilhelm (1951). *Kleine Maus auf Reisen. Eine Tiergeschichte*. Cologne: Hermann Schaffstein.

Zitzelsperger, Helga (2012). "Tierhelfer und der Herr der Tiere. Wie gehen 10- bis 14jährige mit diesem Thema um? Ein Erfahrungsbericht." *Lesen für die*

Umwelt. Natur, Umwelt und Umweltschutz in der Kinder- und Jugendliteratur. Eds. Hans Heino Ewers et al. Baltmannsweiler: Schneider, 31-46.

Christian Ludwig
Elizabeth Shipley

Reading and Creating the Posthuman in the Primary and Secondary EFL Classroom – Report of a Posthuman Teaching Experiment with Graphic Novels, Children's Books and Visual Media

1. Introduction

The desire to become posthuman as well as the horror of becoming posthuman is at the heart of many aspects of today's culture,[1] in particular popular fantasy and science fiction literature, and film. As one example, the comic medium is uniquely helpful in illuminating this fascination with the posthuman within the context of the EFL classroom. The fact that comics have a long history of human, superhuman, transhuman discourse going back right to the Golden Age of comic books since the late 1930s – the period during which comic books were more widely published, their readership increased considerably, and many of today's iconic heroes were created – appears to make them the ideal medium to bring young and adolescent learners of English also closer to the posthuman world. However, while representations of the posthuman in films and TV-series have been the subject of intensive academic research (cf., e.g. Hauskeller et al. 2015), the transgression of the human in graphic narratives – especially beyond the superhero body – still requires further academic investigation. This neglect is all the more surprising as graphic narratives are often innovative in their conceptual design, experimenting with elements such as space-time, dimensionality, and the depiction of the body. The present article attempts to tackle the issue of posthuman existence in graphic narratives, not ignoring the fact that terms such as post-, trans-, super- and metahuman are often used interchangeably in different contexts.[2] Especially for the EFL classroom, a strict separation of these terms is difficult as it would be too complex and theoretical for most young(er) learners of English and would probably use up too much learning time.

For the purpose of exploring the area of concepts beyond what it traditionally means to be human, we have chosen different examples of posthuman existence available from the "zoo of posthuman types" (Gomel 2014, 4) such as the cyborg, the robot, the superhero, the witch and the anthropomorphised animal, represented in comics and picturebooks.

These were the focus of a transatlantic and multimedial posthumanism project initiated by the English Department of Karlsruhe University of Education and conducted at two schools in Germany, one primary and one secondary, as well as a year nine of an American school. The aim of the project discussed in the present article was two-fold: firstly, to investigate how pupils make sense of representations of the posthuman in picturebooks and graphic fiction and, secondly, to draw upon the pupils' personal knowledge of and ideas regarding the posthuman by encouraging them to create their own posthumans, thereby sensitising them for the (post)-human developments currently taking place in society.

This contribution is divided into three major parts: in the first part, we attempt to navigate through the maze of understandings of the posthuman. Based on this, we establish a theoretical framework for representations of the posthuman in media that combine visual and verbal narratives in a book format, namely comics[3] and picturebooks. In the following section, we scrutinise the potential role of those hybrid media in the EFL Classroom when broaching the issue of posthumanist existence. The chapter concludes with a report on the results of three classroom micro-projects, exploring the potential of the posthuman for EFL learning, particularly focusing on the pupils' views of the posthuman.

2. Defining the Posthuman

Attempts at defining the posthuman have resulted in a plethora of understandings of what it means to be posthuman, which can broadly be categorised into two major streams of thought: One important tradition of current posthuman terminology is based on the idea that the human species is in the process of transforming itself through a phase of transhumanism into a final posthuman state of a superior intelligence, in which the human species is both eliminated in its present form and at the same time attains a form of immortality through its transformation.[4] The second tradition we would like to mention, not least because it is very clearly reflected in the project results (cf. section 5), asserts that we have always been or are already posthuman. As Cary Wolfe posits:

> [T]he perspective I attempt to formulate here – far from surpassing or rejecting the human – [....] forces us to rethink our taken-for-granted modes of human experience [...] by recontextualizing them in terms of the entire sensorium of other living beings [...]. But it also insists that we attend to the specificity of the human – its ways of being in the world, its ways of knowing, observing, and describing – by [...] acknowledging that it is fundamentally a prosthetic creature that has coevolved with forms of technicity and materiality, forms that are radically 'not-human' and yet have nonetheless made the human what it is. (Wolfe 2010, xxv)

The essential hybridity of (post)human existence which is implied in the preceding quote can be considered a key element of contemporary posthuman thought. One only has to think of the powerful image of the cyborg as an example. As Donna Haraway writes:

> [A] cyborg world might be about lived social and bodily realities in which people are not afraid of their joint kinship with animals and machines, not afraid of permanently partial identities and contradictory standpoints. (Haraway 1991, 154)

This new form of (post-)human being requires us to reconsider existing labelling and to look beyond traditional concepts. According to N. Katherine Hayles, "the posthuman evokes the exhilarating prospect of getting out of some of the old boxes and opening up new ways of thinking about what being human means" (Hayles 1999, 285). Steen Christiansen agrees with Hayles that "[t]hinking the posthuman is not a matter of thinking the human 'after' the human." However, he goes further to assert that it is more than gaining new perspectives about 'the human.' As he says, "[r]ather, it is a matter of thinking outside the human [...]" (Christiansen 2015, 339). For the purposes of this paper, the term 'posthuman' will be used broadly as an umbrella term to include both traditions that claim a definition of this term, that of its initial transcendent meaning of 'beyond (i.e. superior to) the human' as well as the later use of the term to undercut the privileged and fixed position of homo sapiens in the humanist hierarchy and to redefine homo sapiens as part of a larger community of all sentient beings, from very real nonhuman animals to the speculative aliens and supernatural beings of fantasy and science fiction literature.

Posthuman thought, in classroom contexts often used more broadly than in academic discourse, offers a new perspective important for pupils' lives today as they find themselves in an age of accelerating technological enhancement which makes them doubt the still widely prevailing opinion that humans are and will remain the most important form of existence. Therefore, it represents a topic that should also be addressed in EFL classrooms, whose curricula still largely rely on an anthropocentric view of the world. One way of doing that is using graphic narratives which, through their long tradition of representing existences other than human, can provide a particularly appropriate gateway to critically exploring the posthuman.

3. The Trans- and Posthuman in Visual-Verbal Narratives

'Visual-verbal narratives' is a catchall term which describes any narrative that combines text and images to make meaning. In the following, we will briefly look at those forms of visual-verbal narration which played a role in the classroom projects. We first discuss comics before moving on to the unique way in which comics represent the posthuman. But first a few words on picturebooks. For reasons of brevity, the term picturebooks will not be discussed separately in this article and the term comics will be mostly used hereafter to also include picturebooks. While we appreciate the differences between comics and picturebooks[5] in telling a story, we follow Katja Heim's assessment that

> many of the picturebooks that we use with children can be regarded as comics if we apply McCloud's definition of comics as 'juxtaposed pictorial and other images in deliberate sequence, intended to convey information and/or to produce an aesthetic response in the viewer.'
> (Heim 2013, 72; see McCloud 1993, 9)

Moreover, comics and picturebooks both share language learning suitability (cf. section 4) and, as Heim underlines, although

> we would normally not regard comics and picturebooks as the same thing, their word-picture relations and the fact that sequences of pictures are used to tell stories make them both good means for meaning making and more in the primary English classroom. (2013, 69)

The origin of comics remains uncertain (cf. McCloud 1993, 9-23), and the more recent term graphic novel is still a matter of debate (cf. Wolk 2007, 63-64). Moreover, both comics and graphic novels are, depending on the definition, referred to as genre or medium. Nevertheless, there seems to be consensus that they have become an integral part of contemporary mainstream media and literary culture consumed by children, teenagers, and adults alike. While comics (the term comix[6] appears more suitable here) for a long time have led a counterculture existence, the graphic novel has quickly entered mainstream culture.

For the purpose of this article, we strongly favour the definition of comics and graphic novels as an original medium, as the only defining element the medium shares with literature is that it is "printed and sold in bookshops, and that it contains linguistic sentiments" (Wolk 2007, 63-64). We also follow Mc Cloud's understanding of comics. It epitomises the fact that comics have their own unique way of storytelling based on their "*indigenous* visual rhetorical traditions" (Gomel 2014, 20; original emphasis), which, leaving wordless comics aside for a moment, lies in the combination of words and images, also resulting in a specific form of reading experience.

Due to their hybridity, progressive visual-verbal narratives appear *per se* to be an apt medium for representing the polymorphous and fragmented nature of posthuman existence. The dissolving of boundaries between text and image not only challenges established forms of narrative organisation but also may prepare pupils for imagining themselves in a posthuman world. Furthermore, through the modern superhero comic, humans have entertained themselves with visions of the future as well as alternative realities and engaged with concepts such as transhuman superiority or disability, and related issues such as superpowers since their emergence in the 20th century. The superhero comic, as Scott Jeffery tells us,

> is no longer (if it ever was) an identifiable genre. Rather, the superhero genre is itself an assemblage, made up of heterogeneous, overlapping genres, and characters drawn from the publishers' back catalogues. As Jenkins reminds us, the story of the superhero's dominance of the medium is also retroactive because from the 1940s to the 1970s, superheroes represented just 20 percent of all American comics. (Jeffery 2016, 41)

However, as Dan Hassler-Forest rightly points out,

> the most notable thematic thread that connects even the most diverse superhero figures is the concept of the posthuman. [...] [T]he superhero genre has foregrounded the human body and the desire to overcome its physical limitations. (2015, 67)

This is not to say that representations of the posthuman have not changed. On the contrary, they have been constantly changing since the beginning of the Golden Age (1938-1950) of superhero comics. As Jeffery emphasises:

> 1938 marks the debut of Superman in Action Comics issue [...]. The comic book superhuman was in fact preceded by what Coogan (2006) usefully describes as the Antediluvian Age. At the end of the eighteenth century and the early decades of the twentieth century the posthuman was already manifesting itself in several seemingly disparate realms. In the fantastic fiction [of, not in the original] H. G. Wells for instance, which presented invisible men, human-animal hybrids and highly evolved (and de-evolved) relatives of humankind from the far future. (2013, n.p.)

Superhero comics of course did not end with the Golden Age but went through several metamorphoses resulting in a variety of superhero body types, increasingly moving away from the image of the perfect body and shifting towards a more diverse range of bodies such as RoboCop's military-industrial body of the 2000s, which we will discuss below.

There is an almost unanimous consensus that comics, through their concern with bodies, constitute a corporeal medium. In other words, comics and graphic novels can be read as a 'posthuman body genre.' For example, the transformation of the superhero from man to superman is always marked by morphological change (Batman putting on his cape or superheroes changing at a molecular level) and superpowers are written upon, and performed through, the body.

Closely related to the corporeal concern of graphic narratives is the reconstruction of identities in graphic fiction. Frank Erik Pointner emphasises the fact that while identities are not exclusively constructed through outward appearance, appearance "plays an important role in the construction of identities, and it is here that visual media have their forte" (2013, 53). One may presume that posthuman identities, including their human characteristics such as age, ethnicity, and gender, mainly manifest themselves through physical features (one only has to think of the cyborg or the robot).

However, it is not sufficient to look at the individual superhero body and identity. Superheroes have at least two identities, which, depending on the hero, may intertwine to a certain degree. Superman, who has a civilian as well as a secret identity and who wears his costume under his normal clothes, may serve as an example here. His "altered body is presented as relatively unified and stable, even after his transformation causes him to develop two separate identities" (Hassler-Forest 2015, 70), the one of the shy and sometimes invisible journalist, and the invincible hero.

Moreover, as Pointner emphasises, "[i]dentities always need an 'Other'" (2013, 52). In other words, we can only be posthuman if there is also a human; one can only be a cyborg if there is also robot in opposition. Two of the three panels which we will discuss largely rely on the juxtaposition of different identities. In the third panel, for example, the 'othered human' i.e. the 'real' superheroes such as Spider-Man or Catwoman can only be identified as such by setting them side by side with the daily heroes of human society such as firefighters, nurses, or policemen. The strength of the comic medium when it comes to depicting different identities is to represent them in varying degrees of realism. The more iconic the representation of an identity, something McCloud refers to as "amplification through simplification" (1993, 31), the broader the referential frame and ultimately the more people can partially or fully identify with it, contributing to the immediacy of the comic reading experience. The realism of comics, however, is limited as comics are self-referential or, as Versaci has it,

> one can never completely escape into a comic book because its form – impressionistic illustrations of people, places, and things – reminds us at every turn (or panel) that what we are experiencing is a representation. While comics are very adept at engaging us with their creator's representations of the world, they never allow us to escape completely. (2007, 6)

The ability of comics to express and stage ambiguities is directly related to the aspect of identity construction. To explain this further, let us examine the three panels which were analysed by the secondary pupils through the lens of the posthuman.

RoboCop, who was a leading figure part of the cyborg movie wave during the 1980s and has since become part of popular culture, is the protagonist in the panel from Frank Miller's original storyline in comic form (Miller et al. 2013). The story is set in a near future dystopian version of Detroit. It tells the story of former police officer Alex Murphy, who is murdered by a group of criminals but revived by the Omni Consumer Products (OCP) corporation, subsequently returning to active duty with the police as the cyborg RoboCop.

The panel (see fig. 1) depicts several events and forms, and is a complex web of different human and posthuman identities, for example male vs. female, cyborg vs. human, all juxtaposed to each other. Of particular interest here is the depiction of simultaneity via RoboCop and Alex Murphy through RoboCop's visually externalised memories of his former, (more) human self. Here, both RoboCop's "inside and outside lie on the same continuum of space – that, to reiterate the words of Deleuze and Guattari, 'the self and the non-self, outside and inside, no longer have any meaning whatsoever'" (Brown 2015, 29). With regards to possible classroom discussions of the panel, it can raise the pupils' awareness of how fragile formerly established boundaries can become. Another advantage of comics when it comes to the representation of the posthuman is the comic's ability to externalise the inner life of a character, for example, through thought balloons or the use of graphic objective correlatives in a particularly accessible way

Fig 1: RoboCop (2013: n.p.)

Once again, the RoboCop panel serves as an excellent example. The use of dark, greyish colours evokes the impression of coldness functioning as objective correlatives representing RoboCop's entrapment.

The panel at hand illustrates the representation of (post-)humanism at various levels. RoboCop is a cyborg who was created through the "(often brutal) insertion of machine components into a previously wholly organic entity" (Thomas 2015, 57). The opening page of Chapter 2 of the comic version of Miller's RoboCop sequel, preceding the panel in question (cf. fig. 1), shows the identical scene but with a panel frame of massive automatic metals doors setting the scene and making the viewer aware of the fact that the protagonist is in a laboratory. RoboCop is right in the centre of the panel, emphasising his central function in the panel (sequence) as well as in the narrative as a whole.

In the ensuing panel, the reader's view is expanded and we see a much bigger part of the laboratory. We see RoboCop sitting in a chair and being treated by people who presumably are doctors, nurses, and mechanics working for the OCP cooperation, which points to his cyborgian nature and virtually decentres the human of the first panel. RoboCop's humanoid metal body has nothing of the aerodynamic ease of other cyborgs but looks rather cumbersome. Its clumsy prosthetic attire contrasts with the red cross on the jacket of the nurse in the left part of the panel that identifies her as a human nurse for humans, a connection which is also stressed by the human tissue in the metal box she is holding, pointing at the experimental character of the hybridisation project.

One of the central elements of the RoboCop storyline is Alex Murphy's continuous struggle to balance his humanity with having become a machine after the brutal end of his former life, which is expressed at both the visual and verbal level. For a long time, it has been argued that static images cannot depict the passing of time, or as Lessing put it: "painting employs wholly different signs or means of imitation from poetry, – the one using forms and colours in space, the other articulate sounds in time" (1971 [1766], 340). This assumption needs to be revisited, however, when looking at comics which appear to hold the potential to depict the passing of time graphically. Closely related to this, Charles Hatfield emphasises that the "representation of time in comics can vary considerably: from precise breakdowns that depict a sequence of events in minute detail to single drawings that conflate a whole series of events in one panel" (2005, 52). The frame in question represents both a series of events in one panel as well as a sequence of events in several panels. The fact that protagonists change their position indicates the passing of time.

While RoboCop is being treated, fragmented memories of his former family life are transmitted to the video screens in the background. Apart from the function of this particular scene within the story itself, it also plays with the extended mind thesis which claims that "the physical machinery of mind is not confined to the head. Rather, mental states such as beliefs and memories can be partially realized by artefacts and technologies beyond the boundaries of skin and skull" (Krueger 2015,

176). From a more positive point of view, the technological possibility to separate RoboCop's mind from his body and create a mind-body dualism could be perceived as progress. However, having landed in the wrong hands of the cooperation with its evil intentions, the technology is used to ultimately break RoboCop's will. From a media-analytical perspective, the comic medium appears to be more than suitable to show the audience a long period of time in a relatively short time, for example, through the parallel representation of two or more simultaneous actions.

Furthermore, the scene epitomises the way in which comics are capable of addressing the complex relationship between identity and the self. The speech balloons depict RoboCop's shards of memory at a verbal level, emphasising how much he is struggling with his new existence. He is barely able to speak but is capable of saying his name. Interestingly, RoboCop himself relates his memory of being a man directly to his profession of being a cop. Now he is no longer human, but still a cop, keeping one of the identifying traits of his existence. RoboCop's memories are commented on by Dr Margaret Love, the cooperation's representative and RoboCop's main villain in Miller's original storyline, who discounts them as sentimental attachments to vestigial human memory. The fact that her last comment is printed in larger font emphasises her disgust at RoboCop's sign of human weakness.

Both Dr Love and RoboCop are focalised in the lower two panels which puts them in direct opposition. The two panels are connected to the upper panel by Dr Love's feet transcending the panel border and touching the frame of her 'own' depiction below. RoboCop's tilted head seems to indicate that he has resigned himself to his fate while the villain, the cooperation's representative, is clearly depicted in a fearless and almost aggressive manner. By asking him "Do you know *what* you are?" (Miller et al. 2013, n.p.; original emphasis), she denies his human side by clearly objectifying him through using 'what' instead of 'who.'

One further aspect worth mentioning is the role of the gutter on this particular page. According to Will Eisner (2008 [1985]), there are two frames in comics: the total page and the panel itself (41). Particularly the "frame's shape (or the absence of one) gives it the ability to become more than just a proscenium through which a comic's action is seen: it can become a part of the story itself" (45). In very simple terms, the gutter is the space, "non-space" in Eisner's terms, between two panels. Similar to all other elements on a comic's page, the gutter conveys meaning, triggering a response from the reader to fill the gap or, in the language of comics, complete the act of closure. Moreover, the panel shows the strength of the comic medium, i.e. its ability to visually juxtapose different identities. In the present case, both the human and the cyborg identity become almost tangible. RoboCop is juxtaposed with the clearly human medical and technical staff as well as with mental images of his own past when he was still human.

Furthermore, the doctor's exaggerated femininity in the foreground of the panel also stands in direct contrast to the clumsy medical staff in trainers and laboratory coats and uniforms and, again, RoboCop's experimental cyborg design. The way in which Margaret Love is shown insinuates the "internalized sexism" (Wolk 2007, 70) of comic narratives dating back to the Golden Age of comics. She is a prime example of how female characters are often depicted as the "stereotype of the top-heavy bombshell" (Hatfield 2005, 69), in this particular case contrasting with the nurses.

RoboCop desperately attempts to fill the gaps of his memory: "I was shot… Left for dead. You built… This… So I could keep being a cop …" (Miller et al. 2013, n.p.). Here, the comic adumbrates central ethical concerns. After RoboCop was shot, he was left to die by his murderers and is revived, as the necklace with the Christian cross underlines. In contrast to the idea of Christian resurrection, however, he has been revived by the cooperation and now struggles to find purpose in the unnatural extension of his life, the sole purpose at the moment being a cop again. For that, he is co-dependent on his robot implants to survive as much as the cooperation depends on technology to retain its power.

The second group of examples stems from the plethora of superhero comics, more specifically the realm of post-9/11 comics. While there is nowadays a myriad of literary texts, films, music, and art pieces to support the victims as well as the larger population in dealing with the collective trauma, comics and graphic novels were one of the first media to react to the events. The two selected panels show in an exemplary fashion how the world's superheroes dealt with the attacks and their aftermath.

Fig. 2: Straczynski *et al.* 2002, 22

The panel depicts the Twin Towers in the moment of collapsing. We observe the catastrophe from a bird's eye perspective, not only witnessing the World Trade Centre site but also the surrounding area which was also affected by the explosion and the ash clouds. Spider-Man is shown in the lower left corner of the panel, insinuating his passivity. He stands firmly on the rooftop, his body tilted towards the explosion which takes centre stage. He covers his ears, which indicates that the noise of the collapsing buildings is too much to take for his enhanced sense perception. The intense colours, especially of the fire and the thick, black smoke, which are not visible in the black and white version of the panel, function as objective correlatives. Moreover, the interaction between text and image increases the impression of helplessness with witnessing being the only remaining form of action.

As Maria Eisenmann points out:

> Similar to voice-over in film, the superhero continually states his inability to understand the events. This can already be seen here [...] where words, i.e. Spider-Man's thoughts, do not make the unspeakable speakable: 'God... Some things are beyond words ... Beyond comprehension... Beyond forgiveness.' (Eisenmann 2013, 188)

Spider-Man's posthuman superpowers such as his enhanced reflexes, balance and 'spider-senses,' which he obtained after the bite, are mostly useless here, which is illustrated by juxtaposing a superhero whose main power is to cling to buildings with the collapsing of such buildings. Once again, the colours employed in the panel function as objective correlatives, accentuating the dark, gloomy, and threatening atmosphere of the event.

The third superhero panel (fig. 3) paints quite a different picture. We view a diverse group of superheroes gathered in front of the American flag. It features a wealth of male superheroes, reflecting the long history of male domination of the superhero genre. The same is true for the 'human professions' depicted in the panel. The agencies and groups represented here, such as FEMA, the military, New York City Fire Department (FDNY), or the FBI as well as emergency workers, stand for many first responders to the 9/11 attacks, some of which were killed in their attempt to help the victims. The caption reads "Stand tall" (Straczynski et al. 2002, 22). What stands out in this panel is the diversity of superheroes, including gods, mutants, transformers as well as others.[7] The panel brings together those different superhero types, putting them alongside human superheroes. The positioning of the fictional superheroes in the background of the panel and behind the humans hints at the fact that superheroes often work in secret, supporting the human guardians of the law.

The particular strength of the panel lies in the way in which it seems to "suggest that one can never be sure where the line dividing the 'natural' and the 'unnatural' lies, whether it even exists in any real sense, or whether there are, in its stead, a variety of different permutations and subject positions" (Thomas 2015, 58). Conveying an emotional and even patriotic undertone, 'real' superheroes stand together with the 'superheroes' of daily life such as nurses, firefighters, policemen and others, with unity created by the flag in the background of the panel.

The corporeal concern of comics as well as the embodied reality of the (post)human is increasingly transcended in contemporary graphic fiction, rebalancing the realm of subjectivity and objectivity. It does not appear too far-fetched to say that comics, at least slightly, open a door to alterity (cf. Easterbrook 2009, 384), a property which should not go unnoticed in the EFL classroom.

Fig. 3: Straczynski *et al.* 2002: n.p.

4. Using Comics, Graphic Novels, and Picturebooks in the EFL Classroom to Teach the Posthuman

Pictures have always played an important role in the learning of foreign languages and are gaining even more prominence in our increasingly image-based society. As far as picturebooks are concerned, it is safe to say that they have not lost their status as one of the most frequently used resources in primary English classrooms in Germany as they assist in developing pupils' communicative skills and a positive attitude towards other cultures and school groups as outlined in curricula across Germany and Europe. The same, however, is not (yet) true for comics and graphic novels as their hybridity is still "adduced to derogate the medium which is said to do everything, yet nothing right" (Ludwig and Pointner 2013, 2), while it could easily be argued that comics, as multimodal narratives, are simply too challenging for the contemporary classroom. This is not to say that, from our point of view, the medium does not stand on equal footing with literary texts as well as more contemporary media such as film or internet when it comes to classroom suitability.[8]

If we leave aside possible constraints such as too colloquial language or a high level of referentiality, academic research and classroom practice have identified many advantages of using narratives that combine text and image. To mention but a few, they represent current authentic material (cf. Rüschoff 2013, 8-10), foster cognitive involvement and linguistic (95-124) and cultural advancement, not to forget that the medium's various genres comment on a wide range of issues such as everyday life, racism, sexism, and ageism.

In the following, we focus on one learning aim frequently mentioned in discussions around comics and picturebooks that deserves particular attention with regards to teaching the posthuman: their potential to support the development of visual literacy. Visual literacy can be defined as the ability to situate "an image in its cultural, social, and historical contexts" (Association of College and Research Libraries 2011, n.p.) and to follow visual argumentation, which in the case of comics and picturebooks is closely linked to the information conveyed through written text in multiple manners. In other words, a visual-verbal medium requires students to look more closely at how the visual and the verbal interact. Images always have to be read and interpreted in the cultural context(s) in which they emerged. This ties in with Bland's assertion that picturebooks that

> authentically reflect cultural diversity can move even young readers towards flexibility of perspective, especially in contrast to the often-essentialised illustrations in textbooks [...]. In picturebooks, the pictures are a vital component of the storytelling, and they frequently provide gripping access to empathetic characters as well as individualised cultural details add diversity and illustrating minority perspectives. (Bland 2016, 45)

In the next section, we describe the project design and critically discuss the outcomes of the project, particularly focusing on the pupils' reactions to the representations of the posthuman and on their own concepts of what it means to be posthuman.

Before moving on to a detailed description of the projects, we would like to address the learning objectives. The primary goal was to gain insights into the pupils' concepts and ideas of what it means to be human or posthuman respectively. This very specific topic, however, ties in with various learning objectives mentioned in the curricula for both primary and secondary schools. For example, the curriculum for teaching English at primary level in Baden-Württemberg lists 'body' as one topic area, a topic which is closely related to any discussion of the posthuman. For students at secondary level, the curriculum requires pupils to develop an advanced text and media competence, enabling them to access and analyse authentic texts on topics relevant to today's society. Both receptive and productive language skills form the foundation for the abovementioned text and media competence as they enable pupils to analyse, reflect, and discuss issues relevant in today's society.

5. The Project

5.1 Teaching the Trans- and Posthuman through Picturebooks at Primary Level

The project at beginners' level was conducted in a year-four class of a primary school in a small town in northern Baden-Württemberg.[9] The class consisted of 24 pupils (thirteen boys, eleven girls) three of whom were ill at the time and thus not able to participate in the project. While most pupils were very active during the lesson, some of them were too shy to speak English in front of the class. For the project lesson we used Valerie Thomas' *Winnie's Big Bad Robot* (2016), a story about a cardboard robot which, when turned into a real robot, goes crazy and turns everyone and everything in its surroundings into robot-like beings. One reason for choosing this particular picturebook was the fact that, apart from robots, it also predominantly features beings like a witch and an anthropomorphised cat that, through the students' potential knowledge of fairytales, may be closer to the pupils' reality than robots and stress the fact that there are different forms of existence.

The image of Winnie the Witch, the main character of the eponymous series of children's stories, draws on traditional representations of witches but is good-hearted, chaotic and always creates funny situations. She lives in a big house with her black cat Wilbur, whose ontological status deviates from that of a normal cat, for example, through its ability to speak. At some point, Winnie attempts to create a bear out of an empty cardboard box and tin cans. The result, however, looks more like a robot, which she takes home and brings to life. Unfortunately, the robot turns out to be a nasty being. When Winnie tries to get rid of it, the robot disarms her and, by using Winnie's magic wand, it turns everything around it into robotic beings, including the house and, ultimately, Winnie. Eventually, it is Wilbur's discontent with its new robotic owner that brings the robot's evil doings to an end.

The story not only offers links to the pupils' lives, such as having a pet, but also issues warnings such as 'be careful what you wish for.' Closely related to this, the fact that the robot develops a life of its own shows that one's actions have consequences. From an ethical point of view, Winnie's and Wilbur's actions are at least questionable as their only reason for bringing the robot to life is that they need a household help, being almost entirely ignorant of the personified robot's wishes. However, shortly after having developed a life of its own, the robot turns everyone and everything else into robots and machines, Wilbur ends its life, turning it into a self-unconscious pile of junk. Winnie's and Wilbur's actions urge the pupils to question the finitude of life and ask themselves how they define "what is 'human' and the legal rights of 'personhood'" (LaGrandeur 2015, 111). The 90-minute double lesson was divided into three major parts: an introduction, a storytelling phase, and a design phase. At the beginning of the lesson, the three main protagonists of the picturebook, i.e. the witch, robot, and cat, representing three different types of posthuman existence, together with the key vocabulary, were introduced to prepare the pupils for the demands of the storytelling phase. In order to support the pupils' understanding during the storytelling, key scenes from the picturebook were projected onto the wall. During the post-storytelling phase the pupils were encouraged to create their own robots with black carton and 'magic chalk', encouraging them to express their ideas of their perfect robot.

The pupils' drawings mainly depict their individual visions of their robots' capabilities. Most robots resemble human beings almost to the extent that they appear to be clones of humans only differing from their progenitors in their extra abilities and powers. This was to be expected, because, as Gomel points out: "since the only intelligence we know is our own, fictional aliens are likely to mirror their creators to some degree" (2014, 11). This tendency to anthropomorphism notwithstanding, two general types of robots can be identified in the pupils' drawings: machine-like robots that are characterised by their martial appearance and a variety of weapons, and non-military robots, such as household helps, whose special abilities concentrate on their ability to make their originators' lives more pleasant. It is worth noting, though, that the robot profiles, which the pupils filled in after having completed their drawings, show that most pupils chose abilities which were already known to them in English (e.g. playing football, dancing, cleaning, or playing with the fidget spinner). However, some pupils asked the students for translations of words or concepts they did not yet know, such as the ability to shapeshift. Furthermore, the majority of pupils spontaneously only included information in their profiles directly related to the posthuman identity of their creations, such as colour and size.

Inspired by the robots from the picturebook, most robot drawings share the rectangular shaped heads, torsos, arms, and legs. The fact that the pupils demonstrated notable creativity regarding the robots' hands, which reach from human hands (with a varying number of fingers, over grippers to no hands at all), indicates that their understanding of a robot's purpose is primarily to work. This links back to the ethical dilemma already mentioned above that robots do not constitute equal members of society but are rather considered objects or even equipment. On a reflective note, while it was to be expected that the pupils would create robots similar to the one depicted in the picturebook, it would be a follow-up task to help them call their original views of robots into question. The following three examples (cf. figures 4, 5, 6) each focus on one particular aspect of robotism, such as their sex and gender identities, which we would like to highlight.

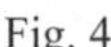
Fig. 4

Fig. 5

Fig. 6

Two robots (figures 5 and 6), both drawn by female pupils, clearly show girlish traits; one is even referred to as robot girl, which lets us surmise that for this particular pupil robots are not neuter but have an assigned sex and gender. This is also reflected in the robots' (human) costumes which add to the impression that the robots function as mirror images of the pupils. Furthermore, the possessive pronoun 'my', in both cases highlighted by a different colour in two of the drawings (figures 4 and 6), reveals another fact about the pupils' understanding of robots. They claim ownership, considering them property. Last but not least, the pupil who drew the robot in figure 4 further humanises the robot by naming it Mäx.

5.2 Teaching the Trans- and Posthuman at Secondary Level

The two classes at secondary level were a year-nine media projects class at Fort Worth Country Day School, a private K-12 school in Texas, USA, and a year-ten group in a *Realschule* in Karlsruhe. Each of these groups had a similar lesson plan and our goal in comparing these two groups was, first of all, to explore the potential of a media project class for this particular topic, for which technology plays such a central role. Secondly, we wanted to have a trial run in a group in which foreign language learning was not an issue and one could concentrate on the posthuman elements themselves. The Fort Worth year-nine media-project group was the first to be taught the posthuman lesson. There were altogether sixteen pupils, four girls and twelve boys, with three absentees on the day of our research project. The 70-minute lesson began with a segment from the series *The Big Bang Theory*, "Sheldon May Be a Robot,"[10] and was followed by the Die Krupps song "Robo Sapien"[11] and a Star Trek clip about the Borg[12], all available as YouTube clips. Afterwards, the comic texts mentioned above in this article were discussed in connection with the question "What is human?"

Pupils then had about fifteen minutes to photoshop themselves as the posthuman they would like to be, present their imagined posthuman selves and engage in a reflection by answering the following questions:

1. *What does it mean to be human?*
2. *What are different types of superhumans/metahumans/posthumans?*
3. *What type of post/super/metahuman did you choose to become and why?*
4. *What powers do you have?*
5. *What does the person in the picture think about the definition of human?*
6. *What's appealing about changing into something non-human?*
7. *What's repulsive about changing into something non-human?*

The answers to Question 5 and the attempts to think "outside the human" "about the human" produced interesting results. Some answers were identical to answers of the question "What is human?" Others expressed a perspective beyond the human, such as "Humans can eat food", "weak", or "He [the posthuman] doesn't think there is a definition because in his time there are no humans."

Somewhat to our surprise, there was no activity that could clearly be said to have been most popular with the group as a whole. In fact, preferences seemed to be very individual. However, the creativity of the responses, both of the photoshopped posthuman images as well as the verbal answers, left no doubt that the topic was of interest and relevance to them. One pupil wrote: "I chose to become a cyborg because I wanted to release my inner robot." The pupils showed interest in the research aspect of their class session and in seeing the article that their class was a part of.

The German secondary level lesson about a month later could in part build on the experiences in Fort Worth. The year-ten class consisted of twenty students, eleven boys and nine girls, who were just finishing their final school leaving exams. On the day of the posthuman project, sixteen of the twenty pupils were present, nine girls and seven boys. As with the primary group, the secondary class had a double lesson of 90 minutes.

Again, the presentation of the *Big Bang* segment marked the beginning of the class. But now, more time than in the Fort Worth group was spent on this short clip, as vocabulary needed to be introduced. A short introduction to Asimov's Three Laws of Robotics[13] was also necessary to make sure that the clip was understandable to all. As there was little response to this activity, we assumed – wrongly, as we later discovered – that the interest was not high.

The class was then divided into four groups that were asked to discuss the comics. Two groups discussed the two RoboCop panels and two groups discussed the 9/11 Spider-Man and Superman panels, with worksheets provided as help. About twenty minutes were allocated and proved sufficient for the pupils to answer all the questions, some of them showing very good skills in observation of detail, thus confirming that this visual medium is particularly appropriate for the classroom. Afterwards, all the comics were projected onto the wall so that the pupils could see all the comic panels while the interpretations of the comics were presented. The pupils seemed to be familiar with the superheroes in the panels and to enjoy working on the questions and discussing them. The answers on the worksheets show that the comic medium was accessible to them. For example, asked what Spider-Man was feeling, pupils wrote: "He has no words and maybe he's afraid." and "He felt powerless and it was to [sic] much to handle." Concerning the question about the meaning of the panel showing a group of superheroes and other people (cf. fig. 3), one pupil wrote: "That their [sic] are heros [sic] without superpowers they work together." There were many similar answers to this question. One pupil, who was otherwise very quiet in class, wrote in great detail about the RoboCop panels, identifying colours and images and their meanings: "Weding [sic] – a big cake, birthday – a present (memorys [sic] in his head/mind)." In answer to the question, "What colours are in the groups? What do the different colours mean?" she wrote "yellow – mechanix/medic's, blue – backroung [sic] & woman, silver – robocop." In addition, the topic of fashion and stereotypes was taken up by many in this group; "The woman is wearing a short dress, "She looks like a typical woman", and "Yes, it's a stereotype, it's a typical agent." One comment in the discussion was: "She's hot." This small sample of pupils' interpretations not only highlights the accessibility of the comic medium to learners of English but also expresses their high degree of empathy and willingness to take risks in sharing their opinions.

The second half of the double lesson began with a slide show of the Fort Worth posthumans that were photoshopped. Enthusiasm for this was immediately tangible. The presentation was also used as an invitation for the pupils to create their own posthumans. Unlike the Fort Worth group, photoshopping was not an option for this class and we had to fall back on traditional materials: pictures from magazines, yarn, coloured pens and crayons, and paper. The pupils surprised us with their creative efforts. In less than 30 minutes, they were able to turn out visually intriguing collages, revealing that electronic media are not always necessary for posthuman effects. In particular, the use of pale blue yarn for energy bolts was very effective.

After creating their posters, pupils presented them by adding a sentence about their powers, which provided an additional language output opportunity. Here are a few examples:

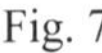

Fig. 7

Fig. 8

Fig. 9

All these posthumans were created by female pupils. "Flying Lady" in Figure 7 is the only one of the three in which the entire body is present and is the most human, although the left arm seems not to be part of the body but artificially attached. She has extensions in dark purple yarn to her feet. This shows the willingness of the pupils to imagine themselves having alternate corporalities and their creativity in expressing posthuman existence with simple and limited means, which can easily be reproduced in any classroom without a lot of resources.

Figure 8, "Mensgender," has only one leg and evidently needs no more to be complete as he/she stands firmly. What is often considered to be a deficit is here a simple alternative way of being. The pupil's sentence reads: "I put a man into women and women into man [sic]," and the Mensgender's power was described as the ability to turn into a man or woman at will. We see this represented in the face of a man and the breasts of a woman. She is clearly a cyborg with a weapon as an extension of one hand. The phrase "Bald im Kino" underlines the importance of films in many pupils' lives.

Figure 9, "Laserwomen," has only half a body. The light blue yarn coming out from eyes and hands captures the effect of photoshopped lasers. It is telling that two of these pupils' posthumans display the "permanently partial identities" that Haraway considers part of the cyborgian condition, an alternative to the traditional human condition. From a pedagogical point of this, creations like these can trigger discussions about the increasing diversity of identity in society. Only a few minutes were left for the evaluation. Yet fifteen out of sixteen pupils returned the evaluation fully completed, four of them even with comments. One pupil wrote, "It was very fun! [sic]" To the question, "Would you change anything?", we received the answers "Nothing", "I don't change anything [sic]" and "No." The overall report was that the project was liked and enjoyed by most pupils. Surprisingly, like the Fort Worth group, no single activity was the most popular one. Two pupils chose the Big Bang clip as their favourite exercise, two others decided for the comics, and five others chose the posthuman project. At the same time, one pupil gave the posthuman project the lowest score. This shows that the variety of activities presented in the lesson addressed the different kinds of learners in the group and that the lesson on the whole was successful if packed. Twelve of the fifteen evaluations gave top or second to top scores for the overall project. Like the Fort Worth group, pupils were interested in being part of the project and in hearing what would become of their work. They also enjoyed the (indirect) connection to pupils close to their age in the US.

The class teacher was particularly supportive of the project throughout and had raised anticipatory interest in the pupils weeks before the lesson already. She told us that she had been sceptical of the topic before but could now imagine teaching this topic in the future in a project and possibly integrating grammar exercises with it, teaching grammar in a contextualised and integrated way and combining it with a topic appealing to the pupils.

6. Conclusion

By motivating pupils to engage with the posthuman we can raise their awareness of their anthropocentric world views and encourage them to question their own views of themselves. The results of the project do not give clear evidence whether or to what degree this happened but the creative products indicate that they at least partially reflected on these issues. By doing so, we prepare the pupils for the increasing number of political, ethical, and philosophical discussions in the future as technological developments increasingly challenge the boundaries of the human body and soul. For this, media such as picturebooks and comics can play an important role. The issues raised by the projects could have been followed up by more in-depth discussions of the topics at hand, which, given the limited timeframe, was not possible here. Both classrooms provided opportunities for language production and authentic language output: in the primary school class, both written and oral language was drawn upon in the form of the pupils' personal descriptions of their robots ('Steckbrief') which was on the other side of the poster as a help when they presented their poster verbally. On the secondary level, working with the comics and answering the questions in groups, in written form on the worksheet and orally in group discussions provided further communicative opportunities. From the perspective of communicative language teaching methodology, this was the most successful part of the lesson because students were already familiar with the comic characters and stories and enjoyed writing down and verbally expressing their ideas based on their pre-existent knowledge.

Especially the creative character of many of the tasks allowed students to be drawn into a discourse that otherwise would have been too theoretical. Moreover, inspiring the pupils' creativity allowed them to give immediate responses to the concepts without thinking about them too much. By doing that, we hope to have called forth the pupils' spontaneous reactions.

The project results indicate that the hybridity and accessibility of the graphic narratives encouraged pupils to transcend their own boundaries at both the visual and verbal level. Moreover, the results from all three groups demonstrate that they developed a clearer understanding of the construction and representation of (idealised) (post-)human bodies and identities. By requiring them to create their own posthuman identities, the creative tasks stimulated the pupils to reflect on their own thoughts regarding posthuman existence and articulate their own understanding of the *conditio (post-)humana*.

Notes

1 As N. Katherine Hayles points out, "the prospect of becoming posthuman both evokes terror and excites pleasure" (1999, 283).

2 The terms metahuman and superhuman, for example, are used, as Jeffery indicates (2016, 12), for the posthumans of DC and Marvel comics respectively.

3 The terms comic, comic book and graphic novel are used interchangeably throughout the chapter.

4 See Jeffery (2016, 17-18) and Raulerson (2013, 31) for excellent definitions of the transhuman and posthuman of this tradition.

5 According to Nikolajeva, "[t]he unique character of picturebooks as an art form derives from their combination of two levels of communication, the verbal and the visual. In this, picturebooks are a synthetic medium, like theatre or film, where the overall meaning is assembled by the receiver in the interaction between the different communicative means" (2002, 85).

6 The term comix refers to self-published underground comic books which, in contrast to mainstream comics, were forbidden under the self-regulation by the Comics Code Authority due to their often explicit content.

7 Cf. Hassler-Forest (2015, 69) for a typology of posthuman superhero bodies.

8 There are a number of recent publications elaborating on the learning potential of comics and graphic novels. See for example Dong (2012).

9 We would like to express our gratitude to our student teachers Yvonne-Jacqueline Muss, Christopher Gerl, Lara Malchow and Mandy Mary, all of whom supported us tremendously in realising the project and especially to the classroom teachers, Klaus Jørgensen at Johann-Peter-Hebel Schule and Gertrud Müller-Lutz at Anne-Frank Schule, without whose steadfast and enthusiastic support these lessons could not have taken place. Particular thanks go to Jonathan Shipley for designing and conducting this posthuman

project in his ninth-year class at Country Day and for providing us with data of results. And our thanks go as well to all the pupils of all three schools for bringing openness and interest to the topic.

10 In the clip "Sheldon May Be a Robot" (2009), the friends of Sheldon Cooper are playing a practical joke on him by using Asimov's Three Laws of Robotics to convince him that he is not human but a robot. The humour of this clip is based on the fact that Sheldon is all too prepared to accept the Three Laws of Robotics as a real law that can be applied to him rather than science fiction.

11 See "Die Krupps. Robo Sapien" (2014). The song describes the enhancement of the human race into robo sapiens, technologically optimised human beings, exploiting the full potential of humans. The accompanying music video depicts a human man in a sterile and technologically more advanced city where normal and enhanced humans live together. The numerous video screens all advertise the same slogan: "Tired of being an ordinary human." Unaware of the man's whereabouts, we gradually learn that he is on way to undergo optimisation treatment. Leaving the facility we experience from his perspective how he tries to adapt to his new body and honed senses. First embracing his new state of being, he malfunctions and 'dies' of systemic failure. In addition to discussing the increasing 'dehumanisation' of the word, the music clip also offers opportunities for critically scrutinising the dark sides of digital work in our 'always on' culture.

12 In this clip, "Star Trek First Contact-Borg Attack" (2013), we see the irony of the android Data, whose biggest desire it is to be human, being captured by the Borg, both artificial intelligence and humans pitted against the powerful cyborgs.

13 Asimov's Three Laws of Robotics are the basis of the science of roboticism in Asimov's fictional universe. In order to prevent robots from causing harm and frightening humans, they are programmed to obey human beings and not to harm them. It is also possible to test whether someone is a human or an android by applying these laws. The Three Laws are described in Asimov (1990, 424).

Works Cited

Abrams, Meyer Howard (2005). *A Glossary of Literary Terms*. 8th ed. Boston, MA: Thomson.

Asimov, Isaac (1990). *Robot Visions*. New York: Byron Preiss Visual Publications.

Association of College and Research Libraries (2011): ACRL Visual Literacy Competency Standards for Higher Education. Web. 14 August 2017 <http://www.ala.org/acrl/standards/visualliteracy>.

Bland, Janice (2016) "English Language Education and Ideological Issues: Picturebooks and Diversity" *CLELEjournal* 4.2, 41-64. Web. 15 August 2017 <http://clelejournal.org/article-3-picturebooks-and-diversity/>.

Brown, William (2015). "DelGuat to ScarJo." *The Palgrave Handbook of Posthumanism in Film and Television.* Eds. Michael Hauskeller, Thomas D. Philbeck and Curtis D. Carbonell. New York: Palgrave Macmillan, 11-18.

Christiansen, Steen (2015). "Posthumanous Subjects." *The Palgrave Handbook of Posthumanism in Film and Television.* Eds, Michael Hauskeller,Thomas D. Philbeck and Curtis D. Carbonell. New York: Palgrave Macmillan, 339-348.

"Die Krupps. Robo Sapien (Official Music Video) [HD]." (2014). *YouTube* Web. 17 August 2017 <https://www.youtube.com/watch?v=4x5YDCj-wiE>.

Dong, Lan (ed.) (2012). *Teaching Comics and Graphic Narratives: Essays on Theory, Strategy and Practice*. Jefferson, NC: McFarland.

Easterbrook, Neal (2009). "Ethics and Alterity." *Routledge Companion to Science Fiction*. Ed. Mark Bould. New York: Routledge, 382-391.

Eisenmann, Maria (2013): "Shadows and Superheroes in 9/11 Graphic Novels." *Teaching Comics in the English Language Classroom*. Eds. Christian Ludwig and Frank Erik Pointner. Trier: WVT, 183-212.

Eisner, Will (1985) [2008]. *Comics and Sequential Art: Principles and Practices from the Legendary Cartoonist*. New York: W.W. Norton.

Gomel, Elana (2014). *Science Fiction, Alien Encounters, and the Ethics of Posthumanism.* New York: Palgrave.

Haraway, Donna J. (1991). *Simians, Cyborgs, and Women. The Reinvention of Nature.* New York: Routledge.

Hassler-Forest, Dan (2015). "Of Iron Men and Green Monsters: Superheroes and Posthumanism." *The Palgrave Handbook of Posthumanism in Film and Television.* Eds. Michael Hauskeller, Thomas D. Philbeck and Curtis D. Carbonell. New York: Palgrave Macmillan, 66-76.

Hatfield, Charles (2005) *Alternative Comics: An Emerging Literature.* Jackson, MI: University Press of Mississippi.

Hayles, N. Katherine (1999). *How We Became Posthuman.* Chicago: University of Chicago Press.

Hauskeller, Michael, Thomas D. Philbeck, and Curtis D. Carbonell (eds.) (2015).
The Palgrave Handbook of Posthumanim in Film and Television. New York: Palgrave Macmillan.

Heim, Katja (2013). "Comics in Young Learners' English Lessons – An Important Aid for Meaning-Making and More." *Teaching Comics in the EFL Classroom.* Eds. Christian Ludwig and Frank Erik Pointner. Stuttgart: WTV, 69-94.

Jeffery, Scott (2016). *The Posthuman Body in Superhero Comics: Human, Superhuman, Transhuman, Post/Human.* New York: Palgrave Macmillan.

--- (2012). "Producing and Consuming the Posthuman Body in Superhero Narratives." Paper presented at the 2011 British Sociological Association Annual Conference. Web. 15 August 2017 <https://nthmind.wordpress.com/posthumanism-and-superheroes-notes-from-phd-land/producing-and-consuming-the-posthuman-body-in-superhero-narratives/>.

Krueger, Joel (2015). "At Home in and beyond Our Skin: Posthuman Embodiment in Film and Television." *The Palgrave Handbook of Posthumanism in Film and Television.* Eds. Michael Hauskeller, Thomas D. Philbeck and Curtis D. Carbonell. New York: Palgrave Macmillan, 172-181.

LaGrandeur, Kevin (2014). "What Is the Difference between Posthumanism and Transhumanism?" Web. 15 August 2017 <https://ieet.org/index.php/IEET/more/lagrandeur20140729>.

---- (2015). "Androids and the Posthuman in Television and Film." *The Palgrave Handbook of Posthumanism in Film and Television.* Eds. Michael Hauskeller, Thomas D. Philbeck and Curtis D. Carbonell. New York: Palgrave Macmillan, 111-119.

Lessing, Gotthold Ephraim (1971). "Laocoon, Chapter XVI." 1766. *Critical Theory Since Plato.* Transl. Sir Robert Phillimore (1874). Ed. Hazard Adams. Fort Worth: Harcourt, 339-341.

Ludwig, Christian, and Frank Erik Pointner (2013). "Introduction." *Teaching Comics in the Foreign Language Classroom.* Eds. Christian Ludwig and Frank Erik Pointner. Trier: WVT, 1-3.

McCloud, Scott (1993). *Understanding Comics: The Invisible Art.* New York: HarperPerennial.

Miller, Frank et al. (2013). *RoboCop.* Los Angeles: Boom!Studios!.

Ministerium für Kultus, Jugend und Sport Baden-Württemberg. "Bildungsplan der Grundschule: Themenfelder." *Ministerium für Kultus, Jugend und Sport Baden-Württemberg.* Web. 25 June 2018 <http://www.bildungsplaene-bw.de/,Lde/LS/BP2016BW/ALLG/GS/E/04>.

Ministerium für Kultus, Jugend und Sport Baden-Württemberg. "Gemeinsamer Bildungsplan für die Sekundarstufe 1: Text- und Medienkompetenz": *Ministerium für Kultus, Jugend und Sport Baden-Württemberg.* Web. 25 June 2018 <http://www.bildungsplaene-bw.de/,Lde/LS/BP2016BW/ALLG/SEK1/E1/IK/10/04>.

Nikolajeva, Maria (2002). "The Verbal and the Visual: The Picturebook as a Medium." *Children's Literature as Communication: The ChiLPA Project.* Ed. Roger D. Sell., Philadelphia and Amsterdam: John Benjamins, 85-108.

Pointner, Frank Erik (2013). "Teaching Comics as Comics." *Teaching Comics in the Foreign Language Classroom.* Eds. Christian Ludwig and Frank Erik Pointner. Trier: WVT, 27-68.

Raulerson, Joshua (2013). *Singularities. Technoculture, Transhumanism, and Science Fiction in the 21st Century.* Liverpool: Liverpool University Press.

Rüschoff, Bernd (2013). "Comics in Language Learning: The Pedagogical, Didactic, and Methodological Framework." *Teaching Comics in the Foreign Language Classroom.* Eds. Christian Ludwig and Frank Erik Pointner, Trier: WVT, 5-26.

Rumlich, Dominik (2013). "The Benefits of Comics for Language Learning at the Lower Secondary Level: A Practical Approach." *Teaching Comics in the Foreign Language Classroom.* Eds. Christian Ludwig and Frank Erik Pointner. Trier: WVT, 95-124.

"Sheldon May Be a Robot." (2009). *YouTube.* Web. 17 August 2017 <https://www.youtube.com/watch?v=BKkEI7q5tug>.

"Star Trek First Contact-Borg Attack." (2013). *YouTube.* Web. 17 August 2017 <https://youtu.be/EYJ9sbM0Hho>.

Straczynski, Michael J. et al. (2002). *The Amazing Spider-Man-Revelations.* New York: Marvel Comics.

Thomas, Rhys Owain (2015). "Terminated: The Life and Death of the Cyborg in Film and Television." *The Palgrave Handbook of Posthumanism in Film and Television.* Eds. Michael Hauskeller, Thomas D. Philbeck and Curtis D. Carbonell, New York: Palgrave Macmillan, 57-65.

Thomas, Valerie (2016). *Winnie's Big Bad Robot.* Oxford: Oxford Children's Books.

Versaci, Rocco (2007). *This Book Contains Graphic Language: Comics as Literature.* New York: Bloomsbury Academic.

Wolfe, Cary (2010). *What Is Posthumanism?* Minneapolis, MI: University of Minnesota Press.

Wolk, Douglas (2007). *Reading Comics: How Graphic Novels Work and What They Mean.* Cambridge, MA: Da Capo Press.

Stefan Herbrechter

What Makes Us Human? Teaching Posthumanism in Secondary School

Posthumanist Education – Taking up the Challenge

In a recent article (Herbrechter 2018; based on Herbrechter 2014), I argue that, from a theoretical and policy point of view, a truly post-*humanist* education would have to deal with the following *double* imperative:

> One cannot help but think that it might be our inveterate humanist reflexes themselves that have led us into the current situation, and that it could be precisely the concealed, posthumanist, potential of an entirely other form of reason, hiding behind the dynamics of new media technology, that we need to do justice to if we want to even begin to tackle the entirely new breed and dimension that future crises may have. Herein lies, in my opinion, the urgency of the posthumanist challenge to rethinking education – namely, in developing a new impartiality outside anthropocentrism, wary of our most strongly and invisibly ingrained humanist reflexes. (Herbrechter 2018, 742-743)

An obvious way in which I was challenged over these claims was: what would this actually mean for teaching and learning *practice*? How would it work in schools, never mind universities? So the following is meant both as a reply to these voices as well as an attempt to prove to myself and others that some form of posthumanism can actually be *taught*, or at least, it shows what would have to happen and what would be at stake for schools as institutions if posthumanism were to properly and consciously enter them.

What follows is a description and analysis of a 10-hour blog-based teaching unit entitled "What Makes Us Human?" carried out with a class of Year 10 (i.e., 15 to 16-year-old) students of English as a foreign language (EFL) at a German secondary school. The class blog can be viewed at <https://whatmakesushuman.edublogs.org>, while the associated individual student blogs are private and will have to remain so for reasons of personal data protection. This very distinction between public and private and the protection of data produced by 'minors' are themselves of course increasingly being undermined by the intrinsic logic of social media like blogs. They are also questionable from a posthumanist point of view in the sense that the private/public distinction maps onto the individual/social opposition, which, in turn, props up the modern idea of the liberal humanist subject. However, present institutional guidelines in Germany are the way they are, which means that this teaching unit had to bracket some of these more radical challenges and instead had to focus on blogging in a 'safe' environment. In this contribution, I will therefore be focusing on the rationale for such an admittedly 'controlled' teaching experiment by discussing some of the methodological questions and evaluating the outcome and further implications for theory and practice.

Context and Rationale

Within the German federal curriculum and given existing content and subject classification, this teaching unit probably falls within the bracket of 'cultural studies' or 'media studies' in the broadest sense, i.e. *Kulturwissenschaft* and *Medienwissenschaft*, although neither of these is actually a recognised subject or discipline at secondary school level. They are subsumed within the established subject discipline of English (media and (inter)cultural competence are prominent learning objectives in EFL). Cultural and media studies have recently turned towards questions that increasingly challenge the dominant, namely anthropological, concept of culture (i.e. Raymond Williams's famous definition of "culture as a way of life," cf. Williams 2013 [1961], *passim*). This development has been taking place in the context of the so-called "nonhuman turn" (see Grusin 2016): a turning to and revaluation of non-human actors (cf. the emergence of theoretical approaches and disciplines like (critical) animal studies, actor-network theory, new (feminist) materialism, and object-oriented-ontology). This theoretical/ philosophical turn towards what has been termed the 'posthuman' or 'nonhuman,' and within which my own work on *critical* posthumanism has also intervened (cf. Herbrechter 2009 and 2013), understands posthumanism essentially in the sense of post-anthropocentrism. This constitutes a reorientation of the question "What is (hu)man?," as well as a re-evaluation of human responsibility in the age of digital technologies, new media, globalization and, more recently, climate change.

My motivation for carrying out this teaching unit with a focus on "What makes us human?" thus lies, on the one hand, in the relevance of this question for education, teaching and learning, and, on the other hand, in my personal expertise in the field of posthumanism or the emerging field of 'posthuman studies.' My *Posthumanism: A Critical Analysis* (first published in German in 2009, revised English edition in 2013), was the first comprehensive work describing this new intellectual landscape. Against this background, the main point of the teaching unit was to explain the urgency of finding new answers to the question of what it means to be human today. The combination of a 'de-centring' of the human from the point of view of non-human actors and environments – say, from micro-organisms to artificial intelligence – together with an increasing ecological and social responsibility for humans (cf. the recent discussion about the Anthropocene and human extinction) poses a double challenge for a *critical* posthumanism.

In a pedagogical context this requires a problematization of traditional notions of the human at both the level of content and form. In terms of content, the unit was designed in such a way that students would learn, through the genre of science fiction, to describe, analyse and evaluate various "constructions of the future." In doing so they would be encouraged to draw conclusions and find possible answers to the question of the human and 'its' present (and future) self-image. In order to do justice to the current media-technological living and learning situation of many students, learning about the new post-anthropocentric challenge also needed to take place in a *form* that is arguably more recognizably posthuman (if not posthumanist). That is why I decided to use teaching through social media to reflect the fact that human communication due to new, digital and social media platforms such as blogs is increasingly being co-constructed by human and non-human actors (e.g., mobile computing devices, algorithms, data mining bots, etc.). The distributive-cognitive environment which represents human-computer-network interaction might therefore be best suited to illustrate what ultimately constitutes a relativization of the special status of humans. As 'textual machines,' blogs provide new communication opportunities that are also particularly attractive for language teaching. However, they equally illustrate how new media are changing human self-understanding as well as the form of human-nonhuman interaction. The thematization of these processes and their effects was thus one of the main objectives of this unit.

The Blog 'Environment'

The learning prerequisites for this EFL teaching unit were first of all practical and media-technological. As opposed to secondary (and even primary) schools in the UK, many schools in Germany still do not have fixed data projection facilities or smart boards, and sometimes even wireless internet is still a problem. The best media-technological environment I was able to book for the duration of the unit was a computer room with just about enough terminals to have one screen per student. Through the teacher's console, I had the possibility to project data (the class blog and its links, film clips, etc.) and also to control what was displayed on the individual screens. Another possibility would have been to borrow a large number of tablets, but the number of devices needed and the length of the loan would have caused some difficulty. In addition, there were no projection facilities in the regular classroom apart from mobile and bookable data projection trolleys, which over a period of three to four weeks would have required too much setting-up time and would have been prone to technical glitches. The equipment in the PC room was therefore the best solution and, fortunately, there were neither major technical problems nor double bookings during that period.

The students were asked about their practical knowledge and experience with social media in advance. Most had a good level of previous experience with the usual platforms such as Facebook, WhatsApp, Instagram and (less frequently) Twitter. However, the students had no specific experience with personal web logs (blogs). The first session was therefore used to discuss the functionality of blogs generally, the blog dashboard and the specific genre of a blog post and its addressees. First, I set up my own Edublogs account and the class blog. To register the students, I asked them to send me an email (an email address is the minimal requirement for opening a student blog). With this minimal amount of personal data information, I added each student to the blog's user list and set up individual blog addresses. The students were then able to log into their individual blogs through their own user account and password, so that each student had access to their own blog as well as the class blog linked to it.

I decided to use Edublogs because they use the familiar WordPress format. Edublogs is an open source platform, based in the US, which has redesigned standard WordPress blogs to specifically cater for educational needs. In its simple version, it is freely available for registered teachers and faculty (see <https://edublogs.org/features/>). Another advantage is that Edublogs does not pass on data for advertising purposes so that students will not be exposed to any online advertising except for messages from Edublogs themselves. To create a 'safe environment,' I made the class blog invisible to search engines (which is an option that you can select during set up to prevent third parties from finding blogs). While this of course defeats the main purpose of blogging, i.e. to communicate with a potentially global readership via the internet, this restriction was important for this educational experiment to be authorised and for the privacy of students to be guaranteed. However, it was possible for the students to surf and link freely from their individual blog platforms, while any traffic to the student and class blogs from other Internet users was restricted. Only the class blog can be viewed 'publicly,' and only for those who know its web address. The students had access to the class blog and, through the 'Reader' function on their own blogs, they could also see all the posts of the other students in class. This way, we created a small 'private' blog community in which everyone could give feedback by using the comment function at the bottom of each post – a feature and experience that was rated very positively in the final student feedback.

As a first step after setting up the blogs, the students received an introduction into security, privacy, netiquette and copyright on the internet. The individual student blog addresses and usernames were anonymised and students were asked to choose nicknames and create avatars that made it impossible (except for the teacher) to associate individual blogs with actual names. In addition, the students were of course asked to keep their own login data (password and username) secret and secure.

Some Preliminary Educational Considerations

In practical terms, the interaction between teacher and student in a blog-taught unit is significantly different from an everyday classroom situation. There are phases in which the students work on their own computer terminals (or mobile devices) before presenting their findings and discussing their results (either verbally in class, or in writing, on their own, or the class blog). Much of the actual work on the blog, however, happens in 'private,' while the students type away on their individual blogs at home. However, these times are of course also 'contact times' since the interactive nature of blogging always also attracts comments from other users including the teacher and thus at least potentially constitutes a radically mixed 'public-private' sphere.

The big advantage of digital social media for teaching foreign languages is the editability of the texts produced in this way. Although a posted blog cannot be easily withdrawn once published, it can be endlessly revised. The second major benefit is the intermediality of the blog post genre, in which virtually all digital file formats can be embedded either via a link or an actual copy (e.g., images, audio files, software, databases, video, etc.). The intermediality of different platforms is usually referred to as (media) convergence and this creates a new kind of multidimensionality and interactivity, and, above all, it promotes intermedial creativity (see Jenkins 2006).

The Class Blog

Setting up a class blog with its content and its learning trajectory requires a significant amount of time. However, it can also be highly rewarding in terms of the enthusiasm and the empowerment and independence students tend to experience. To encourage this, I merely provided narrative feedback on conceptual aspects in the commentary boxes of student posts (i.e., no corrections). Anything else would have been intrusive and a violation of the freedom of expression, autonomy, responsibility and ownership on which blogging as a media-communicational practice is based. As content for the class blog I exclusively selected 'authentic texts' (i.e., unabridged, original 'non-didacticized' material). Instead, I provided help with unknown vocabulary wherever necessary in the blog texts themselves, as well as a permanent link or widget to an online dictionary. There were also some practical help pages on various topics (e.g., How to write a good blog post? How to upload an image or audio file, etc.). The aim was to create a fully immersive language environment for the students.

The theme of the blog, "What makes us human?" with its subtitle "Science – Fiction – Culture," is based on a problematization (or a posthumanist critique) of three important (liberal humanist) principles of knowledge construction:

- the differentiation between science fiction and science fact
- the distinction between humans and (nonhuman) animals, and
- the 'controllability' and 'representability' of the future through narrative and discourse.

The information, texts, pictures and videos selected for the class blog narrative were designed to show breaks and contradictions within accepted 'common knowledge' about what it means to be human. This, in fact, corresponds to one of the classic methodologies of cultural studies, namely (Barthesian) "denaturalisation" of everyday cultural myths (Barthes 2000 [1957]). The class blog narrative begins with an evolutionary and paleoanthropological example (i.e., a timeline of hominization provided by the website of the Smithsonian National Museum of Natural History), which was used in combination with a YouTube music video (Fat Boy Slim's "Right Here, Right Now"– for the educational, participatory, importance of YouTube, see Burgess & Greed 2009), which blurs science fiction with science fact. It thus served as an example of a new genre I referred to as "science faction" (cf. Herbrechter 2013, 114-116). Later examples feeding into the discussion of anthropocentrism included a 'disturbingly' anthropomorphizing animal photograph by Tim Flach (from his series "More than Human"), an analysis of the SF saga *Planet of the Apes* with its latest feature (*War for the Planet of the Apes*, 2017), as well as the Voight-Kampff empathy test in *Bladerunner* and a clip from the 'docufictional' series *Life After*

People. Furthermore, I provided links to a number of both serious and playful quizzes on the question of how to distinguish between a replicant and a human (thus expanding the *Bladerunner* scenario). This also provided an invitation to judge the extent to which smart technologies might turn 'us' into cyborgs (or may indeed have already done so). The educational intention behind this selection was to provoke what might be called 'strategic uncertainty' with the idea to challenge well-established thinking patterns and enable students to provide alternative *constructions* of the future (including the future *as* construction, of course) – a learning objective that in my view is of central importance in an age of uncertainty and of uncontrollable global challenges and risks (esp. but not exclusively with regard to climate change). Needless to say that I am not claiming any originality here. All these are classical devices of the kind of self-reflective approach promoted by cultural studies, whose main aim has always been to question the political motivation of knowledge production (of which education is of course a pivotal example). In this sense, going through the experience of this teaching unit in practical terms also raises the question of the special status normally attributed to humans and what the ethical and implications of abandoning 'human exceptionalism' might be.

Methodology

This certainly cannot be the place to open up a discussion about the relationship between subject-specific educational research (in Germany usually classified as *Fachdidaktik*) and the academic disciplines with which this research is usually associated. The theory-practice divide that often comes with this rather arbitrary (sub)disciplinary knowledge division is extremely unhelpful in the sense that there tends to be little meaningful exchange between academic (i.e. university-based) research-led teaching and teacher training institutions (never mind the actual teaching that is going on in schools) even in a long-established subject like English. And this is even less the place, of course, to start problematizing a categorisation like EFL – English as a *foreign* language – in a time of global English, migration and multiculturalism. Education and *national* curricula (especially if, as in the case of Germany, rolled out at the level of federal states) in times of accelerated globalisation and migration are inevitably going to suffer from a certain degree of provincialism, which, in the face of global challenges for humans and nonhuman alike (cf. the already mentioned digital technologies, new media, globalisation and climate change) is of course less than helpful. This experimental unit cannot address these larger disciplinary and curricular issues. What it does try to do, however, is to show to what extent a combination of language learning and new social media can provide opportunities for conceptual and behavioural changes in students with regard to alternative (i.e., postanthropocentric or posthumanist) constructions of the future.

New media literacy and language learning go hand-in-hand in this process and in this teaching unit. As the BBC – Teaching English website notes: "Blogs offer a hugely exciting platform for learners to express themselves in a new language". A blog in this context constitutes a kind of "public diary" (cf. Ebersbach et al. 2016, 60). Because of their diary-like characteristics, weblogs can support self-reflective processes while also being interactive. For this reason, blogs with their strategic mix of private and public, individual creativity and social participation have evolved into "an alternative information and entertainment system" (2016, 61). In Germany, blogs are being adopted and implemented in schools rather hesitantly. In the Anglo-American context meanwhile blogs have become an important pedagogical platform and learning tool within the last decade or so. Will Richardson's influential *Blogs, Wikis, Podcasts, and Other Powerful Web Tools for Classrooms* was published in 2010. Richardson, one of the pioneers of the pedagogical use of blogs raised the following question with regard to the possibilities and challenges of interactive web education: "What changes must we make in our teaching as it becomes easier to bring primary sources to our students?" (Richardson 2010, 6). And, one might follow up, what kind of "literacy" skills do students need in order to become successful and critical "wreaders [writer-readers]," "prosumers [producer-consumers]" and "produsers [producer-users]" under these new, interactive and multimedia, conditions (cf. Voigt-Virchow 2011, 61)? Richardson cites a study (Fernette and Brock Eide, 2005) according to which blogs not only "promote critical and analytical" but also "analogical" as well as "creative, intuitive and associational thinking" (Richardson 2010, 20). They thus offer the possibility of comprehensive "access and exposure to quality information" and efficiently "combine the best of solitary reflection and social interaction" (ibid.). Blogs also facilitate monitoring student development. As a special skill, students learn to develop a "keen awareness of [the] audience" for whom they write (ibid., 30), the ability to find trustworthy sources through the combination of reading and writing that underlies the blogging process, as well as 'editing skills.' Richardson describes the difference between traditional writing and blogging in these, no doubt somewhat polarizing, terms:

> Writing stops; blogging continues. Writing is inside; blogging is outside. Writing is monologue; blogging is conversation. Writing is thesis, blogging is synthesis... none of which minimizes the importance of writing. But writing becomes an ongoing process, one that is not just done for contrived purposes of the classroom. (30-31)

In this sense, blogging can be understood as a mixed form of creative writing and analytic-interpretive knowledge production. It is thus, in my view, a perfect critical counterpart *and* complement to the genre of *science faction*. With their active and affective involvement, blogs also enhance the students' implication in their own learning process (cf. Jodi Dean's description of blogs as "affective networks" [Dean 2010, 91-126]).

Overview of the Unit

Today's teenagers are often believed to be 'digital natives.' Even though students might have greater intuitive affinity to new digital and social media one cannot presuppose that they will also necessarily have developed an ability to use something like a blog 'critically,' i.e. in an explorative, creative but also analytical way to gather, process, interpret and (re)distribute verified knowledge. At the beginning of the teaching unit, I therefore scheduled an introductory session to sensitize students to the idea of self-reflexivity by encouraging them to frequently ask themselves (or their selves): "why am I doing what I'm doing?"

The overall outline of the sessions looked like this (I am, of course, aware that a radically posthumanist teaching practice would have to get away from this, and eventually any, kind of compartmentalisation of knowledge and from the planification of educational steps usually found in 'lesson plans' altogether, in order to facilitate alternative educational experiences, new non-anthropocentric narratives and nondisciplinary knowledge encounters):

Lesson	**Topic**	**Content**
Introduction	Getting Started	Technical induction; overview of the blog unit; some practical guidelines like netiquette and copyright
1	What does it mean to be human?	Problematization of existing definitions of "human"; practical skill: how to write a good blog post
2 + 3	How did we become human?	Evolution and its problematization and narrativization based on a YouTube video clip of Fat Boy Slim's "Right Here, Right Now"; practical skill: how to do a good analysis of a video clip
4	Nonhuman others	Problematization of the human/animal boundary based on the example of primates (photo by Tim Flach; trailer of *War for the Planet of the Apes*, online article on "Planet Without Apes"); practical skill: how to skim text
5	Science fiction	Science fiction as a genre; the erosion of the boundary between science fiction and science fact; examples (IBM data baby; BBC SF quiz); utopian and dystopian futures: practical skill: fair use of online visual material
6 + 7	Are you a cyborg?	Problematization of the human/machine boundary; the evolutionary role of technology; examples (video clip of Voight-Kampff empathy test in *Bladerunner*; BFI quiz); practical skill: how to make an online quiz
8	Saving the planet? Unlearning to be human?	Discussion of the notions of Anthropocene, climate change and extinction through examples of "science faction" (e.g., *Life After People*)
9	Feedback	Summary and evaluation; practical skill: how to produce and upload an audio file

As homework, at the end of each session, the students were given a practical blog task to complete that involved both analytical and practical skills. In this way, over the course of the unit, each student was able to put together a personal blog portfolio which was then also used as a basis for individual assessment (since, usually and problematically, from a posthumanist point of view, assessment still has to be mapped back onto the 'individual').

The Individual Lessons

The overall narrative of the class blog can be summarised in a few points:

- in order to find new (and less 'exceptionalist,' i.e. not based on the idea of human 'uniqueness') answers to the question "what does it mean to be human?" one has to start by problematizing traditional common sense notions of 'humanness.' One also has to historicize in order to see the constantly changing and thus essentially open nature of the category 'human';
- evolution and science fiction are 'discourses' engaged in specific practices of 'constructions of the future' out of which utopian and dystopian alternative scenarios to contemporary realities can arise;
- traditional definitional oppositions like human versus animal or human versus machine are increasingly being eroded by technology *at the same time* as new global threats and challenges are emerging like anthropogenic climate change, resource depletion, pollution and a dramatic decrease in biodiversity;
- all of this leads both to a '*de*-centring' of the human in relation to the environment and nonhuman others as well as a '*re*-centring' in terms of human responsibility;
- the main political challenge that the ideas of the 'posthuman' and 'postanthropocentrism' pose is: how to act self-reflectively or even self-effacingly *and* responsibly at once?

What does it mean to be human?

The aim of the first blog-based lesson was to get us thinking about and problematizing the question "what does it mean to be human?" We began by looking at Leonardo's Vitruvian man as an example of anthropocentrism and human perfection, followed by a discussion about which scientific disciplines, today, are actually involved in defining the human (e.g., biology, (paleo)anthropology, philosophy, theology etc.). This also served as the starting point for the first blogging task, namely an internet search for 'interesting' definitions of 'human.' The idea was to find examples that could serve to inform students' own attempt at defining what it means to be human. The task thus demanded information retrieval, analysis, as well as affective involvement and additionally had a 'persuasive' component" (i.e., Hello world! Look what I found and was able to come up with). Like most writing tasks in this unit, methodologically, the first blog post was a mixture between guided and 'free' (or creative) writing, or between an open and a closed writing task. The advantage of such an approach is that it is at once a continuation of standard textual analysis, as well as an invitation to self-reflectively thematise personal experience and aspects of self-determination. It also promotes experimenting with language, developing individual writing strategies and expanding active vocabulary.

Researching existing definitions of 'the human' fed into the writing task and was a pragmatic introduction to the affordance of editability that blog posting provides, and which turns blogging into an ongoing and uncompletable, always provisional writing process. The whole unit was designed in such a way that students would constantly be invited to revisit and rewrite their posts (WordPress also offers an 'unpublished draft' function which some students also used to good effect). Furthermore, the final writing task formally required the students to return to their initial definition and revise it in view of the content of the unit and the undergone learning experience. The individual class blog pages accordingly were only 'revealed' as we went along, i.e. at the beginning of the lesson to which they referred.

A particularly engaging example in this respect was the following (very slightly edited) post (let me repeat that my aim, at this stage, was not to correct language mistakes):

> LOVE, DREAMS, DECISIONS? – HUMANITY AND ITS BIGGEST QUESTION

Every toddler knows that it's a human being, but why isn't there anyone that can exactly tell us what it means to be HUMAN.

On my search for an answer to this difficult question I've found the, in my opinion, three most interesting definitions that are trying to explain the state of being a "human individual."

"What makes us human is not our mind but our heart, not our ability to think but our ability to love." (Henri Nouwen)

"Daring to dream what is deepest our collective longings is what makes us most human and fully alive." (Wendy Wright)

"It's the ability to choose which makes us human." (Madleine L'Engle)

So in a nutshell "human" mankind is able to love, dream and choose.

Emotions are the key to a human way of life, to be what we're supposed to: Loving, learning and deciding creatures that should care about each other. This approach is the reason for my personal statement to the biggest question of mankind:

In my opinion it's the ability to feel empathy with fellow man that makes us human.

Mankind wouldn't be capable of understanding needs and emotions if they couldn't develop the skill of empathizing with human beings and that's why they wouldn't associate with anyone else but themselves any longer. Without people caring about each other and without feeling responsible anymore, we wouldn't be better than animals that simply take care of their urges.

My commentary was:

Great definition! It's the ability to empathize that makes us human. Two questions: why do so many humans not empathize (with other humans or nonhumans)? And, do you think (nonhuman) animals don't feel empathy?

And the student got back by saying:

> Empathy is something you have to learn, it isn't an ability you're born with. So if your parents or your environment never thought you how important it is to empathize, you're not the one to blame.
>
> Actually, I do think that animals are able to feel empathy but they can't express it the way humans do.

There were other examples of this kind of exchange between teacher and student and between students themselves which clearly show students' level of affective involvement in their own research process and blog production. After comparing and discussing results in class, students were encouraged to post their definitions on the blog page of the Smithsonian National Museum of Natural History which invites responses by students from all over the world to the question "what does it mean to be human?"

How did we become human?

The second and third lesson were based on an audio-visual task in which a YouTube music video clip of Fat Boy Slim's "Right Here, Right Now" had to be placed within the (previously discussed) context of evolution and then within the wider context of a problematization of the distinction between human and animal. As a first visual stimulus students looked at the banner image of the blog which shows the (science-factual) 'continuation' of natural into artificial evolution (i.e., from ape to cyborg – a theme taken up again in the sixth and seventh lesson). In addition, there were also two preliminary reading tasks, one on the Smithsonian Museum's website, namely a timeline of hominization, and the other, a cartoon depicting a human who 'turns round' to his evolutionary predecessors and says "stop following me." Fat Boy Slim's video shows a mixture of science fiction and science fact and obviously only gives a rather sketchy but thoroughly entertaining account of human evolution, from a single cell organism in the ocean to an obese middle-aged man sitting on a bench in Manhattan. The writing task for the students was to watch the video clip at home as many times as necessary and come up with a description, analysis and interpretation of what they saw.

Again, let me quote an example:

> "Right Here, Right Now" is a song by the British musician Fatboy Slim, released on 19 April 1999 as the fourth single from his second studio album You've Come a Long Way, Baby. The song reached the 2nd placement on the UK Singles Chart for one week.
>
> The video shows us the process of evolution condensed in about three and a half minutes. This story is told by looking from the first living creatures to our species today – the Homo Sapiens. It ends with a fat man sitting down on a bench in a big city at night.
>
> From my perspective the "message" is that we just eat and have only few physical activity all the time and work too less – so it is kind of criticism concerning human acting of today. It should encourage ourselves to do more for *our* world and *our* prospective evolution – and not just living a lonely lazy life.
>
> 
>
> **Somewhere, something went terribly wrong**
>
> [Image: Graham Steel, 2009]

My commentary was this:

> I like the connection you make between the video and the image – something, somewhere went terribly wrong... So, are you saying we need to take care of our own further evolution? How does that work do you think?

There were other, more detailed, solutions but what in my view particularly stands out in this example is the maturity and elegance with which this (15-year-old) student completed a complex writing task (in a 'foreign' language) while making good use of the creative possibilities afforded by a blog post.

Nonhuman Others

A detailed analysis and extensive commentary on each individual task, the students' ideas and responses as well as my interaction would be beyond the scope of this contribution, so my focus will be on what I consider to be the essential steps within the class blog's narrative and how they were translated into student learning tasks. Lesson four probably contained the most difficult task (even though quite a few students said in their feedback that they found the first task, the definition of the human, most challenging). The online articles which the students were asked to skim read and comment on (one about the fact that humans are a lot less "unique" than they think (Hogenboom 2015) and the other, by Craig Stanford, containing a summary comment on his book *Planet Without Humans* (2014)), were quite daunting to some of them. This was due to the texts' length and complexity of argument, as well as the amount of new vocabulary they contained,. Nevertheless, the requirement actually was merely to find the central paragraph in either of these two articles, to explain what was going on and to comment briefly. Most students managed to come up with some well-structured and perceptive thoughts, like these, for example:

> NONHUMAN OTHERS – UNIQUE OR NOT?
> Humans always thought they were unique; the only creatures with emotions, morality and culture. But the more scientists investigate animals, the more they discover that this is not true, because all these traits are also found in animals. Charles Darwin wrote: "There is no fundamental difference between man and the higher mammals in their mental faculties and all the differences are of degree, not of kind."
>
> In the article the author lists some points that had been considered a uniquely human ability, but can be found in animals too:

- Chimpanzees use tools

- Chimpanzees show intricate social behaviours like morality (defined as showing fairness, altruism and empathy)
- They possess mind-reading skills (They can figure out what others are thinking and what their intentions are)
- Chimpanzees even have culture (defined as passing on knowledge, habits and transmission from one generation to the next)
- They use a complex system of communication with gestures and facial expressions

The main argument of the article is that the differences are not absolute, but rather a matter of degree, and by that measure humans are no more unique than any other animal.

In my opinion there are still differences enough to make us unique. Skills and behaviours might be similar, but can you imagine that chimpanzees investigate humans and write articles or books about us? Chimpanzees use a complex system of communication, but we use our language. We don't communicate only by seeing and speaking to each other, we can also communicate by written language like a letter, books or even whatsapp. We use technologies no other mammal was able to develop, because we are rational beings.

In general, students tended, ultimately, to preserve some form of human exceptionalism but they clearly also started revising their initial standpoints and thus potentially opened themselves up to the idea of a 'weak' form of 'postanthropocentrism' while acknowledging an enhanced human responsibility for planetary environmental issues.

Science Fiction

In lesson five, we further problematized the distinction between science fiction and science fact, as well as the one between human and machine. In addition, some more practical and critically creative new media skills were taught, in particular, the embedding of images into blog posts. I used the well-known video clip (again available on YouTube) of IBM's "Data Baby" to ask students to work out a definition of science fiction/science faction in the light of what they saw and to post it on the class blog. This was then discussed in class and used as preparation for the blogging task at home. The idea was for the students to find (or indeed make, mash up, etc.) their 'own'" picture of the future and to explain their choice. This critical-creative task engaged the students in their own 'construction of the future' and, in a sense, invited them to think practically about their implication in something like science *faction*. For the first time, they were also formally required to use the full spectrum of media convergence afforded by their individual blogs. Here, again, is one, in my view, particularly successful example:

> Image of the future
>
> I chose that picture, because I think in the future every electronic device will be connected with each other. They will communicate via the cloud and tell us what we should buy or drive us to our next appointment autonomic. I think this will make our everyday life easier, but it could also be dangerous because of the big concerns having all our data.

[Image: GDJ (2015) Cloud Network]

Are You a Cyborg?

The main objective for lessons six and seven was to get students to think about human ontology. Through a combination of a film clip and an online quiz designed by the British Film Institute they were supposed to consider the idea of a replicant. The clip and the quiz were used because they interacted in the following way: the clip from *Bladerunner* (on YouTube) shows Deckard (Harrison Ford) administering the so-called (and, of course, 'fictional') Voight-Kampff empathy test to find out whether Rachel (Sean Young) is a 'real' human or a replicant (i.e., an android). The BFI quiz then uses exactly the same questions that Deckard asked as a multiple choice test so that the students could test themselves. Quite a few students said in their feedback that this was the highlight (maybe also the turning point) of the unit for them. The quiz then fed into the next practical-creative but also analytical-critical task in which the students were asked to devise their own online quiz with questions that were designed to differentiate between humans and replicants. This was thus another 'learning-by-doing' exercise which contained the deliberate blurring of science fiction and science fact as a heuristic step towards understanding the problematic aspect of defining humans against nonhuman others. Students were directed to a free online (open source) and very easy to handle quiz-making software. The generated quiz was inserted into a blog post in the form of a link and thus made available to other students without anybody having to download or install any of the programmes.

Some sample questions the students devised were:

> Your mother and you had a big argument. You are super angry and go outside to calm down. Where do you go?
>
> 1) to the end of the world. I don't want to see my mother ever again
> 2) to my friends. I need to talk
> 3) to my worst enemy. I need somebody to beat
> 4) I'm super angry, so I kick against street lights and start crying
>
> [The "correct" choice set by the student who devised the quiz was number 4]

You're driving down the street in your huge SUV. Suddenly a deer appears on the road. What are you going to do?

1) I hit the brakes as hard as I can and drive around it!
2) I try to bypass it, that's the best I can do.
3) I stop the car as fast as I can and get out to escort the deer back into the forest.
4) It's just a deer, who cares? I certainly don't!
   [Here the answer that would come up as correct was 3]

Saving the planet? Unlearning to be human?

The topic of the ninth and last lesson was conceptually probably the most demanding but of course also the most important one, since it contained the concluding *ecological* message the previous lessons, by challenging the distinctions or binary oppositions human/animal, human /technology, human/non-human (including the 'environment'), had been building up to. It was also the point at which the notion of the 'Anthropocene' was discussed and illustrated by two video clips (one, purely 'informative' and documentary, available through the *Smithsonian Magazine* site, and the other, 'docufictional' or 'science factionial,' taken from *Life After People*). These provided visualisations of postanthropocentric scenarios that were supposed to lead students towards a revaluation of their initial ideas about and definitions of the human in the light of (science fictional and science factual) constructions of the future.

One such summary expressed the critical role of SF in this process as follows:

> What constructive role plays science fiction if we think about the question what makes us human again?
>
> So what makes us human now?

> My first definition was
>
> Humans are humans because they want to know everything. They will never be pleased if they are not understanding essential questions and one of them/us will always continue asking WHY? or HOW?
>
> And after writing all these blogposts and thinking about what makes us human so much
> In my opinion one of the points that makes us human is that we know that we are polluting and destroying our own world. Some of the Science Fiction movies show that we know that we're compromising the life of many species and even our own, with our way of life. In the movies we can also see the dystopian future and her aftermaths, which threats us. We are able to see clearly what we're doing to our planet and we get warned enough to understand this almost every day and also through Science Fiction. Nevertheless the most of us don't want to see it, and that's why we ignore this fact.
>
> So this is what makes us human, our naivety.

Although this post obviously still hangs on to some form of human exceptionalism it does so in a rather minimalist and possibly even ironic way (in the sense of: humans are exceptionally 'naïve'). In my view, this may serve as a good basis for further discussion about "what makes us human" and what responsibilities this might imply.

Conclusion

Teaching, learning and schools of the future will have to come to terms with new media and their affordances, with all their advantages and disadvantages, and, most of all, with their potential to change realities and futures. Behind the spectre of 'digitalization' lie a variety of fears and desires that often have little to do with everyday experience of educational practice. Unfortunately, these still tend to have a (usually negative) influence. This blog-based 'interdisciplinary' teaching unit, in my view, has provided a small contribution to the shift towards a more practice-oriented and creative-critical approach in foreign language teaching. Of course, even though blogs are no radical innovation by any account anymore, they are still being used quite sparingly and often only in a supportive, instrumentalized function in secondary schools. However, taking blogs seriously as a genre and starting to engage with the multimodal potential of digital media convergence – just like most teenagers are already doing in their everyday life media consumption on their mobile multimedia devices (i.e., their smart phones) – will revive some of the original dynamic of the internet, namely the potential access to the entirety of human (and non-human) knowledge including its global and immediate communicability. As Will Richardson notes:

> Depending on the focus, Weblogs in the classroom have the potential to affect student learning in many positive ways. Blogging can teach critical reading and writing skills, and it can lead to greater information management skills. It can help students become much more media and information literate by clarifying the choices they make about the content they write about, it can teach them about how networks function – both human and computer – and it can teach the essential skill of collaboration. (Richardson 2010, 37)

In addition, the unit presented here has in my view led to a new (self-) understanding at least in some of the students. The fact that this change happened through the 'medium' of English as a foreign language plays an additional, intensifying, namely affective role. Nothing is more enlightening – and this of course goes beyond a merely 'intercultural' perspective – than to become part of a new knowledge community where there are no longer any 'mother tongues' or 'foreign languages,' but maybe only a truly global *lingua franca* (if such a thing exists) that serves to tackle global, 'humanitarian' (i.e., including human and nonhuman actors) and planetary challenges. For this reason, the next, essential, step in the continuation of this experiment would be to open up the blogs to the 'outside' world and encourage students to take advantage of and engage with, precisely, a *planetary* audience. However, this will inevitably turn the *controlled* experiment presented here into an uncontrollable one – which would go beyond the still predominantly humanistic, analogue and anthropocentric default position in most (secondary) education. Language is of course not just any medium, but it too has to adapt to the new communicative conditions like, for example, the fact that in the age of posthumanism and postanthropocentrism communication increasingly takes place not between humans, but between smart media environments, animals and objects, all based on "distributed cognition" (cf. Hayles 2005; and Hayles 1999). As a small contribution to the (re)mediation processes that arise out of this emerging new world picture this teaching unit has without any doubt opened up discussions in this particular class that will, hopefully, lead to a further critical engagement with the ongoing construction of futures, some of which undoubtedly postanthropocentric and posthumanist.

Works Cited

"Are You a Cyborg?" *Quotev.* Web. 21 January 2018. <https://www.quotev.com/quiz/711962/Are-you-a-cyborg>.

"Are You a Replicant?" *BFI.* Web. 21 January 2018. <http://www.bfi.org.uk/are-you-a-replicant/>.

Barthes, Roland (2000) [1957]. *Mythologies*. London: Vintage.

BBC. "Do You Know Your Science Fiction from Your Science Fact?" Web. 21 January 2018. <http://www.bbc.co.uk/guides/zs2sqty>.

Bladerunner. "Voight-Kampff-Test." *YouTube.* Web. 21 January 2018. <https://www.youtube.com/watch?v=g-DkoGvcEBw>.

Burgess, Jean, and Joshua Green (2009). *YouTube: Online Video and Participatory Culture*. Cambridge: Polity Press.

Dean, Jodi (2010). *Blog Theory: Feedback and Capture in the Circuits of Drive*. Cambridge: Polity Press.

Ebersbach, Anja, Markus Glaser, and Richard Heigl (2016). *Social Web*. Konstanz und München: UVK Verlagsgesellschaft/Lucius.

Eide, Brock, and Fernette Eide (2012). *Eide Neurolearning Blog*. 24 September. Web. 21 January 2018. <http://eideneurolearningblog.blogspot.de/>.

Fat Boy Slim. "Right Here, Right Now." *YouTube.* Web. 21 January 2018. <https://www.youtube.com/watch?v=ub747pprmJ8>.

Flach, Tim. "*Monkey Eyes.* More than Human." Web. 21 January 2018. <http://timflach.com/work/more-than-human/slideshow/#33>.

Grusin, Richard (ed.) (2016). *The Nonhuman Turn*. Minneapolis, MN: University of Minnesota Press.

Hayles, N. Katherine (1999). *How We Became Posthuman: Virtual Bodies in Cybernetics, Literature, and Informatics*. Chicago: University of Chicago Press.

--- (2005). *My Mother Was a Computer: Digital Subjects and Literary Texts*. Chicago: University of Chicago Press.

Hayton, Tom. "Using Social Media in the Classroom." *BBC* and *British Council Teaching English*. Web. 21 January 2018. <https://www.teachingenglish.org.uk/article/using-social-media-classroom>.

Herbrechter, Stefan (2009). *Posthumanismus – Eine kritische Einführung*. Darmstadt: WBG.

--- (2013). *Posthumanism: A Critical Analysis*. London: Bloomsbury.

--- (2014). "Posthumanistische Bildung?" *Jahrbuch für Pädagogik*, 267-82.

--- (2018). "Posthumanist Education." *International Handbook of Philosophy of Education*. Ed. Paul Smeyers. Heidelberg: Springer, 727-45.

Hogenboom, Melissa (2015). "Humans Are Nowhere Near as Special as We'd Like to Think." *BBC – The Big Questions / Human*. 3. July. Web. 21 January 2018. <.http://www.bbc.com/earth/story/20150706-humans-are-not-unique-or special>.

IBM Data Baby. *YouTube*. Web 21. January 2018. <https://www.youtube.com/watch?v=7IFtSJ28cJE>

Jenkins, Henry (2006). *Convergence Culture*. New York: Routledge.

Life After People. Part 1. History Channel Special A & E Networks 2008. Web. 21 January 2018. <https://www.youtube.com/watch?v=ahiaSm_kGNc>.

Richardson, Will (2010). *Wikis, Blogs, Podcasts and Other Powerful Web-tools for Classrooms*. Thousand Oaks, CA: Corwin/Sage.

Smithsonian National Museum of Natural History. "Human Evolution Timeline Interactive." Web. 21 January 2018. <http://humanorigins.si.edu/evidence/ human-evolution-timeline-interactive>.

---. "Submit Your Response to 'What Does It Mean To Be Human?'" Web. 21 January 2018. <http://humanorigins.si.edu/about/become-involved/submit-your-response-what-does-it-mean-be-human>.

---. "Human Characteristics: What Does It Mean To Be Human." 3 July 2015. Web. 21 January 2018. <http://humanorigins.si.edu/human-characteristics>.

Stanford, Craig (2014) "Planet Without Apes?" *Huffington Post*, 3 January. Web. 21 January 2018. <https://www.huffingtonpost.com/craig-stanford/planet-without-apes_b_1933073.html>.

Voigts-Virchow, Eckart (2011). "Teaching Web 2.0 and Cultural Studies: The Critical Media Literacy Approach to and with Social Media (Facebook, Wikipedia, YouTube *et al.*)." *Teaching Cultural Studies: Methods, Matters, Models*. Ed. Gabriele Linke. Heidelberg: Winter, 61-81.

War for the Planet of the Apes (Trailer). *YouTube*. Web. 21 January 2018. <https://www.youtube.com/watch?v=qxjPjPzQ1iU>.

"Welcome to the Anthropocene." *Anthropocene.info*. Web. 21 January 2018. <http://www.anthropocene.info/index.php>.

"What Makes Us Human?" *Edublogs.* Web. 21 January 2018. <https://whatmakesushuman.edublogs.org>.

Williams, Raymond (2013) [1961]. "The Analysis of Culture." *Cultural Theory and Popular Culture*. Ed. John Storey. New York: Routledge, 32-40.

Images

GDJ (2015) "Cloud Network." Web. 1 March 2019. <https://openclipart.org/detail/221722/cloud-network >.

Steel, Graham (2009). "Somewhere, Something Went Terribly Wrong." Web. 1 March 2019. <https://www.flickr.com/photos/24236351@N04/2299799840/in/ photolist-4ve5no-7T8TCv-p2yn1p-da6BdT-bnDYGK-21g8DAE-V2ZBph-dPv5a>. (creative commons licence – image not altered).

Christian Schmitt-Kilb
Roman Bartosch

From a Dog's Eye View? Anthropomorphism and Anamorphosis in Eva Hornung's *Dog Boy* (2009) and John Berger's *King: A Street Story* (1999)

Dog Boy

In her brilliant, reality-saturated and astonishingly understudied[1] novel *Dog Boy* (2009), Australian novelist Eva Hornung tells the story of four-year-old Romochka who grows up with his mother and his alcoholic uncle in a run-down district of post-Soviet Moscow as the most vulnerable member of a dysfunctional family. One morning he wakes up abandoned and alone. Everybody has disappeared; not only his mother and his uncle, but the whole apartment block seems to be deserted. Instinctively (rather than desperately, the narration suggests), he walks out onto the street, joins a pack of feral dogs and follows them to their lair. This marks the beginning of a fascinating tale about an interspecies collaboration, about their life together, about affection and adaptation, fear and belonging, rules, hierarchy and power, and, ever-present, the struggle for survival: survival of winters of up to -30°C, of periods of hunger, attacks of rival dogs, and ill-willing humans. If there is warmth to be found in the world for the young protagonist, both literally and symbolically, the dogs rather than Romochka's fellow humans provide it.

The present chapter will investigate fictional engagements with human-animal relationships with a focus on two contemporary novels, Hornung's *Dogboy* and John Berger's *King: A Street* Story (1999). Both texts offer fundamentally different versions of interspecies encounters; but great as the narratological and thematic divide may be, the overlap of the (human) animals' shared physicality, worldhoods, and knowledges provides the basis for an approach that reveals how both make productive use of the fictional means of creating ambiguity through anthropomorphism and through what will be described as moments of anamorphic uncertainty.

This, we argue, is one of the potentials of fiction that literature pedagogies can draw upon in their endeavour to develop a teaching practice that aligns with the posthumanist objective of challenging human exceptionalism. Even though the boy in Hornung's novel is the story's focalizer, it is the life of the pack, and the pack's point of view, which calibrate the reader's sense of empathy and identification. This is no contradiction in a story in which Romochka soon becomes a part of the pack, at times undistinguishable in his urges, wishes and needs from the dogs. We seek to make sense of the novels's convincing blurring of the dividing line between what is human and what is animal or canine and thus constantly questions the nature of humanity or 'normal human behaviour' in light of the pedagogic objectives outlined above. As Romochka approaches the state of 'dogginess' both psychologically and materially, the particular focus which Hornung has created provides a "scenography" (Latour 2005) for him and the dogs, for him as dog, and for the dogs' environment, actions, plans and experiences that we understand as one avenue for imaging a posthuman(ist) teaching scenario.

In the larger framework of his new materialist project, scenographies are a vital element of a "return to the realist attitude" (Latour 2004, 232). They emerge as a result of radical historicizations and contextualizations of everything, every *thing* – human or non-human, living organism or pure matter. Scenographies transform 'matters of fact' ("indisputable, obstinate, simply there") into 'matters of concern' ("disputable…they move, they carry you away"; Latour 2005, Seitenzahlen?), and they are therefore the groundwork for finding new and adequate means of representation for the relationship of the human and non-human world. *Dogboy*'s scenographic mode preempts reductive anthropomorphisms as well as facile allegorization or an impression of incomprehensible difference. Romochka has "crossed a border that is, usually, impassable – not even imaginable" (Hornung 2009, 15). As a result, he acquires a form of human-animal "bicultural fluency" (Garrard 2014, 254) which recognizes – following Garrard's term – the cultural dimension of animal life and opens up a whole new dimension of co-evolutionary experience to him and to the reader.

Donna Haraway describes dogs as "partners in the crime of human evolution" who have been with us "in the garden from the get-go" (Haraway 2003, 5); it is one of literature's many capacities to provide an imaginary concretization of this scenario by decentering the human perspective and unsettling the sense of human self-sufficiency. Hornung's novel achieves just that. She looks at the life of a boy and of dogs, lets dogs and boy look at each other and the boy at himself through the dogs, from a perspective which is neither a dog's eye view, nor a child's perspective, nor a neutral third person's. Ultimately, what emerges from the iridescent, oscillating discourse of the novel is a voice which embodies the acknowledgement that the binary of human and animal is pointless because *homo* is "a constitutively 'anthropomorphous' animal […] who must recognize himself in a non-man in order to be human" (Agamben 2004, 27; see Garrard 2014, 243).

In his review of *Dog Boy* in *The Guardian*, novelist, poet, and essayist John Burnside (2010) praises Hornung's successful attempt at representing the life of Romochka and the dogs which, in comparison with books written from a dog's eye view,

> is a far more difficult challenge. For where a novel with a canine narrator can call upon almost bottomless reserves of wistful charm, light irony and easy humour to carry it along, one whose central character is an abused and neglected child cannot. (Burnside 2010, n.p.)

Ten years before Hornung's *Dog Boy*, John Berger published *King: A Street Story*, a novel which shares with Hornung's the focus on the socially marginalized, homeless, poor, and the central issue of the companionship of human(s) and dog(s). But while in *Dog Boy*, one boy and several dogs live together and the story emerges as a result of their looking at each other, mutually recognizing their common fate and taking action accordingly, *King* reverses the scenario as we follow one dog and several humans through the day. Even though King the dog is the story's first-person narrator, Berger does not exploit this narrative situation in the sense that Burnside claims dog's eye view narratives often do. The brutality of the environment and the hopeless situation of the characters would render any comic relief gained from this peculiar narrative situation cynical.[2] This is why lending a voice to a dog serves a different purpose in the novel, a purpose which needs to be investigated in order to understand Berger's canine poetics. This poetics, explored in

King as well as in Berger's influential essay, "Why Look at Animals" (1977), we argue, can map new educational ground for posthuman(ist) teaching practices. It helps understand forms of interspecies relations that are more than humanistic appropriation but destabilize the clear-cut line between humans and other animals.

"Why Look at Animals?"

Twenty-two years before the publication of *King*, in 1977, Berger wrote a piece which, for our purposes, serves as a theoretical and conceptual framework for his narrative strategy in *King*. The seminal essay, "Why Look at Animals?", anticipates Agamben's idea of man as the "constitutively 'anthropomorphous' animal": "With their parallel lives", Berger claims, "animals offer man a companionship which is different from any offered by human exchange [...] because it is a companionship offered to the loneliness of man as a species" (6). Berger traces the human-animal relationship throughout history from a companionship which was "felt to be so equal that often one finds the conviction that it was man who lacked the capacity to speak with animals" (6) to the gradual disappearance of animals as companion species. In this account, the Cartesian reduction of animals to machine-like existences marks a philosophical and theoretical watershed by internalising, "*within man*, the dualism implicit in the human relation to animals" (11; original emphasis). This made possible a second, more material, watershed: the usage of animals as machines in the early stages of the industrial revolution and their treatment as raw material and commodity until today.

On this basis, Berger argues that due to the cultural and physical marginalization of animals, we can no longer recognize our sameness and difference in an exchange of meaningful gazes. Nowadays, "animals are always the observed" (16): human practices and expertise in observation have led to an ever-increasing objectified scientific knowledge which is an index of our power over animals. But we have paid a high price for the perfection of our faculties to observe, scientifically describe, exploit and commodify animals. The downside of this is the un-learning that animals can and do observe us. They do so still, but we have deprived ourselves of the faculty to "read" their gaze and create an image of ourselves as simultaneously same and different. In other words: "The more we know, the further away they are" (16); and the further away they are, the more difficult it gets for us to address fully the question of what makes us human because without the animal other, it is structurally impossible to think about and imagine ourselves as a species. The result of this broken mirror is our loneliness as a species.

"[S]eitdem wir von dem Baum der Erkenntnis gegessen haben", Mr. C. famously points out in Heinrich von Kleist's *Über das Marionettentheater* (1810), "[ist] das Paradies verriegelt [...] wir müssen die Reise um die Welt machen und sehen, ob es vielleicht von hinten irgendwo wieder offen ist."[3] While, from a critical vantage point, the question as to how to get back into the prelapsarian garden testifies to a naive essentialist nostalgia, it remains critically challenging to investigate how any search for the motives for this journey, or for the means of achieving whichever form of interspecies communion, is thinkable without animals in general and our companion species, the dogs, in particular. Over centuries, the dominant textual trope for bridging the "narrow abyss of non-comprehension" (Berger 1977, 5) were various forms of anthropomorphism. Against the backdrop of the assumption that "what distinguished men from animals was born of their relationship with them" (9), Berger claims that anthropomorphism was, until the nineteenth century, "integral to the relation between man and animal" as "an expression of their proximity" and "the residue of the continuous use of animal metaphor" (11). But the gradual disappearance of animals, the phenomenon of living without them has created a situation of solitude in which "anthropomorphism makes us doubly uneasy" (11).

There are many different forms and degrees of textual anthropomorphism. One strong form, which is often considered naïve, insufficiently sophisticated and therefore relegated to the field of children's stories, consists in giving a voice to animals or other non-human creatures. For some scholars in Critical Animal Studies and elsewhere, though, this narrative strategy counts as potentially valuable and productive because it "disrupts an anthropocentric point of view and breaks with the illusion of a seemingly closed human horizon" (Clark 2011, 197). John Simons claims that the shift of focalization towards a non-human transforms "not only characters [...] but also the very world of the text" because it "offers a transgressive route [...] across species boundaries [and] also between the closed formal universe of the linguistic artefact and into the material world in which it exists" (Simons in Clark 2001, 197). This route may be offering some form of prelapsarian "return into the garden." But it is also an instance of what Jacques Derrida describes as reappropriative "melancholy" that sets in once we assign to an animal "the words it has no need of" (2008, 18). What about literature's potential to decentre the human, to remain open to the incommensurable alterity which needs to be met "on its own terms, not in ours," and thus to approach the recognition of the mystery of the animate Other" (Laycock 1999, 281)? We see educational value in approaches that thrive on this paradox and suggest that literature be taken to explore "a thinking, however fabulous and chimerical it might be, that thinks the absence [...] of the word otherwise, and as something other than a privation" (Derrida 2008, 48).

King. A Street Story

In the novel *King. A Street Story*, Berger confronts the double uneasiness with anthropomorphism he diagnosed in "Why Look at Animals?" on fictional terrain. The novel was originally published without the author's name on front, spine, back or title page in order to prevent its publication from becoming first and foremost a literary event.[4] *King* the novel, and thus the street dog King, tell the story of one tragic day in the lives of the central canine character and the two central human characters, Vico and Vica. Together with a group of other outcasts who have not managed to save for themselves a place in the neoliberal race for a dignified life, they live in a no-place near the "M. 1000" called Saint Valéry in an encampment of self-made shacks – "a zone where people never stop unless obliged [...] because it has been forgotten" (*King*, 5). Appropriate for a text which negotiates liminality on many levels, the story is set in the Edgelands, "empty, yet [...] large" (5).[5] The shacks and huts, sordid as they are, nevertheless constitute a home for their inhabitants. But this home is going to be razed down and their inhabitants attacked with tear gas and driven away at the end of the narrative, assumedly in order to make space for "building a stadium, the biggest ever" (6). In this situation, King is chorus,[6] chronicler and protagonist at the same time. In the meantime, the reader follows the daily activities of King (guarding the huts, fighting off strangers, playing ball with a boy, having "conversations" with Vico and Vica) as well as Vico and Vica who "steal" water (35), try to sell vegetables which they have grown on "stolen" soil (7), drink beer, sleep, and tell each other stories. Everything, even the less terrifying events, happens against the backdrop of deep-felt despair and a hopelessness which has its origins in homelessness and "begins when you cannot imagine anything ever being dry again" (32); it does not yet end when King, after the destruction of Saint Valéry and the dispersal of its inhabitants, finds himself alone with "no arms to lie in" (189).

The structure of feeling (Raymond Williams) which emerges from this novel is familiar to readers of Berger from *Lilac and Flag*, the third volume of his *Into Their Labours*-trilogy, in which the two eponymous protagonists try and tragically fail to make a living in the city of Troy. This structure is based upon what we would like to call Berger's allegorical realism which, to use György Lukács' terms, measures the subjective experiences of individuals against the "living contradictions of life and society" and thus "transcends the limits of immediacy" (Lukács 2007, 33). Berger creates types by inventing individuals, situations and settings which are clearly marked as non-realist and allegorical (the compound global *übercity* of Troy in *Lilac and Flag*, the archetypal motorway M. 1000 with "traffic day and night, nonstop" (5), the unlikelihood of symbolic names, the proximity, in St. Valéry, of Berlin's Treptower Park, the Paris Métro and other European sites, etc.). But he does so in order to reveal "the real factors that relate [characters'] experiences to the hidden social forces that produce them" (Lukács 2007, 33).

King takes de-familiarization and estrangement promoted by these non-realist features a step further by positing a dog as a narrator partaking of and oscillating between both human and animal worlds, but still, realism remains the mode in which the text demands to be read. The rough and merciless environment in which the story takes place is the accompanying nightmare to the consumerist dream in which the ideology of neoliberal capitalism is taken for granted to such an almost religious extent that it is "heresy […] to have no money" (6). In this bleak account, globalisation manifests only in the serial number "ART. NO. 353455B c/NO. 1-700 INHOUD 2 STUKS" (32), imprinted on packaging material which Vico and Vica use as a cardboard ceiling.

Although the point of view is a dog's, there is never a danger that the harshness of the environment is symbolically softened in its devastating effects. Yet what is shown – in a similar move as in Hornung's *Dog Boy* – is that an imaginative renewal of an interspecies companionship between humans and dogs needs the common ground of 'social' status and the experience of 'ferality' – be they those of the street dog or of the homeless human.

This is demonstrated right from the start. "I am mad to try. […] I am mad to try to lead you to where we live." (5) – this is how the novel begins. Georg Zipp reads this opening as an acknowledgement of the impossibility to capture the totality of the world which "Berger's homeless characters live in" (Zipp 2014, 171), and he continues to discuss in detail whether the novel is narrated from a human or a canine point of view, as well as the consequences these respective points of view have for an interpretation of the text. In the context of our approach to the teaching of the novel, it is this impossibility to define clear boundaries that provides educational potential. And it is the 'madness' involved in trying to decipher it that refers to the tripartite perspective introduced by Berger which consists of

a) an inversion of the gaze: Berger presents the story through King and thus turns human beings into objects of observation. King constantly observes his fellow creatures and describes their physical features with his own imagery: Danny has "the pointed face of a fell hound", Liberto "drew himself up as only a short Spaniel can" (12). King reads their behaviour ("I fix my eyes at the two of them sitting on their cardboard… They are sitting close together, casually, unthinkingly, as only the intimate can do," 109) and notices minute alterations in appearance and draws his own conclusions from them ("I watch the ankles of the passersby. […] The sides of all the shoes are a little nearer to the ankle than this morning. […] Everybody is taller when going to work, shorter when going home," 117). Also, King knows about fundamental differences between animals and humans: "The hatred which the strong feel for the weak as soon as the weak get too close is particularly human; it doesn't happen with animals." (22);

b) a suggestion of another form of de-centring, namely that King might indeed be a human being feigning madness because of his devastating situation: "Everyone at Saint Valéry needs a madness to find their balance after the wreck. It's like walking with a stick. Madness is a third leg. Me, for instance, I believe I'm a dog. Here nobody knows the truth." (108)

c) a metamorphosis of the whole group of homeless people into a pack of dogs when they finally have to run for their lives from Saint Valéry, from the Liebherr caterpillars and the FAMAS submachine guns:

> They were barking as they lay there and I listened to the names of their barks: Danny the terrier, Joachim, Saul, Malak, Anna, Alfonso, Liberto the spitz. […] [T]hey had nothing, like I had nothing. We were the same, and we were all barking. (186)

It is impossible to take a final stance on the "species identity" of the narrator, and we believe that this invites relevant readerly investment in textual meaning and ambiguity: "Readers can take their choice. […] Maybe it's a dog […] Maybe it's a person who calls himself a dog, because almost everybody in that group of homeless people change their names. […] [T]hey are no longer the same people that they once were, they have been transformed by this terrible trauma and these hardships" (Koval in Zipp, 177). 'Theriomorphic appropriation' – the ascription of animal traits especially to minority groups and othered humans – is not without grave dangers and needs careful pedagogic attention, of course. And yet, in combining this fictional becoming-pack of King and the (other?) humans in the face of a life-threatening calamity *and* an authorial comment on the transformation brought about by the trauma and hardships of homelessness in a neoliberal environment, the problem of narrative perspective in *King* offers rewarding avenues for thinking animality otherwise. It is ultimately impossible to decide what the status of the animal is, but in the face of the common history, experience and suffering of both species shown in the story it is no longer important to decide:

> Everybody here will tell you the same thing. Suddenly there is no in and out, and you have to survive the next hour alone, and the next and the next and the next. Nobody sees it coming when it comes. For each of us it came differently. And for all of us it happened when we weren't looking. (21)

"The same thing" which "came differently" for each of us: The task to grasp and narrate the nature of this experience must be taken up by a creature who knows "the road between things" (100). King can say "us" and mean a group of beings, an interspecies companionship, united by shared experiences of suffering and social degradation which turn them into "three more plague victims" (115). Empathy, identification and mutual respect grow out of a common knowledge which, in fundamental respects, does not need translation. The momentary powerful, symbolized by passersby and "a man with a telephone in his hand" behave arrogantly and detached but they do so with a deep-seated and ubiquitous "fear of infection" because the non-afflicted are always only the not yet afflicted. "Deep down everybody knows that nobody is telling the truth about this plague. Nobody knows whom it selects and how. […] When the Plague struck Naples in 1656, […] seven out of every ten people died" (ibid).

The "man with a telephone"'s reaction to the sight of three quarrelling creatures is a de-humanizing gaze and an equally de-humanizing muttering: "Flush them out […] they should be hosed off the street" (115). On the one hand, the gaze constructs the group as one which belongs together – King's "us" ("The sight we offer, the three of us.", 115) – and the man's "them" represent a vision on the same group from two opposite poles of a disjointed society. Both promote the construction of the group of dog and humans which then appears as being fundamentally of one kind. On the other hand, this particular construction of the group also reveals the contingency of the opposition.

What does this mean concretely? "Nobody sees it coming when it comes. […] For all of us it happened when we weren't looking" (21): read in context of these statements uttered at the beginning to describe the erratic transition from accepted and seen member of society to its unrecognized, invisible downside, the man with the phone appears in a different light. As long as he is able to direct his anxious and angry gaze at King and his companions, he holds at bay the threat of becoming what he looks at and keeps under control the "fear of infection." The more verbally aggressively he behaves, the greater the imaginary distance between himself and King, Vico and Vica, because "a lack of confidence diminishes immunity" (115). Therefore, subsuming dog and humans in one category is a verbal strategy of enhancing a distance which is felt to be precarious. The apparently clear-cut binary logic of 'us' and 'them' is questioned as it is undermined from both ends: from Vico and Vica's point of view, 'them' signifies a group to which they once belonged themselves, while for the man with the phone, 'them' signifies a group to which he will potentially belong in the future. "What two different people have in common," Berger said in one of his last interviews in 2016, "will always, in all cases, be larger than what differentiates them. And yet for dozens of different reasons, circumstances blind people to that" (Kellaway 2016, n.p.). In the light of "Why Look at Animals?" and *King*, he might have expanded his claim to include different species. The circumstances that blind animals, human or not, to see what they have in common are precisely depicted in *King*, and if there is hope to be gained from the encounter discussed above, or from the novel as a whole, it is to be found on this common ground which, for the time being, only exists as a photographic negative.

The identification and the separation of the imaginary social groups to which people and dog belong is not the only instance in the novel where the reader is called upon to constantly shift perspective in the process of reading. The anthropomorphic change of perspective and the ensuing undecidability concerning the novel's narrative situation is another such instance. It produces several effects which are important for the reception of the text: as human readers, we are 'with' the human characters in the novel in so far as we may be inclined to empathize with our own kind. At the same time, we are prone to sympathize with and feel proximity towards the voice of the narrator, a result of the conventional regulation of empathy as it happens in narratives of all kind. To complicate things further, the human world described by King is one that is as alien to the average reader of novels as the world of King himself, even though his voice is full of wisdom and insight and thus posits him in an almost extra-diegetic position vice versa the human (or canine) individuals of whom he tells.

These narratological features and the readerly activity they demand plus the thematic volatility concerning social class and identity described above transform the experience of reading the text into the experience of looking at a more-dimensional *Kippfigur* in which the reader has to constantly negotiate position, self-understanding and the basis for value judgments. Our understanding of the term *Kippfigur* takes its cue from Ludwig Wittgenstein's reflections upon the ambiguous rabbit-duck image on which he elaborates in *Philosophische*

Untersuchungen.[7] It is an image which, depending on what one sees, appears as a rabbit or as a duck, but never at one and the same time as both. Important in this context is Wittgenstein's notion not only of the switch between rabbit and duck, but of the earlier switch between an initial *seeing* of either rabbit or duck without yet knowing about the alternative meaning of the figure, and *seeing as*, which makes sense only once the two versions have been seen. Only then is it possible and meaningful to speak about a change of aspect ("Aspektwechsel," 1028) which reveals a paradox: it is the solution to a picture puzzle ("Vexierbild," 1028) in which we now detect a *non-simultaneous co-presence* of figures. The object has not changed and yet the image appears categorically different once both aspects have been revealed to the observer – "as if the object had changed in front of my eyes" (1028). Wittgenstein concludes: "The expression of change of aspect is the expression of a *new* perception, together with the expression of an unchanged perception" (1028; original emphasis).

In "Das Kippen der Figuren," Thomas Fries has underlined the potential of this paradox to irritate and to disturb (2012, 27), an irritation which originates in the suspicion that all of our perceptions may take place in a realm prior to an initial switch, and that we may therefore unknowingly be stuck in an environment of which we perceive only one of several aspects while mistaking this aspect for the totality of being. Novels such as *King* and *Dog Boy*, read as literary instances of the *Kippfigur*, make productive usage of this disturbance in order to delineate a field of experience which is common to dogs and humans. The irritation consists of a perspectival switching which is not at all comparable with multi-perspectivity because in this case, two perspectives, human and dog, 'happen' while the narrative discourse does not change. The switch takes place in the reader's imagination, and once it has taken place, it cannot be stopped. De-familiarization and familiarization are aspects which are realized in that paradoxical mode of non-simultaneous co-presence – we both are and are not of one kind with the canine (*King*) or human (*Dog Boy*) bearer of the narrative voice, and we both are and are not one with the human characters (*King*) and the pack (*Dog Boy*). In *King*, this issue loses its classificatory importance when ultimately, there is only one cross-species voice to be heard: the voice of the outcast who is considered as waste which needs to be "flush[ed] out" (115). On the grounds of a common fate and a common potential to suffer, the text demands and produces a multi-dimensional openness to alterity and creaturely sameness (see Herman 2016; Ohrem and Bartosch 2017). The loneliness of King is the transcendental loneliness of the creature, but also prerequisite for posthuman(ist) understanding.

We suggest using the term 'anamorphosis' for making sense of this ambivalence that complexifies the role and meaning of human-animal stories. As a "type of picture that requires the beholder to view it from an oblique angle, rather than head on," anamorphism affords that "pleasure and surprise result when a confused, perplexing image [...] suddenly assumes a proper form before one's eyes as one discovers the correct angle from which to view it" (Shickman 1977, 67). From our posthumanist angle, then, readers of literary fictions such as the ones discussed here are constantly required to negotiate their perspectives and to experience how anthropomorphic narratives constantly puzzle and complicate interpretive closure.

Understood in this sense, both *Dog Boy* and *King* demand and promote anamorphic readings. In conjunction with what has been termed 'theriomorphic appropriation' above, both novels make a strong case for the necessity to look at posthumanist concepts through the prism of class or intersectionality, and at social concerns with an awareness of questions and problems raised by posthumanist thought. The reader's identification with dog boy Romochka's perspective necessarily literally tips into identification with the pack of dogs and back until both blend into each other; King's status as a speaking dog (or is he?) and fellow sufferer in a group of social outcasts equally blurs the line between human and animal experiences. In both cases, anamorphosis produces a perspectival dynamics which includes the reader who, in the course of reading the novels, almost instinctively begins to identify with the struggling, neglected and mistreated creature – be it human or animal.

Affordances of Anthropomorphism

In recent years, numerous works in human-animal studies have engaged with the notion of the creaturely to describe the forms of relationality our readings have analysed, too (Santner 2006; Vermeulen and Richter

2015; Herman 2016; Ohrem and Bartosch 2017). One of the conceptual and discursive means of narratively establishing such relationalities is anthropomorphism. Notoriously, anthropomorphism is understood as either a simple category mistake, or as one possible means of negotiating possible points of access to non-anthropocentric forms of thought (Crist 1999). As one of us has argued elsewhere, for literary studies and pedagogies, it is not at all necessary to take sides; rather, the question whether anthropomorphic representation and language are helpful, adequate, and apposite depends on the stories woven around it. This suggests we understand anthropomorphism "not as a correct or flawed idea but as a stance and perspective that unfolds in the narrative sequence of a story" (Bartosch 2017, 156). In the educational contexts at the heart of this volume, we could therefore speak of 'affordances' of anthropomorphism, which we have described as anamorphic. The pedagogic objective of reading human-animal stories in class is not to find out whether the tale is overly anthropomorphic, or whether anthropomorphism is a good or a bad thing. It rather lies in cultivating a productive sense of ambivalence and (de)familiarization, and in engendering a more inclusive tolerance of ambiguity.

This could mobilize the helpful but sometimes rather static typologies of anthropomorphism, developed by Sasha Matthewman and Greg Garrard, respectively. While Garrard distinguishes four types of anthropo- and theoriomorphism, depending on their being 'critical' rather than 'crude' (2011, 152-69), Matthewman suggests no less than seven categories, from "theriomorphic representation" to "scientific description," all of which can help analyze forms of discursively construing animal alterities or identities for the benefit of classroom work (2011, 64-65). While conceptual clarity and such typologies do have their unquestionable merit, instead of one-on-one correspondences between texts and typology, a posthumanist education might do well in getting to terms with the ambivalence of anamorphism: What happens in the course of the narrative, who sees what in which way? And what happens if we shift our own epistemological grounds – can we see (animal) others differently, once we identify, and eventually try to let go, of our own anthropocentrism? There is ample space for communicative work on these questions as well as numerous points of departure for productive tasks, creative writing, or drama-pedagogical approaches to explore such ambivalences hands-on.

With regard to the changes of perspective discussed above, it is possible to assign such 'anamorphic' tasks on reversions of the gaze, the ambivalence of human or animal identity, and processes of becoming-animal. Rewriting a story, or writing alternative endings and so forth, is common practice in creative classrooms. Why not include nonhuman perspectives and have pupils ponder the changes in epistemology and phenomenology? Thinking like a bat might trouble philosophers – but pupils might be very sensitive when it comes to such questions and are probably willing to explore them with great fun. (Besides, they are not required to find watertight answers to be presented on academic conferences – an enjoyable role play or little poem might do.) In order to create situations in which 'humanimal' ambivalence is crucial, teachers can make productive use of cooperative methodologies: Instead of having pupils pace a task and arrive at 'the' solution at some point, why not create tasks with numerous possible answers and have pupils negotiate how to deal with that? Not only is this closer to our actual engagement with difference and diversity as well as to the demand of communicative classroom practice. It moreover prepares pupils for a democratic practice in multispecies worlds. Finally, both the affordances and dangers of theriomorphism and becomings-animal could be discussed by minute analyses of the languages used to render animal intelligible (or not). After all, English is about languages and the use of languages. Watching documentaries about animals, reading picture books that make use of anthropomorphism, or reading about practices of degradation of othered humans through the use of animal imagery – all these endeavours are enriched by rhetorical and discourse analysis that aim at the workings of the 'anthropological machine' (Agamben 2004). Our point is not to suggest one over the other approach. It is to identify the numerous affordances of ambivalence and uncertainty, gauged and experienced by reading literary fiction, that benefits a posthumanist take on education.

Coda: Anamorphism and Indistinction

In his most recent book, *Thinking through Animals* (2015), the US-American philosopher, Matthew Calarco, presents a brief overview of the current state of philosophical debates in human-animal studies, reviewing approaches that emphasize radical difference (from Adorno to Derrida) as well as sameness and identity (neo-Darwinian, rights-based, and so forth). He suggests 'indistinction' as a third category, linking this line of thought with "ways of thinking about human beings, animals, and ethics in a manner that radically displaces human beings from the center of ethical reflection and that avoids many of the exclusions associated with lingering forms of anthropocentrism" (50). This has clear connections with the posthumanist project discussed in the context of the present volume and surely has implications beyond the original field of philosophical inquiry. In education too, especially in areas such as gender studies or critical disability studies, indistinction plays an important role in the dyad of "dramatization" and "de-dramatization," for instance (Budde 2006; Debus 2012). The idea behind it is that dealing with diversity thrives on the ambivalence generated by a direct analysis of strategies of exclusion, and linguistic repertoires or cultural practices for retaining it, and an attempt to enable experiences and ideas beyond the binaries underlying such exclusions (see Debus 2012, 151).

Needless to say that human exceptionalism and speciesism are based on comparable exclusionary strategies, and that an educational practice informed by posthumanist research especially in language and literary pedagogies would benefit from a discursive analysis that tackles their inherent ambivalences. We believe that our notion of anamorphism can "help us work our way to the edges of language in order to catch sight of that which exceeds our conceptual mastery," as Calarco suggests (2015, 56). What is more, an approach to teaching literature that thrives on ambivalences and needs different perspectives for collective and communicative negotiations links easily not only with conventional tenets of neo-communicative teaching methodologies, it also offers opportunities for a truly inclusive and cooperative pedagogy.

Notes

1 The novel is inspired by the real-life story of four-year-old Moscovite Ivan Mishukov who joined a pack of wild dogs in 1996 and lived with them for two years until he was found and reintroduced to human society. Greg Garrard's essay in *The Oxford Handbook of Ecocriticism* (2014),"Ferality Tales," includes a subchapter on *Dog Boy*. This is the only scholarly discussion of the novel of which we are aware.

2 To be sure, there are comical moments in the novel, but the comedy does not result from the fact that the narrator is a dog.

3 "Since we have eaten from the tree of knowledge, Paradise is locked…; we must make the journey around the world and find out if perhaps somewhere there is an opening at the back side." (Our translation of Kleist [1810] 1952, 885.) We are quoting Kleist because this famous sentence is uttered in a context which offers huge ground for a Haraway-inspired discussion of cyborgs, animals and other post-humanist issues, but this would be another essay.

4 "The story claims to be told by a dog so it's not me. […] When the author's name is on the cover and especially if it's an author like me who has written quite a lot of books, the book is first seen as a kind of literary event. […] I wanted it to be announced as a street story rather than as a new novel by John Berger." (Berger in Zipp 2014, 176.)

5 Edgelands is a term first launched by Marion Shoard in 2002 to describe the undefined "interfacial landscape" between the urban and the rural. The poets Paul Farley and Michael Symmons Roberts have explored these regions and further developed the concept in an attempt to find a language for this hitherto "untranslated landscape" (2011, 5). *King* can be read as a novel which also contributes to the imaginative opening up and the translation of the *Edgelands*, but while Farley and Symmons Roberts want to clothe these places in metaphors so that they can be recognized and appreciated as "places of possibility, mystery, and beauty" (6), Berger is interested in the lives being lived there which are as much marginalized, overlooked and untranslated as the land itself. And yet, contrary to the beautifying gaze on the land, these lives are largely characterized by limits of possibility and lack of "beauty."

6 Not only does King provide background information. He also functions, in the classical sense, as a kind of mediator between the diegetic world of the action and the world of the reader, a function which August Wilhelm Schlegel called a mitigation of the impression provoked by extremely shocking and moving representations and a lifting up of the reader to the level of experience and perception of the characters. ("Er lindert den Eindruck einer tief erschütternden oder tief rührenden Darstellung [und führt den Zuschauer] in die Region der Betrachtung hinauf." Schlegel 1809, 51.)

7 As far as we are aware, Wittgenstein does not mention the term. His notion of a "Vexierbild" comes close to our meaning of *Kippfigur* (Wittgenstein 2001, 1028).

Works Cited

Agamben, Giorgio (2004). *The Open. Man and Animal.* Trans. Kevin Attell. Stanford, CA: Stanford University Press.

Bartosch, Roman (2017). "Storying Creaturely Lives." *Beyond the Human-Animal Divide. Creaturely Lives in Literature and Culture*. Eds. Dominik Ohrem and Roman Bartosch. Basingstoke: Palgrave Macmillan, 153-65.

Berger, John (1977). "Why Look at Animals?" *About Looking*. New York: Vintage International, 3-28.

--- (1999). *King. A Street Story.* New York: Vintage International.

Budde, Jürgen (2006). "Dramatisieren – Differenzieren – Entdramatisieren." *Der Deutschunterricht* 1, 71-83.

Burnside, John (2010). "*Dog Boy* by Eva Hornung", *The Guardian*, 13 February 2010, n.p. Web. 31 August 2018. <https://www.theguardian.com/ books/2010/ feb/13/dog-boy-eva-hornung> .

Calarco, Matthew (2015). *Thinking through Animals. Identity, Difference, Indistinction.* Stanford, CA: Stanford University Press.

Clark, Timothy (2011). *The Cambridge Introduction to Literature and the Environment*. Cambridge: Cambridge University Press.

Crist, Eileen (1999). *Images of Animals. Anthropomorphism and the Animal Mind.* Philadelphia, PA: Temple University Press.

Debus, Katharina (2012). "Dramatisierung, Entdramatisierung und Nicht-Dramatisierung in der geschlechterreflektierten Bildung. Oder: (Wie) Kann ich geschlechterreflektiert arbeiten, ohne geschlechtsbezogene Stereotype zu verstärken?" *Geschlechterreflektierte Arbeit mit Jungen an der Schule. Texte zu Pädagogik und Fortbildung rund um Jungen, Geschlecht und Bildung*. Ed. Dissens e.V. (2012). Berlin, 149-58.

Derrida, Jacques (2008). *The Animal that Therefore I Am.* Ed. Marie-Louise Mallet. Trans. David Wills. New York: Fordham University Press.

Farley, Paul, and Michael Symmons Roberts (2011). *Edgelands. Journeys into England's True Wilderness*. London: Jonathan Cape.

Fries, Thomas (2012). "Das Kippen der Figuren. Auerbach, Baudelaire, Nietzsche, Keller". *Figurationen: Gender, Literatur, Kultur*. 13.2 (Kippfiguren/Figures réversibles, Ed. Hans Georg von Arburg, Marie Theres Stauffer), 26-46.

Garrard, Greg (2011). *Ecocriticism.* 2nd ed. London and New York: Routledge.

--- (2014). "Ferality Tales." *The Oxford Handbook of Ecocriticism*. Ed. Greg Garrard. Oxford: Oxford University Press, 241-59.

Haraway, Donna (2003). *The Companion Species Manifesto. Dogs, People, and Significant Otherness*. Chicago: University of Chicago Press.

Herman, David (2016). *Creatural Fictions. Human-Animal Relationships in Twentieth- and Twenty-first-Century Literature*. Ed. David Herman. Basingstoke: Palgrave Macmillan.

Hornung, Eva (2009). *Dog Boy*. London et al.: Bloomsbury.

Kellaway, Kate (2016). "Interview John Berger: 'If I'm a storyteller it's because I listen'." *The Guardian*, 30 October 2016. Web. 19 September 2018 <https://www.theguardian.com/books/2016/oct/30/john-berger-at-90-interview-storyteller>.

von Kleist, Heinrich. "Über das Marionettentheater" [1810]. *Sämtliche Werke*. München: Droemersche Verlagsanstalt 1952, 882-88.

Latour, Bruno (2004). "Why Has Critique Run out of Steam? From Matters of Fact to Matters of Concern." *Critical Inquiry* 30, 225-48.

--- (2005). *What Is the Style of Matters of Concern? Two Lectures in Empirical Philosophy* (Spinoza Lectures presented in Amsterdam 2005). Assen: Royal van Gorcum.

Laycock, Steven W. (1999). "The Animal as Animal: A Plea for Open Conceptuality." *Animal Others. On Ethics, Ontology, and Animal Life*. Ed. H. Peter Steeves. New York: State University of New York Press, 271-284.

Lukács, Georg (2007). "Realism in the Balance." *Aesthetics and Politics*. Ed. Ronald Taylor. London: Verso, 28-59.

Ohrem, Dominik, and Roman Bartosch (eds.) (2017). *Beyond the Human-Animal Divide. Creaturely Lives in Literature and Culture*. Basingstoke: Palgrave Macmillan.

Matthewman, Sasha (2011). *Teaching Secondary English as if the Planet Matters*. London and New York: Routledge.

Santner, Eric (2006). *On Creaturely Life: Rilke, Benjamin, Sebald*. Chicago: Chicago University Press.

Schlegel, August Wilhelm (2018) [1809].. *Vorlesungen über dramatische Kunst und Literatur. Kritische Ausgabe der Vorlesungen*. Ed. Stefan Knödler, Leiden: Ferdinand Schöningh.

Shickman, Allan (1977). "'Turning Pictures' in Shakespeare's England." *The Art Bulletin* 59.1, 67-70.

Shoard, Marion (2002). "Edgelands." *Remaking the Landscape*. Ed. Jennifer Jenkins. London: Profile Books, 117-46.

Vermeulen, Pieter, and Virginia Richter (2015). "Introduction: Creaturely Constellations." *European Journal of English Studies* 19.1, 1-9.

Wittgenstein, Ludwig (2001). *Philosophische Untersuchungen. Kritisch-genetische Edition*. Ed. Joachim Schulte. Frankfurt/M: Suhrkamp.

Zipp, Georg (2014). "Life on the Streets: Parallactic Ways of Seeing Homelessness in John Berger's *King: A Street Story*." *Narrating Poverty and*

Precarity in Britain. Eds. Barbara Korte and Frédéric Regard. Berlin: De Gruyter, 167-185.

Gigi Adair

Postcolonial and Indigenous Posthumanism

1. Introduction

While critical debate and thinking between scholars in postcolonialism and/or indigenous studies and posthumanism has been marked by some mutual scepticism, recent work in these fields shows an increasing belief that it is possible to develop "a nondichotomic approach to posthumanism and postcoloniality" (Luisetti 2016, 217). Nonetheless, significant criticisms and differences remain. Understanding these debates and criticisms, as well as the points of common interest between postcolonial and posthumanist thinkers, is one way to approach critical posthumanism whilst simultaneously learning about long-standing philosophical debates on the 'human' and other key concepts in the Western philosophical tradition, anti- and postcolonial thinkers' criticisms of these concepts in the light of the colonial exploitation and atrocities that they were often called upon to sanction, and ongoing indigenous resistance to colonialism and insistence upon indigenous governance and knowledge. A consideration of posthumanist debates can be a valuable way to understand the range of responses of indigenous and postcolonial thinkers to the legacies of historical European colonialism and current global inequality and neoimperialism. It is important to note that there are quite stark differences between postcolonial studies and indigenous studies in regard to posthumanist thinking. While both areas have formulated criticisms of posthumanism, these tend to be quite different; likewise, they may understand posthumanism's potential quite differently. It is important, therefore, not to conflate indigenous thinking with postcolonial studies.

For some scholars of race, the value of humanism is clear and indisputable, and posthumanism suspect: Lewis Gordon writes, for example, that most African-American thinkers "consider themselves humanists for obvious reasons; dominant groups can 'give up' humanism for the simple fact that *their humanity* is presumed, while other communities have struggled too long for the humanistic prize" (Gordon 1998, 39). Echoing such concerns, Severin Fowles speaks for a range of scholars when he reveals some unease with the recent scholarly enthusiasm for objects: "as human subjects increasingly protested against being treated like objects – anthropologists began to explore the advantages of treating (non-human) objects like (quasi-human) subjects" (Fowles 2016, 12). Recent versions of these and other critiques are taken up in section 5. Some postcolonial scholars in the late 1990s and 2000s did indeed call for a return to some form of humanism, and particularly the work of Paul Gilroy and his call for a 'planetary humanism' (Gilroy 2000, 15) caused Rosi Braidotti, in her *Transpositions* to position postcolonial studies as a "non-Western" perspective pursuing concerns similar to posthumanism (dubbed a "Western-situated perspective"), but in parallel with and bound to humanist paradigms, thus essentially incompatible (Braidotti 2006, 56).

Against such claims of incompatibility, as early as *Posthuman Bodies* (Halberstam and Livingston 1995), at least some scholars acknowledged that posthumanism had not yet accounted for the politics of race and colonialism, and that it needed to do so. Neil Badmington's important edited collection *Posthumanism* (2000), for instance, foregrounds questions of posthumanism's links to feminist and postcolonial thought. Recent introductions to posthumanism tend to at least cite postcolonial studies as a pre-cursor of posthumanism or briefly note the role of race in defining the less-than-human within humanist thought (Braidotti 2013, 1-2; Castree and Nash 2006, 501-02; Ginn 2017, 5269). Interestingly, Braidotti has successively moved from a diagnosis of incompatibility to one of vital imbrication in her understanding of the relationship between posthumanism and postcolonial thought in her subsequent writing: in recent work she posits postcolonial studies as not only compatible with, but central to, posthumanist thinking on a range of topics (Braidotti 2017, 92). Nevertheless, numerous examples can be found of posthumanist scholarship which is oblivious to race and colonialism,[1] while other influential work in posthumanism continues to ignore or discount the potential use of postcolonial studies, even when exhibiting some interest in race (e.g. Wolfe 2010). Other scholars use the language and analytical apparatus of postcolonial studies and indigenous studies, but do not seriously engage with those fields (e.g. Shotwell 2016; Greenfield 2017).[2] Calls for posthumanist scholars to engage more fully with questions of race and colonialism therefore remain common (e.g. Hinton, Mehrabi and Barla 2015).

Marie Lathers dates the beginnings of an interest in posthumanism among postcolonial scholars to the 1990s, as a means "to pass beyond the philosophical barrier of the subject – as always already human and only human" (Lathers 2006, 433). She rejects the position that posthumanism and postcolonialism are incompatible, arguing instead that they are closely related. Similarly, Sidonie Smith writes that

> feminist and postcolonial theorists have been 'doing' posthumanist critique for years as they have labored to destabilize the notion of the humanist subject as autonomous, bounded, free, and rational; to insist on the historical racialization of the human, or liberal subject, as 'white' and male; and to expand the concept of the human to incorporate collective, environmental, ecological, technological, and material features and flows. (Smith 2012, 141)

Meanwhile, posthumanist ideas and the work of Deleuze have prompted new work on race, such as that by Amit Rai (2012), and postcolonial studies and posthumanist ideas have come together particularly in collections such as *Postcolonial Ecologies: Literatures of the Environment* (DeLoughrey and Handley 2011) and *Global Ecologies and the Environmental Humanities: Postcolonial Approaches* (DeLoughrey, Didur and Carrigan 2015) and in other work in the field of ecocriticism (Huggan 2004; Huggan and Tiffin 2010).

Another approach is taken by a group of scholars who employ classic anticolonial theory – in this case the work of Albert Memmi – to argue that "the beings that comprise the 'natural world' are colonized" and to consider "how we might enact solidarity with other beings as anti-colonial allies" (Blenkinsop et al. 2017, 349-50). All of these scholars, therefore, see great potential in bringing postcolonial and posthumanist ideas together. In the following, I will focus on several key areas in which postcolonial studies and indigenous studies have taken up posthumanist thought: in critiques of humanism and colonialism, in response to climate change, and in animal studies. I will look at these first before summarizing the key points of contention that postcolonial and indigenous thinkers have raised. Then I will turn to a range of literary texts to explore how these issues are explored in the literature and how these theoretical debates can be read and taught in dialogue with a range of fictional works.

2. Postcolonial, Indigenous and Posthumanist Critiques of Humanism

Some first points of crossover and divergence between postcolonial and indigenous studies, and posthumanism can be identified by examining the critiques of humanism that scholars in these fields have offered; this also allows students to come to grips with key aspects of European humanist thought. An introductory text by Neil Badmington offers a concise summary of influential posthumanist critiques of humanism and compares these to a key text of Enlightenment humanism: Descartes's *Discourse on the Method* (Badmington 2011; Descartes 2006, e.g. 28-29, 46-49, 51-52). In this short text, however, Badmington does not address questions of colonialism or race).

These can be profitably compared to postcolonial and indigenous critiques of humanism. Leela Gandhi's chapter "Thinking Otherwise" is perhaps closest to posthumanist critiques when she notes the postcolonial adoption of the poststructuralist critique of anthropocentrism "on account of its indifference to difference, and consequent refusal to accommodate that which is not human" (Gandhi 1998, 39). Linda Tuhiwai Smith notes that "[c]olonized peoples have been compelled to define what it means to be human because there is a deep understanding of what it has meant to be considered not fully human, to be *savage*" (Smith 1999, 26), but that this process cannot simply involve an inversion of colonial binaries nor an acceptance of essentialist accounts of 'nature'. This, too, is a position compatible with many strains of posthumanist thought. Robert Young's account occasions more caution: He too argues that critiques of humanism by anticolonial thinkers such as Aimé Cesaire and Frantz Fanon reveal the complicity of humanism with colonialism, that is, the way "humanism was utilized as a form of ideological control of the colonized peoples" (Young 1992, 246),[3] and that this critique lies at the centre of poststructuralism and antihumanism. He also argues, however, that "humanism found genuinely revolutionary echoes in Third-World struggles" (249) and that this tradition of critical humanism, exemplified, for instance, by Fanon's attempt to reformulate humanism "as a non-conflictual concept no longer defined against a sub-human other" (ibid.) lies at the heart of anti-colonialist thought. Dipesh Chakrabarty has also argued that "Fanon's struggle to hold on to the Enlightenment idea of the human – even when he knew that European imperialism had reduced that idea to the figure of the settler-colonial white man – is now itself a part of the global heritage of all postcolonial thinkers" (Chakrabarty 2000, 5). This argument has been taken up more recently by Paul Gilroy in his criticism of the concept of the Anthropocene, and will be discussed below.

3. Climate Change: Postcolonial and Indigenous Responses

The most prominent postcolonial scholar writing about climate change, and the attendant changes to postcolonial thinking and writing that it demands – alongside other, more widely discussed changes – is Dipesh Chakrabarty. Starting in 2009, he has argued that climate change deserves more serious attention from historians, in particular, as it has consequences for historiography, as well as for human life on Earth (Chakrabarty 2009). He has also explored how these historiographical questions are relevant to understanding, comparing and identifying the misunderstandings between the work of climate scientists and policy makers (Chakrabarty 2014). Chakrabarty has also argued that post-colonial studies should pay more attention to climate change, not only because it is likely to exacerbate global inequality, but also because the work of postcolonial scholars in formulating a "doubled and contradictory" (Chakrabarty 2012, 8) conception of the human subject – oscillating between "normative and onto-existential images of the human" (6), between an ideal of universal justice and the recognition of lived subalterneity – is precisely the conceptual armoury needed to understand the conceptual challenge of climate change, in which the human must be thought on multiple scales at once.[4] In this article, Chakrabarty provides a valuable summary of anticolonial and post-colonial thought on the notion of the subject and the category of the human which is useful for tracing these developments, and he argues for the relevance of this work to a range of contemporary – and not only strictly postcolonial – challenges (ibid., 1-8). Perhaps surprisingly, therefore, Chakrabarty's latest work argues that climate change is *not* "inherently – or logically – a problem of past or accumulated intra-human injustice" (Chakrabarty 2014, 11). The relevant question of justice concerns the "near-complete human appropriation of the biosphere" (16), leading to a question familiar to any scholar or student of postcolonialism studies, due to its "striking similarity to the question that Europeans often asked themselves when they forcibly or otherwise took over other peoples' lands: by what right or on what grounds do we arrogate to ourselves the almost exclusive claims to appropriate for human needs the biosphere of the planet?" (16). For Chakrabarty, it is in intervening in debates such as this that postcolonial studies can best serve the pressing questions which anthropogenic climate change poses.

Chakrabarty's attempt to think the human at multiple and incommensurate scales at once touches upon a key debate in posthumanism: the reconceptualization of agency. For Chakrabarty, the recognition that humans now act as a geophysical force on the planet indicates a "nonhuman, forcelike" (Chakrabarty 2012, 13) mode of agency in which humans are neither subjects nor objects, and which our typical (Western) conceptual framework cannot stretch to accommodate. He thereby critiques the posthuman model of agency and politics presented by Bruno Latour (Latour 2004; 2014): unlike Latour, who in Chakrabarty's reading calls for "a new idea of politics that brings together – as active partners into our arguments – both humans and nonhumans" (Chakrabarty 2012, 13), Chakrabarty argues for the recognition of a "pure, nonontological agency" (ibid.) when humans collectively act as a geophysical force. Mark Jackson offers a concise and incisive critique, informed by postcolonial studies, of what he views as Chakrabarty's misreading of Latour; this can be very profitably read alongside both Latour and Chakrabarty's work to generate a fine-grained understanding of the conceptual issues at stake (M. Jackson 2014, 76-77). Jackson suggests that much postcolonial studies is unable to overcome, or even to recognize, its own ongoing dependence on the (Western) nature-culture distinction; of more value in trying to disrupt such thinking, Jackson suggests, are a range of aboriginal and indigenous cosmologies which "begin from a multifaceted relational account of embodied becoming, and not from an assertion that nature is fundamentally other to culture" (M. Jackson 2014, 83). As particularly valuable and influential sources of these types of thinking he points to the ethnographic work of Philippe Descola (1996, 2013a, 2013b) and

Eduardo Viveiros de Castro (1992; 2012). For students, however, shorter examples of such indigenous concepts of land, nature, humans and agency may be more accessible (e.g. Coulthard 2010; Watts 2013).

While Jackson identifies Latour as one of several "sympathetic interlocutors" (M. Jackson 2014, 82) of indigenous conceptualizations of agency and nature, other scholars have been more critical of the tendency to return to Eurocentrism and to erase indigenous thinking in his work. Zoe Todd notes both her admiration for Latour's work and her disappointment with his continual failure to acknowledge the indigenous concepts, philosophies and knowledges that have shaped posthumanist thinking like his own; her article provides abundant resources to introduce students to indigenous theory and activism on climate change, including the Inuit concept of *Sila* (Todd 2016, 4-7).[5] An accompaniment to such discussions might include a consideration of how such non-indigenous students and scholars can approach indigenous knowledge without repeating the appropriation and erasure which Todd identifies in Latour and others. Todd and Sarah Hunt both argue that indigenous thought must be understood as an embodied and practised, living body of thought, linked to indigenous legal governance and sovereignty, not simply as a "well of ideas to draw from" (Todd 2016, 17; see also Hunt 2014).

4. Animal Studies in Postcolonial and Indigenous Thought

The next topic within posthumanism that has witnessed a large degree of crossover with postcolonial scholars and areas of interest is animal studies. Cary Wolfe argues, for example, that "our stance toward the animal is an index for how we stand in a field of otherness and difference more generally" (Wolfe 2003, 5). Furthermore, he insists,

> as long as it is institutionally taken for granted that it is all right to systematically exploit and kill nonhuman animals simply because of their species, then the humanist discourse of species will always be available for use by some humans against other humans as well, to countenance violence against the social other of whatever species – or gender, or race, or class, or sexual difference. (8)

For Wolfe, therefore, challenging humanist concepts of nonhuman animals and overcoming human exceptionalism is a way to combat racism. Similarly, Giorgio Agamben argues that the attempt to separate human and animal can only function by "animalizing the human, by isolating the nonhuman within the human" (Agamben 2004, 37). Examples of such figures include "the slave, the barbarian, and the foreigner, as figures of an animal in human form" (ibid).

Fayaz Chagani's claim that postcolonial studies "has not fully interrogated its own anthropocentrism" and thus "perpetuates both epistemic and corporeal violence" (Chagani 2016, 620) against non-human animals largely aligns with the project set out by Wolfe. His article provides an overview of postcolonial thought – or lack thereof – on the question of the animal and argues that postcolonialism's critique of universality ends at the species boundary. For Chagani, recent work in ecocriticism or postcolonial ecocriticism which is "committed to the idea that a rethinking of the postcolonial project is linked to a rethinking of the exploitation by humans of nonhuman beings" (631) marks an important, but still too rare, development in postcolonial thought.[6]

Other postcolonial scholars have seen quite different forms of potential in 'the question of the animal'. Philip Armstrong argues that "the most promising collaborations between postcolonial and animal studies lie in the production of sharp, politicized, culturally sensitive, and up-to-the-minute local histories of the roles that animals have played – or been make to play – in colonial and postcolonial transactions" (Armstrong 2002, 416). Examples of this might include Clapperton Chakanetsa Mavhunga's work on the crossover between human and non-human "vermin beings" in colonial Rhodesia (Mavhunga 2011), or Timothy Mitchell's work on the *Anopheles gambiae* mosquito in 1940s Egypt (Mitchell 2002).

All of these thinkers are aware of the lingering unease which animal studies can create when it comes into contact with histories of racialization and colonialism. Julie Livingston and Jasbir K. Puar's introduction to a special issue of *Social Text* – the same issue in which Mavhunga's essay appears – makes this argument very clearly: "much of posthumanist thought as well as animal studies suffers from an often unmarked Euro-American focus and through that, ironically, a philosophical resuscitation of the status of 'the human' as a transparent category" (Livingston and Puar 2011, 5). It is clear, however, that the answer to this, for all these writers, is not for postcolonial scholars to disengage from animal studies, but rather to bring the historical understanding and conceptual tools of postcolonial studies to bear on these questions.

Indigenous studies approaches to animal studies exhibit both similarities and divergences from those of postcolonial scholars. Much indigenous thinking on animal-human relations demonstrates quite different conceptual underpinnings: there is no need to overcome a strict human-animal division, for example, or to begin to consider whether animals might have agency or consciousness when starting from a conceptual frame which does not include that division or which has always attributed these properties to non-human animals. Short excerpts from ethnographies such as Deborah Bird Rose's *Dingo Makes Us Human* (on the Yarralin people of Northern Australia) can illustrate a cosmology in which humans are not defined in opposition to nonhuman animals, but in terms of similarity and relatedness (Rose 1992, 42-47, 58-63, 106-110). The description of a moose hunt by a Native American hunter quoted by Glen Coulthard "emphasizes the consciousness and individual agency of the raven, but also depicts the relationship between the hunter and the bird as a mutually interdependent one" (Coulthard 2010, 80). Kim TallBear offers a short reflection on the importance of indigenous standpoints to non-indigenous scholars interested in "interspecies" thinking (TallBear 2011); the same argument has been made more recently and at greater length by a group of non-indigenous scholars interested in "multispecies studies" (Dooren, Kirksey and Münster 2016). Perhaps the most interesting, and for students most valuable, example is the collaborative work of Annette Watson and Orville H. Huntington. This article describes a moose hunt in Alaska from the (overlapping) perspectives of Watson, a non-indigenous geographer, and Huntington, an Athabascan hunter. They offer summaries of the philosophical and epistemological foundations of each of their thinking, and Watson's efforts to grapple with the conceptual differences of Indigenous Knowledge and the bloody reality of the hunt are likely to resonate with students who are also encountering these ideas for the first time. Watson and Huntington's piece also clearly differs from that work in animal studies that is concerned with stopping the human killing of non-human animals: it makes a strong argument for an ethical practice of hunting which attributes agency to the animals (Watson and Huntington 2008).

5. Postcolonial and Indigenous Criticisms of Posthumanism

Who counts as the 'human' that posthumanism seeks to decentre? Or the 'human' in 'humankind' (let alone the 'Man' in 'mankind')? Such general categories have become particularly prevalent in recent discussions of the Anthropocene, in which posthumanist thinking plays a significant role. Andreas Malm and Alf Hornborg, however, argue that important distinctions are lost in these discussions, including distinctions of global power and inequality. As they insist, "the fossil economy was not created nor is it upheld by humankind in general" (Malm and Hornborg 2014, 62). The use of the species category in Anthropocene studies, they suggest, is "analytically flawed, as well as inimical to action. Intra-species inequalities are part and parcel of the current ecological crisis and cannot be ignored in attempts to understand it" (62). This point is an important one, yet it is not the focus of the majority of either post-colonial or indigenous criticisms of posthumanist scholarship.

Many postcolonial and indigenous critics of recent work in posthumanism are less critical of the theories and concepts advanced by that work than they are of the framing of posthumanism: as a new development, emerging from the Western academy, and aligned with a largely white, European philosophical tradition. Zakiyyah Iman Jackson identifies a blindness among some posthumanist scholars to the work of their postcolonial and indigenous colleagues: "It has largely gone unnoticed by posthumanists that their queries into ontology often find their homologous (even anticipatory) appearance in decolonial philosophies that confront slavery and colonialism's inextricability from the Enlightenment humanism they are trying to displace" (Z. Jackson 2013, 681). On a different but related note, Tiffany Lethabo King notes the common assumption that black and indigenous scholars, and the fields of Black and Native studies, are often assumed to reify categories such as 'the human' unless these scholars prove otherwise:

> Black and Indigenous academics, as well as Black and Native studies scholars, are expected to perform a commitment to a Deleuzian brand of posthumanist and nonrepresentational theory as proof that they are critical and postmodern scholars and disciplinary formations. (King 2017, 163)

Both Jackson and King argue that the tradition of critical black humanism, particularly the work of Sylvia Winter, may provide more valuable resources than Eurocentric versions of posthumanism.

This is the position advanced by Paul Gilroy is his recent attack on much contemporary work concerned with the Anthropocene (Gilroy 2018). Gilroy criticizes approaches to the Anthropocene which too quickly turn away from humanism and particularly the history of critical humanism developed by anti- and postcolonial writers. Returning to the history of race and its distortions of humanism, he suggests, might provide other ways of thinking about nature and culture, time and modernity. Gilroy instead advocates a "reparative humanism" or a "planetary humanism"; toward the end of his essay he writes of "a cautious, post-humanist humanism capable of grasping the relationship between human and non-human" (Gilroy 2018, 16). Thus, although Gilroy is combative in his rejection of posthumanism and the Anthropocene and sets quite different aims from posthumanist thinkers in his desire for "humanism's re-enchantment", the critical humanism he proposes has much overlap with critical and postcolonial post-humanisms, all of which are concerned with "grasping the relation between human and non-human" in a radically unequal world (ibid.).

In Timothy Brennan's recent book on the mutual interdependency of European philosophy and modern anti-colonial thought, he argues that posthumanism emerged from European anxieties about the global restructuring of power threatened by post-war decolonization, and that it can be understood as an imperial ideology. It is important to note, however, that Brennan means a different version of posthumanism than the one primarily under discussion here: he refers to "the positing of a posthuman condition" (Brennan 2014, 224); a posthumanism reliant "on tropes of technoscience" (19). *This* version of posthumanism, he writes, is not "a rejection of the humanism of the Enlightenment, [but] it is a devotion to one rather than another Enlightenment legacy" (225): a privileging of the natural sciences over philosophy and the humanities. This recalls Ferrando's critique of those who understand 'posthumanism' to mean 'human enhancement', but whereas Ferrando argues that such ideas are opposed to the aims of critical posthumanism and should not be understood as posthumanist (Ferrando 2013, 27-28), Brennan argues that critical posthumanist thinkers such as Latour and Wolfe are also overly attached to scientific versions of posthumanism, and that their ideas therefore work to obscure global inequalities and the West's responsibility for colonial exploitation, to disable critical argument, to discount "all expression and intentionality", "to deprive of choice that being which they contend has no choice" (Brennan 2014, 232). He thus concludes that posthumanism, which "rest[s] ambiguously on the authority of contemporary cultures of control" (232), cannot offer conceptual tools for an emancipatory or decolonial politics or philosophy. Brennan's argument is clearly polemical and does not account for many variants of posthumanist scholarship – most obviously and damningly, perhaps, the indigenous scholarship discussed in this chapter – yet it provides a bracing critique and much material for discussion about the political uses or consequences of posthumanism. Brennan's reading of Latour could be compared to the more favourable interpretation of Latour by Luisetti, who finds resources for a decolonial politics in Latour's thought despite his Eurocentrism (Luisetti 2016).

Numerous indigenous scholars who have published critiques of posthumanist scholarship argue that their criticisms are not of posthuman ideas per se, but of the way in which those ideas are discussed and contextualized, and the structures of the academy in which such scholarly discussions take place. Those academic structures, however, which tend to silence indigenous thinkers, also shape the scholarship and concepts produced within them. Thus, despite its affinity with – and indeed too often unacknowledged dependence upon – much indigenous thought, posthumanist scholarship as currently practised in the Euro-American academy may contribute to the ongoing exclusion, marginalization and colonisation of indigenous peoples (Hunt 2014; Sundberg 2014; Todd 2016). Zoe Todd's article makes the various layers of this problem very clear. She notes the way in which (usually white, Euro-American) posthumanist scholars continue to erase or ignore the work and the vital contributions of indigenous scholars and activists in fields including anthropology, posthumanist theory, climate change activism and more. Indigenous thinkers are not cited as philosophers and intellectuals – much less frequently invited to speak themselves – but figure in Euro-American scholarly discourse at most as "research subjects or vaguely defined 'collaborators'" or as "disembodied representatives of an amorphous Indigeneity that serves European intellectual or political purposes" (Todd 2016, 7). Todd argues that it is the structures maintained by "the European academy's continued, collective reticence to address its own racist and colonial roots, and debt to Indigenous thinkers in a meaningful and structural way" (10), that enable those within that academy to continue "to advance and consume arguments that parallel discourses in Indigenous contexts without explicitly nodding to them, or by minimally nodding to Indigenous intellectual and political players" (8). The consequences of this erasure are not only that indigenous intellectuals are silenced or ignored, but that this scholarship contributes to the ongoing colonization of indigenous peoples:

> [I]t is so important to think, deeply, about how the Ontological Turn – with its breathless 'realisations' that animals, the climate, water, 'atmospheres' and non-human presences like ancestors and spirits are *sentient* and *possess agency*, that 'nature' and 'culture', 'human' and 'animal' may not be so separate after all – is itself perpetuating the exploitation of Indigenous peoples. (Todd 2016, 16)

The solution, however, is not simple:

> [T]he appropriation of Indigenous thinking in European contexts without Indigenous interlocutors present to hold the use of Indigenous stories and laws to account flattens, distorts and erases the embodied, legal-governance and spiritual aspects of Indigenous thinking. [...] However, there is a risk as well, to Indigenous thinking not being acknowledged at all. (ibid., 9)[7]

Despite the risks of non-Indigenous scholars appropriating Indigenous thought without accounting for its context, Todd believes that this is better than ignoring and erasing it; she calls her article "a 'cite this, not that' cheat-sheet" to direct scholars to Indigenous thinkers, urging all those working in posthumanist studies that

> every time you want to cite a Great Thinker who is on the public speaking circuit these days, consider digging around for others who are discussing the same topics in other ways. Decolonising the academy, both in Europe and North America, means that we must consider our own prejudices, our own biases. (19)

This point is also made by Cutcha Risling Baldy: while settler colonialism "relies on the continued erasure and silencing of Indigenous epistemologies and knowledges to prevent challenges to settler colonial claims to land and history", this project may also be furthered, possibly unwittingly, by "(perhaps) well-meaning scholars and theorists engaged in 'decolonization as metaphor'" (Risling Baldy 2015, 4). That is, when only the language of decolonization is adopted within the Euro-Western academy, disconnected from indigenous "struggles for land and life", it cannot advance that project and may in fact hinder it via "'settler moves to innocence' that hide ongoing settler culpability in colonialism" (4).[8] The superficial use of indigenous knowledge by non-indigenous posthumanist thinkers (without challenging the structural factors which marginalize that knowledge) may operate as a form of "colonial parallelism": "The settler aims to move toward innocence by embracing this knowledge but only in so far as they are able to draw parallels between this knowledge and western ideologies" (5).

6. Literary Responses

Postcolonial literary (and non-fiction) responses to and imaginings of posthumanist ideas and futures take a wide range of forms and genres, and they interrogate or mobilize posthumanist ideas to quite different ends: some criticize post- or transhumanist tendencies and advocate a return to humanism, others use posthumanism to support a postcolonial critique of global inequality, others again employ posthumanist ideas to undo both anthropocentrism and Eurocentrism. It is here that we find various resources for teaching, including texts that themselves can be read as forms of posthumanist theory and can be used as examples in class for illustrating and critiquing posthumanist ideas.

In nonfiction works such as Arundati Roy's essay on the building of the Sardar Sarovar dam, "The Greater Common Good", the posthuman seems to play a limited role. Roy describes the fight against the dam project as a "war for the rivers and the mountains and the forests of the world" (Roy 1999, n.p.), and she talks briefly about the ecosystem and wildlife destruction that the dam will entail, but her focus is very clearly on the human cost of the dam: the 25 million people who live in the valley, and the human societies and ways of life that will be destroyed. Yet, although the human remains centred, questions emerge about who counts as human:

> [T]he Government of India does not have a figure for the number of people that have been displaced by dams or sacrificed in other ways at the altars of 'National Progress'. [...] The millions of displaced people don't exist anymore. When history is written they won't be in it. Not even as statistics. (ibid.)

Rob Nixon's essay on the same dam project, and others like it, reveals the subtle workings of Enlightenment notions of humanity and nature, and their consequences today. Megadam projects are portrayed as "spectacular symbol[s] of rational deliverance from irrational rivers and irrational cultures": a sign of Man's mastery over nature, of rational modernity over irrational nature and premodernity (Nixon 2011, 172). Those who oppose the dam – mostly tribal people and Dalits – are revealed as barely human:

> In Lockeian (and in Jeffersonian) terms, to dwell in movement is an unacceptable, uncivilized, irrational contradiction: you are improving neither the physical land nor yourself and, by extension, you're failing to advance the national interest. (165)

Nixon makes clear the particular postcolonial paradox at work here: while postcolonial studies has often criticized the way in which Enlightenment notions of the human justified colonialism, in many postcolonial nations, the same definition of the human and the same understanding of the relationship between humans and nature was put to work to assert postcolonial nationhood:

> [T]o erect a megadam was literally to concretize the postcolonial nation's modernity, prosperity, and autonomy. [...] Each dam was simultaneously an act of national self-assertion – independence writ large across the landscape – and an act of natural conquest. [...] Yet ironically, in economiç and political terms, these glamorous hydrological regimes of independence doubled as invisible statements of dependence that threw into question the very condition of postcolonialism itself. (166-67)

Here, both the postcolonial political dependence on a certain humanism and its nefarious consequences for postcolonial independence (such dam projects always depend on large loans from the World Bank or from Western countries, miring postcolonial nations in debt) become clear, even if a fuller ecocritical or posthumanist perspective is yet to emerge. Nixon's analysis of Roy also emphasizes questions of form and style, of writerly aesthetics: he argues that her use of the essay form "allowed her to take on the weighty, leaden genres that gave ballast to the culture of the megadam and, beyond that, to the culture of developmental gigantism", and that her style stands in stark contrast to "the uninhabited language of forum speak, policy speak, boardroom speak, and environmental impact speak" (168-69). This focus on literariness and textuality will prove a recurring theme in almost all of the works discussed here.

Many works of speculative fiction engage explicitly with posthumanism in the sense of future technological developments and their effect on humanity and society. Precisely this focus on humanity and (human) society, however, means that these works rarely avoid anthropocentrism. Nonetheless, some offer a postcolonial critique of posthumanist tendencies in line with criticisms voiced by postcolonial scholars. Tobias S. Buckell's short story "Necahual" echoes anticolonial critiques of humanism and the use of the categories of human/subhuman to justify imperialism, but it clearly adheres to and advocates traditional humanist values – including for those who, in this universe of interplanetary war and colonization, are not 'pure' humans (Buckell 2004).[9] Similar themes can be found in contemporary popular culture, such as in the "Men Against Fire" episode of the series *Black Mirror* (Brooker 2016). Manjula Padmanabhan's play *Harvest* takes place in a speculative near future, in which its Indian characters cannot find work except for selling their bodies: in sex work or as organ donors for Westerners who appear only in virtual form via a surveillance device (Padmanabhan 2003). It is critical of social and technological developments towards simulacra and cyberspace, ending instead with an insistence on the resistance of the colonized and exploited (female) body against its commodification. This insistence on embodiment echoes numerous postcolonial feminist critiques, but in the play these are not synthesized with or brought into dialogue with a posthumanist questioning of, for example, the boundaries of the body in a highly technologized world, but rather placed in opposition to such post- (or more properly trans-) humanist developments.

In contrast, Keri Hulme's short story "Floating Words", in her collection *Stonefish*, incorporates elements of fantasy in its imagining of a world radically changed by rising sea levels, but in ways that are less attached to either humanist values – including human survival – or traditional definitions of human characteristics such as language (Hulme 2004). As Elizabeth DeLoughrey writes, Hulme's story "complicates the individuated speaking subject (and species)" (DeLoughrey 2015, 355); in this world, where climate change is "profoundly ordinary", the protagonist must "[read] the signs of an always dynamic nonhuman nature" and "her mode of interpretation and of narrative must change" (353) – recalling Chakrabarty's demand for new modes of narrative and historiography to understand climate change, but departing from his insistence that human survival should be a, or the only, priority.

Somewhat similar narrative and aesthetic interventions are also at work in another work of speculative climate change fiction, Alexis Wright's *The Swan Book* (Wright 2013). Adeline Johns-Putra argues that the novel uses silence – its protagonist Oblivia is mute – to resist the anthropocentrism of realist fiction and particularly the novel form; the decentring of the anthropos is, in this novel, aligned with a decentring of voice (Johns-Putra 2018). Its posthumanism operates not only on the aesthetic level; rather, it explicitly links postcolonial and posthumanist politics: "the alignment of racial with environmental exploitation is crystallized in Oblivia's special affinity with the nonhuman" (Johns-Putra 2018, 34), particularly the black swans driven from southern to northern Australia by climate change. For Jean Skeat, it is this posthumanist poetics, in which nature is not inert or passive, which drives the political force of the text, so that posthumanism here supports and furthers a postcolonial aesthetic and political project (Skeat 2016, n.p.).

Another novel engaged with questions of reading, silence and the role of literature in a posthuman future is Amitav Ghosh's *The Calcutta Chromosome* (1995). According to Mike Frangos, the text "figures machine reading as an imaginative device enabling the recovery of subaltern histories and the construction of a posthuman future" (Frangos 2013, para. 1). Here again, postcolonial, posthumanist and literary questions are brought into close dialogue.[10] In this novel, the borders of the human and the question of human interdependence on parasites and viruses, as well as on subjectivity in cyberspace, enables reflection on embodied (post)humanity – scholars have variously read the novel as recording the threats or promises of modern technology and cyberspace (Nayar 2009; Shinn 2008). Perhaps more interestingly, however, the novel's vision of a posthuman future is related to technological developments, but not focused on the technologically upgraded human body, but on digital archiving enabling a posthuman and postcolonial historiography. This can therefore be read productively alongside the work of a postcolonial historian such as Chakrabarty (2000).

A wide range of literary texts can be read in productive dialogue with theoretical work in animal studies. Some of these challenge anthropocentrism, some the perceived cultural divisions between animals and humans – and the ethnocentrism behind assuming such divisions – while others imagine new forms and ethics of relationality between human and non-human animals.

Barbara Gowdy's *The White Bone* is narrated by a group of elephants and set in a mythic, yet clearly post-imperial landscape that evokes East Africa. It makes a range of narrative alterations and stylistic choices to convey a sense of elephant embodiment, consciousness and sociality, thus thematizing and attempting to creatively overcome the question of human-animal understanding and communication (Gowdy 1998). Huggan describes Gowdy's project as "a narrative that attempts to break with anthropocentric/anthropomorphic conventions by presenting the experience of creatures in a language that can never fully be theirs, nor yet unequivocally our own" (Huggan 2004, 718). The postcolonial context of the novel and its commentary on the parallels of speciesism and racism is further explored by Huggan and Tiffin elsewhere (Huggan and Tiffin 2010, 149-59).

Gowdy's novel has frequently been read in dialogue and comparison with J.M. Coetzee's *The Lives of Animals*, which Allison Carruth describes as "a foundational text for postcolonial ecocriticism [...] and critical animal studies" (Carruth 2011, 201). The two lectures of which the book consists, delivered by the (fictional) novelist Elizabeth Costello, closely echo some of the arguments of Wolfe and Chagani; Costello attacks the way in which Enlightenment 'reason' justifies the exploitation of and dominion over all non-human animals and many colonized or devalued people (Coetzee 1999, 22-23). In her second lecture, she takes on literary conventions for the representation of animals, criticizing both "fabular abstraction" and "romantic primitivism" (Huggan 2004, 713); she argues instead for "sympathetic imagination", arguing that there is "no limit to the extent to which we can think ourselves into the being of another" (Coetzee 1999, 35). Thus while the paradoxes of animal rights become clear in Coetzee's text – including the reliance upon and simultaneous denunciation of reason, the return to abstraction when representing animals – it makes a strong argument for literature and imagination in overcoming some of these barriers. Gowdy's *The White Bone* might be analysed as one example of the approach which Elizabeth Costello recommends, while the next example turns away from written language to visual depiction to imagine forms of ethical relationality between human and non-human animals.

Shaun Tan's graphic novel *The Arrival* (2006) is, on first glance, a story of human migration. The protagonist, evidently under threat from some monstrous force, leaves his home and family and eventually resettles in a new country. There, he must navigate immigration bureaucracy and an unfamiliar language to find a place to live, work, and new friends. Life in this new place is strongly marked by experiences of migration – each new friend tells the protagonist their own story of flight and arrival – but it is also characterized by intimate relations between humans and non-humans: every human has a companion creature, apparently native to the place, and no two alike. Bidisha Banerjee therefore reads the novel as a story of diasporic 'companion species' (drawing on the concept from Donna Haraway) (Banerjee 2016; Haraway 2003, 2008). The novel offers a "posthuman ethics of care", Banerjee suggests, in which the well-being of radically different creatures is nonetheless interrelated (Banerjee 2016, 412). Banerjee argues that Shaun Tan's earlier graphic novel, *The Rabbits* (written with John Marsden), can also be read as an exploration of the "posthuman contact zone" created by the British colonization and settlement of Australia (Banerjee 2013, 419). Beyond this, the form of the graphic novel, in which the only texts are written in an invented language unknown to the protagonist (or reader), offers a different solution to Gowdy's aesthetic innovations in confronting the question of animal language (or lack thereof) and the possibility of animal-human communication.

The question of the animal is addressed in a very different way in Indra Sinha's *Animal's People* (2005), a fictional retelling of the Bhopal disaster and its long aftermath. It is narrated by Animal, a 19-year-old man who is severely disabled as a result of the poison: his spine is twisted and he walks on all fours. From his position at 'crotch level' rather than "eye level" (Sinha 2005, 2), Animal repeatedly claims that he is not human – but it is also clear that, despite his claimed name, he is not fully animal.[11] Instead, Animal occupies a liminal position between these categories that throws their borders and relations to each other into relief and into question. As Pablo Mukherjee argues, Animal "embodies exaggerated human and nonhuman qualities. We might say that he is the location where these meet, and, as such, his very existence is an argument for their continuity and their ontological equality" (Mukherjee 2011, 227). (Mukherjee's assignment of various qualities as either typically human or typically animal is debatable and might be seen to emphasize the contingent and historical nature of such characterizations.) For Mukherjee, Animal's liminal position enables him to become a mediator between human and non-human worlds and lends him "a transpersonality, an ability to experience the objective existence of the entire environment of Khaufpur as a network composed of related subjects, including himself" (226). The political potential of the "postcolonial consciousness of resistance" (229) thus created is limited, nonetheless, by the historical reality of neoimperial and postcolonial state greed, corruption and neglect that the text also narrates. Roman Bartosch argues that the novel is "humanist in its ethical impetus" but posthumanist in its rejection of certain tenants of humanism, including disembodiment and autonomy (Bartosch 2012, 14). As was the case in Arundhati Roy's essay, posthumanism here tends to be limited to exposing and questioning the definition of the human and the uses to which it is put in postcolonial context, rather than fully decentring the human. Nonetheless, the interaction of postcolonial and posthumanist ideas in the novel is interesting in the light of debates over the usefulness of posthumanism to postcolonial thought or postcolonial politics. In Sinha's novel, posthumanism is seen to support and further postcolonial aims, suggesting their compatibility.

Pauline Melville's *The Ventriloquist's Tale*, set in an inland Amerindian community and in the capital city, Georgetown, of Guyana, combines a remarkable range of posthuman themes and debates (Melville 1997). It not only introduces readers to an indigenous world in which animals and people have common traits, plants and rocks are vibrant and play an active role in shaping events, and language and narration emerge from a complex ecology, rather than being understood as distinctly human traits. The tension between this cosmology and a European one – variously visible in the novel in the guise of Mr McKinnon, a Scottish settler on the inland savannahs, the missionizing Catholic priest, Father Napier, or the neoimperial oil company wreaking devastation in the contemporary sections of the novel – is used to repeatedly question ethnocentric epistemological divisions, such as between myth and science. The novel is, among other things, a reckoning with the European anthropological tradition, and with the 'colonial fracture' described by Luisetti:

> The colonial fracture between political society and premodern states of nature, the Western Hemisphere and the rest, is the other side of the coin of the nature/culture *dispositif*, a fictional and yet concrete universal, keeping together the violence of colonial domination and an ethnographic museum of animisms and totemisms, idolatry and epistemic confusion. (Luisetti 2016, 216-217)[12]

It offers the opportunity to discuss topics from posthuman sexuality – in line with Halberstam and Livingston's assertion that "sexuality is a dispersed relation between bodies and things" (Halberstam and Livingston 1995, 5)[13] – to indigenous (and possibly posthuman) science (De Line 2016; DeLoughrey 2007).

7. Teaching Ideas and Challenges

The themes and debates discussed here could either be treated as a stand-alone topic in a course on postcolonial posthumanism, or integrated into other theoretically oriented courses, such as on animal studies. It would also be possible to discuss many of these theoretical works, and the topic of postcolonial posthumanism, in a course focused on metafiction, narrative, language and writing. Another option would be to introduce posthumanism, or some posthumanist ideas, within a course on, for example, contemporary Australian writing or Native American literature. A course on postcolonial science fiction would also offer a good opportunity to discuss debates on posthumanism and postcolonialism.

Students who are already somewhat familiar with postcolonial studies need to be introduced to posthumanism and the similarities and differences between the fields. This tends to be challenging for some students because posthumanist thought is not necessarily well defined – or definitions of posthumanism differ significantly from each other. Students who are uncomfortable with a field full of ongoing debates and fuzzy definitions may find this frustrating; on the other hand, students more comfortable with theoretical debates may find it exciting to be working with ideas that are clearly being developed by scholars and by ongoing discussions in the present moment. It is potentially good training for students to learn to write, for example, not "posthumanism is ..." but "according to Badmington, posthumanism is ...". Students who are familiar with neither posthumanism nor postcolonial studies will need more extensive preparation to understand both fields; nonetheless, many of the theoretical texts cited here provide good critical summaries of important developments in anti- and postcolonial thought, and post-humanist ideas, so that these texts can be used either to introduce students to major tenets of postcolonialism and posthumanism or to refresh their knowledge of the fields.

In many cases, both the theoretical and literary texts discussed here allow students to come into contact with at least some posthumanist ideas without extensive background knowledge. In class discussions of many of the literary texts here, it would be possible first to identify features of the text – such as the attribution of agency to non-human actors – and then to lead on to a discussion about, for example, whether this should be considered anthropomorphism or a posthumanist perspective that questions human exceptionalism and the human-animal divide. The theoretical background and history of ideas behind such debates could then be introduced as contextualization, rather than confronting students with an enormous body of theory to begin with. Such decisions – about whether to begin with fiction and work back to theory, or to introduce the theoretical debates and then bring these into dialogue with the fiction – will depend both on the desired focus of teaching and the theoretical fitness and level of the students.

Notes

1 For example, Martin Kurthen (2009) proposes a rather unfortunate categorization of "white" (benevolent) and "black" (destructive) posthumanism.

2 Alexis Shotwell's work on purity, toxicity and the Anthropocene conceptualizes the process of clearing pollution from one area or city as a process of colonization, in which toxins are offloaded onto another land or population. Adam Greenfield speaks of the "colonization of everyday life by information processing" (2017, 32) – a conceptual link that his book, unfortunately, takes as a transparent metaphor rather than an opportunity to investigate how the "radical technologies" and their transformation of the world that he discusses might be differentially affected by racialization and colonialism.

3 This text is a slightly shortened extract from *White Mythologies. Writing History and the West* (Young 2004, 157-65).

4 A similar critique of work on the Anthropocene that does not, however, complicate the figure of the human in the way demanded by Chakrabarty is offered by Malm and Hornborg (2014).

5 On *Sila*, Todd points in particular to the work of Rachel Qitsualik (1998).

6 Chagani points to several exemplary essays in DeLoughrey and Handley (2011); and Huggan and Tiffin (2010).

7 Todd draws here on Watts (2013). Similar points are raised by Hunt (2014).

8 Risling Baldy takes the concept of "settler moves to innocence" from Tuck and Yang (2012).

9 Several other stories in the same collection *So Long Been Dreaming. Postcolonial Science Fiction and Fantasy* (Hopkinson and Mehan 2004) rehearse similar themes.

10 For another analysis of the connections between postcolonialism, posthumanism, genre and form in the novel, see O'Connell (2012).

11 For a reading of the novel via reflections on the rejection of human status non-fictional survivors of environmental catastrophe, see Nixon (2011, 45-67).

12 Luisetti is here reworking ideas from Latour (1993).

13 Posthuman sexuality is a topic which has, so far, received less attention than might be expected. Some other references include Lingis (1997); Luciano and Chen (2015); and Muñoz (2015).

Works Cited

Agamben, Giorgio (2004). *The Open: Man and Animal*. Trans. Kevin Attell. Stanford, CA: Stanford University Press.

Armstrong, Philip (2002). "The Postcolonial Animal." *Society & Anima*ls 10.4, 413-19.

Badmington, Neil, ed. (2000). *Posthumanism*. Houndmills, Basingstoke: Palgrave Macmillan.

--- (2011). "Posthumanism." *The Routledge Companion to Literature and Science*. Eds. Bruce Clark and Manuela Rossini. New York: Routledge, 374-84.

Banerjee, Bidisha (2013). "Utopian Transformations in the Contact Zone: A Posthuman, Postcolonial Reading of Shaun Tan and John Marsden's The Rabbits." *Global Studies of Childhood* 3.4, 418-26.

--- (2016). "Kinship Between 'Companion Species': A Posthuman Refiguration of the Immigrant Condition in Shaun Tan's The Arrival." *Journal of Postcolonial Writing* 52.4, 399-414.

Bartosch, Roman (2012). "The Postcolonial Picaro in Indra Sinha's Animal's People – Becoming Posthuman through Animal's Eyes." *Ecozon@* 3.1, 10-19.

Blenkinsop, Sean, Ramsey Affifi, Laura Piersol, and Michael De Danann Sitka-Sage (2017). "Shut-Up and Listen: Implications and Possibilities of Albert Memmi's Characteristics of Colonization Upon the 'Natural World'." *Studies in Philosophy and Education* 36, 349-65.

Braidotti, Rosi (2006*). Transpositions: On Nomadic Ethics*. Cambridge: Polity.

--- (2013). *The Posthuman*. Cambridge: Polity.

--- (2017). "Critical Posthuman Knowledges." *South Atlantic Quarterly* 116.1, 83-96.

Brennan, Timothy (2014). *Borrowed Light: Vico, Hegel, and the Colonies*. Vol. 1. Stanford, CA: Stanford University Press.

Brooker, Charlie (2016). "Men Against Fire." Directed by Jakob Verbruggen. *Black Mirror*, season 3, episode 5, Netflix. 21 October 2016.

Buckell, Tobias S. (2004). "Necahual." *So Long Been Dreaming: Postcolonial Science Fiction and Fantasy*. Eds. Nalo Hopkinson and Uppinder Mehan. Vancouver: Arsenal Pulp Press, 251-67.

Carruth, Allison (2011). "Compassion, Commodification, and The Lives of Animals: J. M. Coetzee's Recent Fiction." *Postcolonial Ecologies: Literatures of the Environment*. Eds. Elizabeth DeLoughrey and George B. Handley. Oxford: Oxford University Press, 200-15.

Castree, Noel, and Catherine Nash (2006). "Posthuman Geographies." *Social & Cultural Geography* 7.4, 501-04.

Castro, Eduardo Viveiros de (1992). *From the Enemy's Point of View: Humanity and Divinity in an Amazonian Society*. Trans. Catherine V. Howard. Chicago: University of Chicago Press.

--- (1998). "Cosmological Perspectivism in Amazonia and Elsewhere." Masterclass Series 1. Four Lectures Given in the Department of Social Anthropology, University of Cambridge, February-March 1998. *HAU Books*. Web. 19 November 2018. <https://haubooks.org/cosmological-perspectivism-in-amazonia/>.

Chagani, Fayaz (2016). "Can the Postcolonial Animal Speak?" *Society & Animals* 24.6, 619-37.

Chakrabarty, Dipesh (2000). *Provincializing Europe: Postcolonial Thought and Historical Difference*. Princeton, NJ: Princeton University Press.

--- (2009). "The Climate of History: Four Theses." *Critical Inquiry* 35.2, 197-222.

--- (2012). "Postcolonial Studies and the Challenge of Climate Change." *New Literary History* 43.1, 1-18.

--- (2014). "Climate and Capital: On Conjoined Histories." *Critical Inquiry* 41.1, 1-23.

Coetzee, J.M. (1999). *The Lives of Animals*. Princeton, NJ: Princeton University Press.

Coulthard, Glen (2010). "Place against Empire: Understanding Indigenous Anti-Colonialism." *Affinities: A Journal of Radical Theory, Culture, and Action* 4.2, 79-83.

De Line, Sebastian (2016). "All My/Our Relations: Can Posthumanism Be Decolonized?" *Open! Platform for Art, Culture & the Public Domain* 7 July. Web. 13 April 2017. <www.onlineopen.org/all-my-our-relations>.

DeLoughrey, Elizabeth (2007). "Quantum Landscapes: A 'Ventriloquism of Spirit'." *Interventions* 9.1, 62-82.

--- (2015). "Ordinary Futures: Interspecies Worldings in the Anthropocene." *Global Ecologies and the Environmental Humanities: Postcolonial Approaches*. Eds. Elizabeth DeLoughrey, Jill Didur and Anthony Carrigan. London and New York: Routledge, 352-72.

---, and George B. Handley, eds. (2011). *Postcolonial Ecologies: Literatures of the Environment*. Oxford: Oxford University Press.

---, Jill Didur, and Anthony Carrigan (2015). *Global Ecologies and the Environmental Humanities: Postcolonial Approaches*. London and New York: Routledge.

Descartes, René (2006). *A Discourse on the Method of Correctly Conducting One's Reason and Seeking Truth in the Sciences*. 1637. Trans. Ian Maclean. Oxford: Oxford University Press.

Descola, Philippe (1996). *The Spears of Twilight: Life and Death in the Amazon Jungle*. Trans. Janet Lloyd. London: Harper Collins.

--- (2013a). *Beyond Nature and Culture*. Trans. Janet Lloyd. Chicago: University of Chicago Press.

--- (2013b). *The Ecology of Others*. Trans. Geneviève Godbout and Benjamin P. Luley. Chicago: Prickly Paradigm.

Ferrando, Francesca (2013). "Posthumanism, Transhumanism, Antihumanism, Metahumanism, and New Materialisms: Differences and Relations." *Existenz* 8.2, 26-32.

Fowles, Severin (2016). "The Perfect Subject (Postcolonial Object Studies)." *Journal of Material Culture* 21.1, 9-27.

Frangos, Mike (2012). "The End of Literature: Machine Reading and Amitav Ghosh's The Calcutta Chromosome." *Digital Humanities Quarterly* 7.1. Web. 19 November 2018. < http://www.digitalhumanities.org/dhq/vol/7/1/000152/000152.html>.

Gandhi, Leela (1998). *Postcolonial Theory: A Critical Introduction*. New York: Allen & Unwin.

Ginn, Franklin (2017). "Post-humanism." *The International Encyclopedia of Geography: People, The Earth, Environment and Technology* 10. Eds. Noel Castree et al. Oxford: Wiley-Blackwell, 5269–77.

Gilroy, Paul (2000). *Against Race: Imagining Political Culture beyond the Color Line*. Cambridge, MA: Harvard University Press.

--- (2018). "'Where every breeze speaks of courage and liberty': Offshore Humanism and Marine Xenology, or Racism and the Problem of Critique at Sea Level." *Antipode* 50.1, 3-22.

Ghosh, Amitav (1995). *The Calcutta Chromosome. A Novel of Fevers, Delirium and Discovery*. Avon: Ravi Dayal Publishers.

Gordon, Lewis R. (1998). "African-American Philosophy: Theory, Politics, and Pedagogy." *Philosophy of Education Archive*, 39-46.

Gowdy, Barbara (1998). *The White Bone*. New York: Metropolitan Books.

Greenfield, Adam (2017). *Radical Technologies: The Design of Everyday Life*. London and New York: Verso.

Halberstam, Judith, and Ira Livingston, eds. (1995). *Posthuman Bodies*. Bloomington and Indianapolis, IN: Indiana University Press.

Haraway, Donna J. (2003). *The Companion Species Manifesto: Dogs, People, and Significant Otherness*. Chicago: Prickly Paradigm.

--- (2008). *When Species Meet*. Minneapolis, MN: University of Minnesota Press.

Hinton, Peta, Tara Mehrabi, and Josef Barla (2015). "New Materialisms/New Colonialisms." *Proceedings of ISCH COST Action IS1307* New Materialism Working Group Two: New Materialism on the Crossroads of the Natural and

Human Sciences, 2015. Web. 19 November 2018. <newmaterialism.eu/content/5-working-groups/2-working-group-2/position-papers/subgroup-position-paper-_-new-materialisms_new-colonialisms.pdf>.

Hopkinson, Nalo and Uppinder Mehan, eds. (2004). *So Long Been Dreaming: Postcolonial Science Fiction and Fantasy*. Vancouver: Arsenal Pulp Press.

Huggan, Graham (2004). "'Greening' Postcolonialism: Ecocritical Perspectives." *Modern Fiction Studies* 50.3, 701-33.

---, and Helen Tiffin (2010). *Postcolonial Ecocriticism: Literature, Animals, Environment*. London and New York: Routledge.

Hulme, Keri (2004). "Floating Words." *Stonefish*. Wellington, NZ: Huia Publishers.

Hunt, Sarah (2014). "Ontologies of Indigeneity: The Politics of Embodying a Concept." *Cultural Geographies* 21.1, 27-32.

Jackson, Mark (2014). "Composing Postcolonial Geographies: Postconstructivism, Ecology and Overcoming Ontologies of Critique." *Singapore Journal of Tropical Geography* 35, 72-87.

Jackson, Zakiyyah Iman (2013). "Animal: New Directions in the Theorization of Race and Posthumanism." *Feminist Studies* 39.3, 669-85.

Johns-Putra, Adeline (2018). "The Rest Is Silence. Postmodern and Postcolonial Possibilities in Climate Change Fiction." *Studies in the Novel* 50.1, 26-42.

King, Tiffany Lethabo (2017). "Humans Involved: Lurking in the Lines of Posthumanist Flight." *Critical Ethnic Studies* 3.1, 162-85.

Kurthen, Martin (2009). *White and Black Posthumanism. After Consciousness and the Unconscious*. Trans. Robert Payne. Berlin and Boston: Ambra Publishing. TRACE Transmission in Rhetorics, Arts and Cultural Evolution.

Lathers, Marie (2006). "Toward an Excremental Posthumanism: Primatology, Women, and Waste." *Society & Animals* 14.4, 417-36.

Latour, Bruno (1993). *We Have Never Been Modern*. Trans. Catherine Porter. Cambridge, MA: Harvard University Press.

--- (2004). *Politics of Nature: How to Bring the Sciences into Democracy*. Trans. Catherine Porter. Cambridge, MA: Harvard University Press.

--- (2014). "Agency at the Time of the Anthropocene." *New Literary History* 45.1, 1-18.

Lingis, Alphonso (1997). "Animal Body, Inhuman Face." *Social Semiotics* 7.2, 113-26.

Livingston, Julie, and Jasbir K. Puar (2011). "Interspecies." *Social Text* 106, 29.1, 1-14.

Luciano, Dana, and Mel Y. Chen (2015). "Has the Queer Ever Been Human?" *GLQ* 21.2-3, 182-207.

Luisetti, Federico (2016). "Decolonizing the State of Nature: Notes on Political Animism." *Critical Posthumanism and Planetary Futures*. Eds. Debashish Banerji and Makarand R. Paranjape, New Delhi: Springer India, 215-24.

Malm, Andreas, and Alf Hornborg (2014). "The Geology of Mankind? A Critique of the Anthropocene Narrative." *The Anthropocene Review* 1.1, 62-69.

Mavhunga, Clapperton Chakanetsa (2011). "Vermin Beings: On Pestiferous Animals and Human Game." *Social Text* 29.1, 151-76.

Melville, Pauline (1997). *The Ventriloquist's Tale*. London: Bloomsbury.

Mitchell, Timothy (2002). *Rule of Experts: Egypt, Techno-Politics, and Modernity*. Berkeley, CA: University of California Press.

Mukherjee, Pablo (2011). "'Tomorrow There Will Be More of Us': Toxic Postcoloniality in Animal's People." *Postcolonial Ecologies: Literatures of the Environment*. Eds. Elizabeth DeLoughrey and George B. Handley. Oxford: Oxford University Press. 216-31.

Muñoz, José Esteban (2015). "Theorizing Queer Inhumanisms." *GLQ* 21.2-3, 209-48.

Nayar, Pramod K. (2009). "The Informational Economy and Its Body in Amitav Ghosh's The Calcutta Chromosome." *Kunapipi* 31.2, 52-69.

Nixon, Rob (2011). *Slow Violence and the Environmentalism of the Poor*. Cambridge, MA: Harvard University Press.

O'Connell, Hugh Charles (2012). "Mutating Toward the Future: The Convergence of Utopianism, Postcolonial SF, and the Postcontemporary Longing for Form in Amitav Ghosh's The Calcutta Chromosome." *MFS Modern Fiction Studies* 58.4, 773-95.

Padmanabhan, Manjula (2003). *Harvest*. London and Sydney: Aurora Metro Publishing.

Qitsualik, Rachel. (1998). "Word and Will – Part Two: Words and the Substance of Life." *Nunatsiaq News*. 12 November 1998. Web. 19 November. 2018. <www.nunatsiaqonline.ca/archives/nunavut981130/nvt81113_09.html>.

Rai, Amit S. (2012). "Race Racing: Four Theses on Race and Intensity." *WSQ: Women's Studies Quarterly* 40.1-2, 64-75.

Risling Baldy, Cutcha (2015). "Coyote Is Not a Metaphor: On Decolonizing, (Re)claiming and (Re)naming Coyote." *Decolonization: Indigeneity, Education & Society* 4.1, 1-20.

Rose, Deborah Bird (1992). *Dingo Makes Us Human. Life and Land in an Aboriginal Australian Culture*. Cambridge: Cambridge University Press.

Roy, Arundati (1999). "The Greater Common Good." *Friends of River Narmada*, April 1999. Web. 19 November 2018 < www.narmada.org/gcg/gcg.html>.

Shinn, Christopher A. (2008). "On Machines and Mosquitoes: Neuroscience, Bodies, and Cyborgs in Amitav Ghosh's The Calcutta Chromosome." *MELUS* 33.4, 145-66.

Shotwell, Alexis (2016). *Against Purity: Living Ethically in Compromised Times*. Minneapolis, MN: University of Minnesota Press.

Sinha, Indra (2005). *Animal's People*. New York: Scribner.

Skeat, Jean (2016). "Political Poetics and the Power of Things: Nonhuman Agency and Climate Change in Alexis Wright's The Swan Book." *Transformations* 27. Web. 19 November 2018. <www.transformationsjournal.org/issue-27/>.

Smith, Linda Tuhiwai (1999). *Decolonizing Methodologies: Research and Indigenous Peoples*. London: Zed Books.

Smith, Sidonie (2012). "Reading the Posthuman Backward: Mary Rowlandson's Doubled Witnessing." *Biography* 35.1, 137-52.

Sundberg, Juanita (2014). "Decolonizing Posthumanist Geographies." *Cultural Geographies* 21.1, 33-47.

TallBear, Kim (2011). "Why Interspecies Thinking Needs Indigenous Standpoints." *Cultural Anthropology* 24 April 2011. Web. 19 November. <culanth.org/fieldsights/260-why-interspecies-thinking-needs-indigenous-standpoints>.

Tan, Shaun (2006). *The Arrival*. Melbourne: Lothian Books.

Todd, Zoe (2016). "An Indigenous Feminist's Take on the Ontological Turn: 'Ontology' Is Just Another Word for Colonialism." *Journal of Historical Sociology* 29.1, 4-22.

Tuck, Eve and K. Wang Yang (2012). "Decolonization is Not a Metaphor." *Decolonization: Indigeneity, Education & Society* 1.1, 1-40.

Van Dooren, Thom, Eben Kirksey, and Ursula Münster (2016). "Multispecies Studies: Cultivating Arts of Attentiveness." *Environmental Humanities* 8.1, 1-23.

Watson, Annette and Orville H. Huntington (2008). "They're Here – I Can Feel Them: The Epistemic Spaces of Indigenous and Western Knowledges." *Social & Cultural Geography* 9.3, 257-81.

Watts, Vanessa (2013). "Indigenous Place-Thought and Agency Among Humans and Non-Humans (First Woman and Sky Woman Go on a European World Tour!)." *Decolonization: Indigeneity, Education & Society* 2.1, 20-34.

Wolfe, Cary (2003). *Animal Rites: American Culture, the Discourse of Species, and Posthumanist Theory*. Chicago: University of Chicago Press.

--- (2010). *What Is Posthumanism?* Minneapolis, MN: University of Minnesota Press.

Wright, Alexis (2013). *The Swan Book*. London: Constable.

Young, Robert (1992). "Colonialism and Humanism." *'Race', Culture and Difference*. Ed. James Donald and Ali Rattansi, London: Sage. 243-51.

--- (2004) *White Mythologies: Writing History and the West*. 2nd ed. London and New York: Routledge.

Alessandra Boller
Eckart Voigts

"What counts as a liveable life and a grievable death?" – Critical Posthumanism and Cloning in Kazuo Ishiguro's *Never Let Me Go* and Caryl Churchill's *A Number*

Introduction

After the first successful cloning of monkeys in 2018, this branch of biotechnology seems to be at the forefront of genetic engineering – or at least of its media coverage – again. Together with the recent biotechnological revolution of CRISPR/Cas, cloning is – again or still – controversially discussed, at least by the rather new field of bioethics and ethical criticism in literary and cultural studies. Since these technologies might be able to modify the human body, they fuel current anxieties and insecurities about posthumanism (cf. Vint 2007, 8. 182), which also tie in with notions of (human) identity.

In their introduction to *Clones and Clones*, Martha Nussbaum and Cass Sunstein stressed the impact of the "arrival of Dolly" (1998, 11). While the figure of the clone had already been prominent in science fiction before 1997, Dolly made this technology famous and produced a "tsunami" of speculation and speculative fiction (Dann and Dozois 1998, ix). Cover stories about the possibility of adapting cloning techniques for the production of human clones appeared in newspapers and magazines all over the world (cf. *Time Magazine* March 1997, February 2001; *Newsweek* October 1997) and contributed to a change in the public perception of the applicability of this technique; cloning seemed to have become reality overnight. Discussions about the legality and morality of cloning human beings (cf. Dann and Dozois 1998, ix) arose and according to Nussbaum and Sunstein, it has been the idea and apparent possibility of human cloning "far more than the reality of animal cloning, that has caused public anxiety" (1998, 11). This insight already alludes to the power of ideas and metaphors, and to humanity's schizophrenic connection to the creation of 'artificial' beings: Humankind is commonly regarded as the only world-building species; and creating new life, a subject of human fascination not only since Mary Shelley's paradigmatic novel *Frankenstein* (1818), would be the ultimate proof of humanity's capacities, on the one hand. On the other hand, the ontological status of such beings bears disruptive potential: If fully-fledged human beings can be artificially created, instead of springing from the (sacred) union of man and woman,, does that make mankind less exceptional?

Biotechnology thus challenges the "immutability of boundaries between humans, animals and machines, artificial and natural, 'born' and 'made'" (Graham 2002, 1-2). It consequently questions the stability of 'human nature' along with the Enlightenment conception of 'man' as an autonomous, rational and unique subject (cf. Simon 2003, 1, 4) who can improve himself and society through education and self-reflection (cf. Didur 2003, 98). This idea points to the discursive and educational production of 'the human', and the risks and benefits the rapid progress of biotechnology poses or offers. The term 'cloning,' coined in 1903 by Herbert J. Webber, who drew on O.F. Cook, was first only used for plants but has now covered "semantic distances[,] and the degree of abstraction [...] in popular and scientific language seems rather astonishing" (Camenzind 2015, 28-29). Thus, the figure of the clone, mostly employed in dystopian narratives, can serve as a space and metaphor that helps to reassess humanity, its construction of and claim to an exceptional position, and the pitfalls of such human exceptionalism.

"What is all the emotion about?," Nussbaum and Sunstein rhetorically ask: "Human beings have always been afraid of their own creative power, and the idea of man-made life was scary long before science was in any position to think of procedures that might make it reality" (1998, 11). Greek mythology features various living beings that "were human bodies without regular souls," for example (12). "To the Greeks [...] the idea that [...] creatures who bypassed [the 'natural' way of reproducing] were a little peculiar, came quite easily, without science to back it up" (ibid). However, since at least Dolly, cloning resides in the liminal sphere between scientific possibility and imagination. Pointing out some of the nightmares connected to artificially created life-forms, Nussbaum and Sunstein, like so many others before and after them, refer to *Frankenstein* which still serves as a common ground and seems to interlink science, everyday discourse, and bioethics, for example, when genetically modified crops are termed 'Frankenstein Food' (Gray 2001, 117). Nussbaum and Sunstein explain that science can answer many questions of cloning and set things straight, but it

> doesn't give us the answers to the ethical, political, social, and religious questions raised by cloning. These answers need to be worked out, ultimately, in the course of public debate. But the humanities and the social sciences can help us lay out the options in a clear way, and give us some good arguments to ponder. (14)

Some of the questions raised by Nussbaum and Sunstein are also crucial thematic foci in Caryl Churchill's play *A Number* and Kazuo Ishiguro's novel *Never Let Me Go*, two influential contemporary British dystopian texts which serve as an entry point to bioethical discussion and are thus also valuable for the university and EFL classroom. Approaching the clone from different viewpoints, they reveal the potential of this figure or metaphor. Our article examines how they deal with ideological bias and the malleability of 'the human' within the framework of critical posthumanism. Advocating a non-anthropocentric[1] approach, this article will focus on the re-evaluation of concepts of humanity in posthumanist dystopias by centring two common denominators of humanity: language, which also ties in with world-building (culture) and definatory power, on the one hand, and death as well as Judith Butler's concept of grievability, on the other.

Critical Posthumanism and Its Potentials

'The human' is not only a biologically defined species but also an idea or concept which determines the behaviour of 'the human' towards other beings in ecological relations, including those people not regarded as fully-fledged human beings or persons. This concept "functions to domesticate and hierarchize difference within the human (whether according to race, class, gender) and to absolutize difference between the human and the non-human" (Halberstam and Livingston 1995, 10).

Inseparably connected to anthropocentrism, human exceptionalism thrives on this basic distinction between human and nonhuman animals. Halberstam and Livingston describe 'the human' as an "exclusive club [...] complete with all the rights and privileges pertaining thereunto (for example, to eat non-members of the club and the privilege not to be eaten)" but "some of the some that we are have been excluded" (ibid.). So while human exceptionalism distributes power and value on the level of species membership, it also serves as a basis for intraspecies discrimination, i.e. the practice of denying dignity, the right to life, or equal consideration of needs to so called minority groups who are, in the logic of human exceptionalism, degraded to the realm of 'the animal.' Thus, the term 'the human' actually is a matter of definition and of discursive production which ties in with the exploitation of other beings; it is the result of the process of discrimination against women, homosexual, or non-western people, for example.

Critical posthumanism allows for the complication of basic western notions of (post)humanism. It may be characterized by its "critique, both of an essentializing conception of human nature, and of human *exceptionalism*" and

> by discourses of the dissolution or blurring of the boundaries of the human, whether conceptual and philosophical (as in the 'decentring' of the human in 20th-century structuralist and poststructuralist thought) or scientific and technological (as in biotechnologies, genetics and cybernetics). (Wallace 2010, 692-93; original emphasis)

Due to its deconstruction of the objectification and commodification of some lives by capitalist science and neoliberalism, critical post-humanism helps to move towards a more biocentric, and thus non-anthropocentric, approach to life.

Hence, critical posthumanism can function as a counterweight to anthropocentric demarcation strategies, and helps discuss and evaluate notions of 'the non/post/human.' In this context and in dystopian fiction, posthuman figures such as the clone become sites of both hope and concern. They are helpful screens or projected images to turn to (cf. Halberstam and Livingston 1995, 3) as they enable reflection on humanity and ingrained ideologies from a vantage point which takes bioethics and the concomitants as well as bases of human exceptionalism into account. Besides, they offer the opportunity to realise the need for a re-evaluation of 'the human' by stressing the instability of its traditional definitions in a biotechnological age which renders science ever-more capitalist and neoliberal. The posthuman therefore does not imply just another evolutionary step forward. It rather offers a new view on humanity and its discriminatory practices as it follows in the tradition of various former 'others' (such as monsters or aliens) used to draw attention to the instability of "the ascribed and not essential nature of human nature" (Graham 2002, 13). As 'fabulations,' dystopian narratives can be counted among the "forms of popular culture that disrupt certainties or explode ideologies" (Barr qtd. in Graham 2002, 13). Understood as spaces to (re)negotiate what counts as human and grievable life, they play a crucial role in reconstructions of ideology and thus bear educational potential in line with non-anthropocentric pedagogy. All these ideas are thus integral to a form of pedagogy which is urgently needed to raise awareness of western society's discriminatory practices and tendencies.

Pieter Vermeulen's idea that "the human creature has a future beyond the liberal humanist subject, and that future has already begun" (2017, 394) becomes obvious in the unspecified spatial and temporal setting of *A Number* and even more so in Ishiguro's novel: published in 2005, it spans the time from the 1970s to the 1990s, thus employing an alternative history scenario which appears both nostalgic and futuristic and creates an eerie effect of immediacy. These texts do not promote a return to humanist definitions and ideals, which are exposed as harmful demarcation strategies, but instead invite readers to ponder the meaning of being human while acknowledging humanity's embeddedness in ecological and technological structures. Therefore, they rethink and complicate basic western structures of living and thinking instead of only promoting a shift of the definition of 'the human' within given frameworks of anthropocentric and capitalist thought.

'The Human,' the Clone and Judith Butler's Concept of "Grievable Life"

Traditionally established and ideologically anchored dichotomies (e.g., the human/animal divide) and specific concepts which establish differences among human beings, such as grievability, inform the discussion of ethically determined questions of human exceptionalism and anthropocentric discourse in this article. Situated at the intersection of these processes and discourses, 'the posthuman' acquires functions crucial for a reimagining of 'the human' and the lives constructed as its 'others' and foils. A posthumanist discussion of harmful exclusions benefits from Judith Butler's concept of grievable life, which she first developed in *Precarious Life*, a collection of essays she wrote as a reaction to 9/11 and to the ensuing social and legal circumstances within the US and in the whole world. This caesura in western history has triggered various forms of engagement with human lives. Butler's essays reveal the (political) impact of normality and normativity, when she emphasises that

> [s]ome lives are grievable, and others are not; the differential allocation of grievability that decides what kind of subject is and must be grieved, and which kind of subject must not, operates to produce and maintain certain exclusionary conceptions of who is normatively human: what counts as a liveable life and a grievable death? (Butler, 2004, xiv-xv)

The notion of grievability – constructed and maintained from a powerful western position – produces categories of stable, safe, and normative lives on the one hand. On the other hand, it constructs other lives as not grievable and unliveable (cf. 2004, xv). Accordingly, "normative conditions for the production of the subject" (Butler 2009, 3-4) are established and maintained but can also be modified according to the circumstances. Such norms and conditions have tangible effects, especially on lives which are not acknowledged as grievable subjects and consequently regarded as lacking inherent value.

Thus, Butler emphasises that the binary 'us versus them' ties in with the idea that only certain lives are and must be highly protected, often at the expense of lives not regarded as valuable (cf. 2004, 32). Such classifications might also partly regulate the population's sympathy with some human beings on the one hand, and the lack of it on the other.[2] The same observation applies to other groups that are protected through the death of seemingly inferior ones, an idea taken up in *Never Let Me Go*, for example, in which a biopolitical society creates clones to harvest their organs in order to cure those people who are regarded as human beings, the citizens.

The dichotomy human/clone established in many dystopian scenarios also evokes the dichotomy original/copy. The figure of the clone, often depicted as a copy of a 'real' human being and hence of lesser value, reveals that the two sides of a dichotomy actually rely on one another. It therefore draws attention to definitions of 'the human,' the benefits this definition seems to bring, but also the negative aspects it produces – for those excluded from the definition and as a second step, for 'the human' itself. The clone raises awareness of 'the human' as an instable idea which is maintained through performative re-enactment only, which brings us to ideas of identity, in various ways, as the two examples from dystopian fiction will prove. Part of this instability derives from the false universalism critiqued by critical posthumanism and from the undermining of human value and the ends to which allegedly positive, outstanding, human characteristics are used. Cary Wolfe, among others, draws attention to the impossibility of defining 'the human' without 'the animal' (2003, xiii). Camenzind points out a different dependency by stating that

> it only makes sense to speak of the concept of an original if a copy exists. The original depends as much on the copy as the copy depends on the original. It can even be claimed that the original does not generate the copy, but the copy generates the original, conceptually speaking. (2015, 31-32)

The reliance of 'the human' on its alleged others even raises questions about humanity's special status as the only form of life with inherent value. The clone as a copy threatens the exceptional status of 'the human,' and thus its claim to sovereignty, by commodifying it. For example, in *Never Let Me* Go, the clone is an organ donor raised in isolation to guarantee harvests of maximum benefit and hence is exploited as a biological factory, while *A Number* rather revolves around the raising of clones and the question of originality and ownership.

In terms of grievability, cloning and the figure of the clone are insightful with regard to ethics and values. Although debates revolving around the moral dimension of cloning are launched regularly and although cloning human beings is still forbidden, Gray claims that "[e]ventually these technologies will be accepted because there are cures and money to be made. There is no threshold in sight" (2001, 123). In 2018, the media coverage of the birth of two monkeys directly turned towards the effects this might have for human beings, instead of pondering the number of nonhuman lives lost in the process (cf.

Cyranoski 2018, n.p.). Camenzind also points out that cloning, in contrast to public perception, still is risky (2015, 27), and therefore, only 'the animal' is subjected to cloning since the risks "are not reasonable for humans, but for animals" (27; 34), or: only humans are grievable.

We may thus, with Maximilian Probst in the German newspaper *Die Zeit*, call for a form of education which transcends anthropocentric thought. Probst claims that the ideal of Enlightenment has destroyed the planet and therefore demands mankind not to focus on its own freedom only. Challenging the strong links between education and neoliberal economic thought, and discussing the problematic linkage with industrialisation, Probst also invokes notions of individual growth and progress of the individual prevalent in German idealism. Probst claims that with fossil fuel instead of watermills, for example, mankind suddenly seemed to oppose externalised nature and thus to stand above it. This process of understanding mankind and the culture that seems to define it as the opposite of nature has led to many other dichotomies and informs contemporary issues such as the loss of species diversity or climate change.

As Probst states, some, but still too few, areas of the humanities and social sciences have started to react to this insight; there seems to be a new turn towards an understanding of ecology as a web of relations that mankind is also part of. It is in this context that Probst returns to his call for a new aim and concept of education: arriving at an understanding of a network which interconnects (and is co-produced by) human and nonhuman agents. Literature and the arts might become a means of reconciliation – various dystopian texts have offered scenarios which appear dystopian but actually also offer a utopian core and might provide valuable food for thought in university and high school education.

The re-evaluation of monstrosity in *Frankenstein* or the reassessment of humanity in *Never Let Me Go*, for example, challenge anthropocentrism and "[o]nce the centrality of *anthropos* is challenged, a number of boundaries between 'Man' and his others go tumbling down, in a cascade effect that opens up unexpected perspectives" (Braidotti 2013, 65-66). Such a destabilisation offers opportunities, even though it threatens human exceptionalism and is hence mostly evaluated as dystopian. Thus, the thought experiments offered to us in fiction (which draw on the physical reality of scientific experiments) do have a tangible value when it comes to society, education, and the survival of a species – even though the new understanding of humanity might considerably depart from the Enlightenment concept.

The Clone and Clone Narratives

Stressing that the idea of the clone as copy is a metaphor only, Camenzind emphasises that metaphors are not neutral tools but tie in with the language of objectification and have a normative component: "They carry values, express how the world is experienced, and literally shape the world," they inform and transform it (2015, 29, cf. 25). The metaphor of the clone as genetic copy has "some inevitable short-comings in highlighting some aspects but hiding others and may include some normative aspects, which should be handled very carefully in a descriptive field of science such as biology" (29). This necessitates pondering norms and ideologies as well as the point of view from which a reader approaches a text. Challenging ideology thus also means taking hierarchically structured dichotomies into account; an insight which should be taken into consideration in an educational context. As feminist criticism, for example, has pointed out, hierarchical dichotomies follow a patriarchal logic, viewing the allegedly more valuable first half of the dichotomy as male. This underlines that the respective demarcation strategies vilify the discriminated parts.

The metaphor of the clone helps to scrutinise the differential allocation of value to lives, visualising both the dichotomy original/copy and the current problems which can be traced back to such binary thinking. Following the logic of human exceptionalism, the maintenance of definitions and hierarchical dichotomies seems to be regarded as the most important problem in the dystopian texts mentioned: (cloned) human beings become capitalist commodities in a neoliberal world order and a text such as *Never Let Me Go* reveals how the production of the clone in a framework of humanist traditions produces cruelty and an updated form of vivisection reminiscent of Wells's Dr. Moreau.

Since the late 1960s, science fiction and speculative fiction has increasingly revolved around the figure of the clone. The ethical concerns voiced by texts revolving around replicants (e.g., Philip K. Dick's *Do Androids Dream of Electric Sheep*? (1968)) or AI (artificial intelligence; e.g., Alex Garland's *Ex Machina* (2015)), for example, bear some resemblance to the discourse of the clone. Christina Brandt claims that the clone's various literary precedents, such as the doppelganger, the automaton, the android, or other creatures can be likened to Frankenstein's creature (cf. 2008, 128).

Marking the amalgamation of fact and fiction, the clone stands at the intersection of biotechnology and imagination (cf. Caduff 2004, 230-31). Dystopian novels and plays can be interpreted as thought experiments, or as allegories on present realities fiction; reading such texts as an extension of reality (cf. Camenzind 2015, 29) offers perspectives on present-day life and the directions it is taking.

A common reading of clone narratives focuses on identity issues on a personal level, but such questions can easily be extended: What about the uniqueness of a species which relies on morality and concepts such as death (or killing) and language? It is in the interrelation of such concepts that grievability re-emerges as a pattern with tangible consequences. Both *Never Let Me Go* and *A Number* serve as ideal examples to discuss some of the effects of the figure of the clone in this light.

Language

Language has frequently been described as one of the most essential attributes of human beings. While stressing that "[l]anguage has always been [...] the defining mark of human uniqueness and its lack has traditionally determined the inferiority and exclusion of the nonhuman other," philosophers such as Carlo Salzani have also claimed that the "posthuman decentering of 'the human' means therefore also a decentering of language and its exclusiveness" (2017, 101).

Martha Nussbaum's concept of the species norm might even prove to be more valuable than Salzani's explanation that the "turn to the animal" highlights "the necessity of bypassing language, of exiting the representational cage, in order to make sense of animals (and of human animality), and thus of going beyond the 'human' as defined by Western tradition" (2017, 102). The "species norm [...] tells us that certain abilities are not equally valuable in all species" (Nussbaum 2008, 364) and thus constitutes a different approach to definitions of 'the human' and the role of certain properties. In this regard, Nussbaum asserts that "[l]anguage is an extremely valuable capacity for life in the human community" (2008, 364) but also underlines that for other species, it is not. Thus, even if 'the animal' did not possess language, this would not render the life of 'the animal' less valuable than human animal life.

Dystopian narratives reveal and scrutinise the power of language and the process of naming. The human power to define ties in with the common practice to summarise all nonhuman animals in the term 'the animal,' which bears testimony to this employment of power. In *Frankenstein*, the creature is defined as nonhuman and internalises this labelling, which results in his self-evaluation as not being of the "same nature as man" (Shelley 1971, 120). The same technique is mirrored in Ishiguro's novel, when clones are defined as not-quite-human and therefore do not qualify as (precarious and grievable) lives. Miss Emily, one of the few citizens featured in the novel, eventually reveals that most people consider clones to be "less than human" and soulless beings, which in the logic of human exceptionalism legitimises their exploitation and suffering from an organ donation programme which has their vital organs removed for transplantation purposes. The clones thereby help to secure a healthy 'human' population, which they are, by this society's understanding, not members of.

The clones' alleged deficiencies account for their definition as less than human and tie in with a presumed absence of feelings and their status as non-persons. This is also symbolised by their lack of a last name (Kathy's 'full name' is Kathy H.; there are two Bernards in *A Number*) which reveals that they are socially and culturally constructed as not fully-fledged human beings. The practice of refusing clones a complete name resembles the case of Victor Frankenstein's creature that is labelled demon, fiend, or monster. As Graham explains with regard to Shelley's novel, being nameless means being denied an entry into human subjectivity (cf. 2002, 70), but the clones apparently do not notice this disparaging practice (see Boller 2018, 251-53).

In *Never Let Me Go*, the clone protagonist and narrator Kathy's subject position and narration disclose that the border established between the clones and the citizens is merely arbitrary. Difference is a human construct and, thus, the definition of the clones as less than human is biased. Although Kathy seems to take language and world-making into her own hands, she cannot help employing the euphemistic language and the dominant people's diction she was trained to use. Kathy's voice and thought patterns are caught in a system and symbolic order which form a metaphorical imprisonment that also accounts for the lack of an escape route and the clones' inability to rebel; their language normalises their situation and renders it correct. Many of the words Kathy uses are only gradually revealed to be euphemisms: In Hailsham, where the clone children grow up and are educated, Kathy and her friends are labelled either 'students' or 'special' children, but never 'clones.' The clones 'donate' their organs and 'complete' eventually. As Toker and Chertoff observe, the "careful choice of new terms that take advantage of old positive connotations emphazises the link between ideological propaganda and marketing" (2008, 164). The word 'complete' implies success and hence has an utterly different connotation than the term 'die.'

In contrast to *A Number*, there are no parents who want to shape their children according to their own ideals or to revive somebody lost. This society operates on a different level, creating living beings who are literally drained or worn out when they fulfil the others', i.e. the citizens', ideals. The biopolitical society of Ishiguro's novel effectively indoctrinates the clones, who internalise its norms and values, and gives them a symbolic order that prevents rebellion. However, in contrast to the clones, the reader can understand the ideological structures which hurt them and eventually see the forces at work in western society, which, based on the notion of grievability, sacrifices some lives for the sake of others. This process allows for a general reassessment of apparently naturalised ideological structures.

The importance attributed to language becomes especially evident in *A Number* when it is linked to the notion of the copy. The cloned son Bernard 2 notices that Salter, the father, calls the other clones "things" (Churchill 2008, 166). He challenges Salter ("I think we'll find they're people," 166), reproaching his father's devaluing of them. Subsequently, the play raises the issue of the monetary value of these lives – ten or one hundred thousand or a million pounds (cf. ibid., 168-169). Just like the metaphor, language in general is not neutral and it can have tangible effects: For example, Bernard 2 is deeply hurt by the term 'things' since he suddenly notices that he might also be such a thing due to his artificial production. The "copy metaphor not only is a rhetorical tool, but also contributes, or at least mirrors, objectification tendencies"

(Camenzind 2015, 34), an insight often foregrounded in Churchill's play. When "metaphors actively shape the world, calling a clone a genetic copy is already an act of objectification" (ibid). This happens to the initially unknown clones in *A Number*, which are identified only as numbers.

The dialogues between Salter and his son Bernard 1, the clone Bernard 2, who is devastated by the revelation that he is not an 'original,' and another clone called Michael Black often revolve around similarities and differences, the genetic make-up of the clone and his original, and the question of personal identity. Bernard and his clone brother hate the idea of someone "indistinguishable" (B1, Churchill 2008, 178), "identical" to, or "like" them existing (B2, 186). One of the clone Michael's first questions is "Do I look like?" (199), significantly leaving out the parameter for his comparison. While the clones in Ishiguro's novel believe that finding their 'possibles,' the people they were cloned from, could reveal "who you were deep down" (Ishiguro 2005, 138), Salter tells his clone son Bernard 2 that the scientist, who produced a number of clones without permission, "damaged [his] uniqueness, weakened [his] identity" (Churchill 2008, 169). Salter and Bernard 2, in the first act of the play, use all the keywords of the clone rhetoric when they ponder who is 'real,' who was born in the 'normal' way, and who is a 'thing.' Bernard 2, at the end of act 1, states that "I'm just a copy. I'm not the real one" (174). "By attempting to quantify the value of his uniqueness, Salter reduces him to exchange value and thus reiterates the hideous rationale behind the son's laboratory beginnings" (Gobert 2014, 114). Besides, he consoles Bernard 1 with the same words, thus betraying the very idea of uniqueness (cf. 115).

Though the short play stays with Salter, his son, and his clones and thus on an individual level, the concerns raised here can easily be applied to a more general sense of threat that the clone still seems to trigger. However, due to its portrayal of the cloned lives as individuals on stage, the play also challenges the metaphor of the copy. As Camenzind stresses, the copy metaphor conceals certain normative aspects but simultaneously makes other, ethically relevant normative considerations visible: "These new normative aspects concern the way scientific language is used as an instrument or indication of *objectification tendencies* in biotechnological research" (2015, 32, emphasis original) which again points to the euphemisms employed in

Never Let Me Go. The fear evoked by cloning "lies in the idea that humans are dehumanized (or in the case of animals, deanimalized) and treated as copies and, therefore, things" (ibid). The (il)logic of human exceptionalism thus threatens the human, the world-building animal that erases itself by rendering itself non-unique: Paradoxically, the ability to create life (using the same methods to create human, animal, and plant life) and to model oneself can be seen as the world-building capacity of the human being which is, in the form of culture, one of its claims to exceptionalism. At the same time, however, the creation of a life which is commonly understood as being a copy also deconstructs the claim to human individuality and uniqueness. 'The human' is thus threatened to vanish in a puff of logic, like God in Douglas Adams' *Hitchhiker's Guide*; as soon as it actualises its unique abilities, it gets rid of itself. The clones in *A Number* seem to show that we have never really been ourselves – at the same time, the clone offers a possibility to see the human from a new viewpoint, which has become increasingly necessary.

Death

Gobert reads *A Number* as a dystopian play which focuses "acutely on the relationship between the self and the body that houses it";

> the doubling of Bernard, Bernard, and Michael Black works powerfully to embody Churchill's thesis about the unique value of each human being even in an age of biotechnological reproduction, when our reducibility to chromosomal patterns renders us vulnerable in a corporatized world. (2014, 120)

When Bernard 1 reports to his father that he has killed Bernard 2, the grievability of (clone) lives is foregrounded. The particular question if Salter grieves for the clone Bernard 2 is answered differently by various critics (and depends crucially on the staging of the play). For example, Gobert (cf. 2014, 115) says Salter is destroyed while Wilkinson states that he "seems unimpressed" by the murder of Bernard: "His strong trust in his own human-manufacturing abilities renders his sons replaceable" (2013, 40).

Immanuel Kant claimed that human beings are above all price, while things, including nonhuman animals, have a value – this value, however, is not intrinsic. Only when 'the human' uses these things as a means to an end, they are attributed a specific value (cf. Rachels and Rachels 2011). It is in this logic that human beings have exploited what they styled as their 'others': nature, animals, and also other human beings not considered equals. When Bernard becomes a problematic child after his mother's suicide, Salter acquires Bernard 2 as a means to an end since he wants to prove to himself that he can be a good father. Churchill gives Salter a long monologue which serves to rationalise his decision. Salter confronts his 'original' son with his decision not to kill him ("though you were this disgusting thing" (Churchill 2008, 198)) – now objectifying the supposedly 'original' son – and interprets his desire for a clone identical to his son (rather than a different, new child) as testament to his true, intense love. In *Never Let Me Go*, on the contrary, the clones are objectified and treated as a means to achieve a new physiology and immortality – but not for the clone but for the lives considered human. In fact, the relation to death is one aspect that makes the human human/e since it ties in with personhood, a precondition of grievability, and is thus linked to consciousness and identity. Ishiguro's clones die while the human citizens continue living which reveals that the rules mankind establishes are based on an unstable footing. The dying clones hold up a mirror to the humans and expose false universalism, double standards and demarcation strategies at work. What is more, their death (in addition to further characteristics, see Boller 2018) renders them more human/e than 'the human'.

However, since the clones' lives are not considered grievable, Ishiguro's biopolitical society can easily sacrifice them. Drawing on Derrida, Vint explains that the pervasive logic of the sacrifice is hidden in biopolitical regimes in which living beings in general can be put to death or human beings are allowed to

> die of hunger or disease [...] without any legal tribunal ever being considered competent to judge such a sacrifice, the sacrifice of others to avoid being sacrificed oneself... The smooth functioning of [a society's] moral discourse and good conscience presupposes the permanent operation of this sacrifice. (Derrida qtd. in Vint 2010, 452)

Thus, the sacrifice is ingrained in the logic of many actions and basic processes of quotidian (western) life. In order to protect one life, a 'less valuable' one is sacrificed. This argumentation is partially reminiscent of Butler's theory of grievability: only some lives can be mourned and are therefore worth preserving while others can be sacrificed in order to protect the former ones. In *Never Let Me Go*, a state-run breeding programme generates an almost limitless organ supply through the production and destruction of posthuman lives that constitute the supporting pillars of a society which is "made healthier through the biotechnological intersection of organ transplantation and artificial human reproduction" (Jennings 2010, 18). For the reader, Kathy and her friends appear and are human/e and grievable but they are not even considered human in the storyworld. This has severe consequences, because if the clone, analogous to 'the animal,' perishes but never dies,[3] it cannot be murdered or treated cruelly. Vint's claim that the logic of the sacrifice is rooted in the human/animal boundary is thus updated as human/clone boundary in Ishiguro's novel because the clones' lives are not regarded as lives according to anthropocentric norms (cf. Butler 2009, 16) but in terms of the sacrifice. Based on this differential allocation of grievability, linked to exclusionary practices and the normative construction of 'the human,' a clone's death is rather interpreted as a benefit instead of a loss. While the citizens are classified as grievable, human lives, the clones are constructed as bare lives whose only value consists in their deaths.

In *A Number*, Salter's two Bernards die, as the original son, Bernard 1, kills the clone, Bernard 2, and subsequently commits suicide. Confronting another one in a set of clones secretly produced by the doctors, Salter states that when he lost the cloned son "it wasn't so bad as you'd think because it seemed fair. I was back with the first one" (Churchill 2008, 205). Salter in fact claims he grieves his two dead sons, whereas the rest of the set, represented by Michael Black, are no compensation because they never lived with him and he never got to know them. Can he still mourn them when there are still "nineteen more of us," (ibid.) as the unfazed Michael claims, other cloned 'things' that might be identical. Are their lives grievable and precarious? In this regard, the clone again asks basic questions about the human being not only as a species but as an idea and concept. Gobert emphasises that Salter "conceives of clones as commodities," and even links him to

Monsanto and Harvard ('Oncomouse'), since he "reduces life to an acquisition" (2014, 115). "In a speech that underscores the clones' fungibility," Bernard 2 laments that a number of clones were made from the same genetic material and Salter was "one of the people who acquired" – the importance of agency and autonomy is highlighted when people are thus defined as "those who acquire instead of being acquired" (Gobert 2014, 115). "It is a patriarchal habit, but not exclusively male," Gobert (115) explains in view of the male linearity addressed by feminist playwright Churchill in *A Number*, but it might be more pertinent to point out that acquiring something is an anthropocentric habit which stresses power and agency. However, patriarchy and anthropocentrism are interlinked since anthropocentrism relies on a false universalism which actually favours the white, male, heterosexual, and thus European norm.

Salter suggests he deserves to be murdered by his son (cf. Churchill 2008, 197). His obvious crime is that he does not only acquire a clone, raising him without informing him about his origin. In so doing, he also abandons his first son and has him cloned to be able to start anew. When he thus exchanges his son for a new, hopefully improved version, he denies his individuality. Therefore, Bernard only seems to have an instrumental, but not an inherent or individual value. This is also stressed by the name that Salter's two sons share and by the third clone introduced: Michael Black is not defined in relation to Salter and even denies Salter's search for a core that all the clones share, after Bernard 1 and Bernard 2 have died. Loss is Salter's punishment for his failure to accept his son, abandoning him for a new start with a clone – a resonant echo of Mary Shelley's *Frankenstein*.

Individuality, consciousness, and the idea of a human or individual core are often connected to the notion of the soul. Nussbaum and Sunstein, referring to *Frankenstein*, state that the

> idea that we might make a human being without a soul was a source of horror; equally horrible, however, was the thought that we might make a being who *did* have a soul, but who, by virtue of its strange origin, would be doomed to live without love. (1998, 12-13)

What is more, an artificially created being that has a soul would symbolise a threat to what is considered human and could also not be sacrificed in line with anthropocentric norms and ethics. *Never Let Me*

Go shows this in form of the fictional Morningdale scandal: When the scientist James Morningdale designs human children with "enhanced characteristics" (Ishiguro 2005, 258), he reminds people of their fears: "a generation of created children who'd take their place in society? Children *superior* to the rest of *us*? Oh no" (259). Ishiguro's citizens apparently do not want to be confronted with genetic engineering and its scarier possibilities (and products) even though they still desire to benefit from the cures it provides. Moreover, Morningdale's use of genetic engineering highlighted that genetic engineering can produce both allegedly 'mechanical' clones and human children and thus threatened to dissolve the already instable boundaries drawn between human citizens and subhuman clones, between 'us' and 'them.'

Never Let Me Go, like many works of speculative fiction, confronts the reader with both utopian and dystopian elements. A world that has apparently achieved almost complete health could easily be considered utopian from the point of view of those whose pain and suffering are nearly abolished. However, the foregrounding of the clones' perspective makes readers side with the clones, but also requires its readers' critical engagement with regard to the evaluation of the society's ethical principles and value systems. Thus, it can serve as the ideal text to introduce such questions and categories to young readers and make them reflect on ideological constructs.

The two dystopian texts emphasise the constructedness of various demarcation strategies and corresponding ideological bases, and challenge fixed definitions of grievable or sacred lives. When biotechnology and ethics meet in the context of critical posthumanism, the idea of the clone as mechanical body as well as the sanctity of the human body are deconstructed. These two kinds of bodies are revealed to be almost the same and Kathy's narration even raises the question if the allegedly subhuman clones behave in a more human/e way than the beings defined as human. This idea does not end discussions revolving around clones but rather asks wide-reaching questions such as: When the clone is, just like the animal, not a mechanical body, can it then be defined as a person? How does this re-classification tie in with (bio)ethics and western practices or views of human morality and value systems?

Camenzind (cf. 2015, 31) states that Dolly overthrew a common hierarchy because, as a copy, she was more valuable than 'the original' (whoever counts as original). In the logic of commodification and capitalist science, rendered highly visible by the clone body, the same holds true for the clones in Ishiguro's and Churchill's texts: the clones in *Never Let Me Go* save the lives of various citizens and thus are worth various lives – but as sacrifices only. Salter tries to label the momentary value of the clones in terms of compensation. As he has a clone produced for his unsatisfactory Bernard, he learns that grievability results from the intimacy emerging between entities. Both texts establish grievability as a form of measurement which deconstructs the inherent value traditionally ascribed to 'the human' in humanist ideals. Ishiguro treats the clones throughout as grievable entities who establish their own emotional networks, and in Churchill's play, it does not matter if you are an original (Bernard 1) or a clone (Bernard 2).

Camenzind stresses that cloning is not entirely determining, that it is rather a process of splitting than of copying (cf. 2015, 31), and so Salter ultimately (and desperately) tries to find something he can relate to in the identity of his son's clone, Michael Black. The issue of ownership is prevalent in ethical debates about cloning and in clone narratives; Michael Black's final happiness in *A Number* suggests a person free from slavery for Salter. The clones in *Never Let Me Go*, however, are not acknowledged as persons, a term apparently inseparably connected to human beings, even though they are biologically human. However, Kathy's friend Ruth once claims that the clones are "modelled from *trash*. Junkies, prostitutes, winos, tramps. Convicts, maybe, as long as they aren't psychos" (Ishiguro 2005, 164; original emphasis). Thus, they suffer from a two-fold inferiority which again emphasises the interconnection of all lives on the 'wrong' side of hierarchical dichotomies. The narrative perspective and the quiet empathy the novel generates for the clones attack the arbitrary definition of humanity in the context of neoliberal slavery. Ishiguro's novel and Churchill's play expose that simple dichotomies of human/clone or human treasures/human trash do not hold: a separation of human- and personhood is necessary and has occurred in philosophy, animal studies, and eventually has found its way into legal discourse which the case of the orangutan Sandra, who was established as the first nonhuman person (cf. Lough 2014, n.p.), in Brazil shows. We might question, with Powell, if humanising clones makes for a properly posthuman narrative: "These cinematic clones, then, be they vengeful rebels, melancholy romantics or passive capitalist dupes, attest to the survival of humanism by role-reversal, as clones become surrogate humans and humans become monsters" (2015, 81).

Challenging naturalised definitions, connections, and, thus, also ideologies is the key to create an understanding for the network interconnecting human and nonhuman agents. Contemporary dystopian fiction testifies to the crucial role that culture can play in this new pedagogy called for by Probst and others. For example, *Never Let Me Go*, just like *Frankenstein*, rather focuses on how culture could possibly be seen as a factor of reconciliation if viewed outside of the framework of human exceptionalism. A more inclusive understanding of culture, of personhood, or of sympathy and empathy could lead to a new recognition of cultures and (grievable) lives. Categories facilitate common world structuring processes and can, therefore, hardly be entirely abolished but they can be rendered more inclusive through redefinitions. This less discriminatory categorisation process can take groups that do not fit into constructions of western normativity as well as "non-human agency and [...] subjectivity" (Feder 2014, 2) into account. Furthermore, Feder claims that "[r]ecognizing the existence of other animal cultures – and, in so doing, rejecting various ideologies of nature, particularly that of human supremacy – challenges structures of power that oppress both human and non-human animals" (ibid) – the clone as a posthuman figure helps discuss these ideas. As the editors of *Clones and Clones* stress, "cloning, so far, is still in our future. Like the Greeks, therefore, we also feel the need for fiction and fantasy, to map out some alternative futures for us with the imagination's flexibility and precision" (Nussbaum and Sunstein 1998, 15). Dystopian, speculative fiction can serve as critical posthumanism's space to speculate on notions of 'the human' and its alleged exceptionalism, to reassess and renegotiate humanity and to engage in a rhetoric of inclusion. Such texts challenge structures of power and of the supremacy of one specific human group – and approaching them from a non-anthropocentric perspective, we can recognise that they do not only confront us with nightmares but actually make us ponder alternatives when western conceptions of 'the human' and its 'others' are in urgent need of revision. If mankind does not want to fall prey to its own logic of uniqueness, it needs a new pedagogy that takes leave of definitions based on humanist ideals. This process of education might come at the expense of alleged privileges but could eventually help the human survive – as a species and as individuals. Both 'the human' and lives excluded from exceptionalism can benefit from this reassessment. In contrast to defenders of human exceptionalism, texts such as *Never Let Me Go*, which deconstructs the anthropocentric belief in specific human superiority by emphasising the often arbitrary denial of dignity to various other forms of life, argue that human beings do not need to concentrate on the preservation of human exceptionalism in the age of biotechnology and that fragile boundaries are not inevitably dangerous. Instead, they can be embraced and offer a chance for ethical coexistence. Consequently, such narratives do not only point towards a process of overcoming anthropocentrism and speciesism but simultaneously introduce the possibility of a new, positive multiculturalism which transcends the limiting anthropocentric idea of 'the human.'

Notes

1 Anthropocentrism is firmly embedded in western religion and philosophy. It describes the belief that human life is the most significant form of life and the only one that has intrinsic value.

2 For a more detailed discussion of Butler's concept in connection to anthropocentrism and posthumanist dystopias, see Boller 2018.

3 Heidegger claimed that only man has an "experiential relation to death, to dying," whereas 'the animal' perishes but never dies (Derrida 2009, 307).

Works Cited

Boller, Alessandra (2018). *Rethinking 'the Human' in Dystopian Times: Modified Bodies and the Re-/Deconstruction of Human Exceptionalism in Margaret Atwood's* MaddAddam *Trilogy and Kazuo Ishiguro's* Never Let Me Go. Trier: WVT.

Braidotti, Rosi (2013). *The Posthuman.* Cambridge: Polity Press.

Brandt, Christina (2008). "*Cloned Lives*: Literarisches Experiment und biowissenschaftliche Narration im Klondiskurs der 1970er Jahre."

Engineering Life: Narrationen vom Menschen in Biomedizin, Kultur und Literatur. Eds. Claudia Breger, Irmela M. Krüger-Fürhoff and Tanja Nusser. Berlin: Kulturverlag Kadmos, 123-143.

Butler, Judith (2004). *Precarious Life: The Powers of Mourning and Violence*. London: Verso.

--- (2009). *Frames of War: When Is Life Grievable?* London: Verso.

Camenzind, Samuel (2015). "On Clone as Genetic Copy: Critique of a Metaphor." *Nanoethics* 9.1, 23-37.

Caduff, Corina (2004). "Experiment Klon." *Science & Fiction: Über Gedankenexperimente in Wissenschaft, Philosophie und Literatur*. Ed. Thomas Macho and Annette Wunschel. Frankfurt: Fischer Taschenbuch Verlag, 230-241.

Churchill, Caryl (2008). "A Number." 2002. *Plays: Four*. London: Nick Hern Books, 161-206.

Cyranoski, David (2018). "First Monkeys Cloned with Technique That Made Dolly the Sheep." *Nature* 24 January 2018. Web. 3 April 2018.

Derrida, Jacques (2009). *The Beast and the Sovereign*. Vol. 1. Eds. Michel Lisse, Marie-Luise Mallet and Ginette Michaud. Trans. Geoffrey Bennington. Chicago: University of Chicago Press.

Dann, Jack and Gardner Dozois (1998). "Preface." *Clones*. Ed. Jack Dann and Gardner Dozois. New York: Ace Books, ix-xi.

Didur, Jill (2003). "Re-Embodying Technoscientific Fantasies: Posthumanism, Genetically Modified Foods, and the Colonization of Life." *Posthumanism*. Spec. issue of *Cultural Critique* 53, 98-115.

Feder, Helena (2014). *Ecocriticism and the Idea of Culture: Biology and the Bildungsroman.* Farnham: Ashgate.

Gobert, R. Darren (2014). *The Theatre of Caryl Churchill*. London: Bloomsbury.

Graham, Elaine L. (2002). *Representations of the Post/Human: Monsters, Aliens and Others in Popular Culture*. New Brunswick, NJ: Rutgers University Press.

Gray, Chris Hables (2001). *Cyborg Citizen*. New York: Routledge.

Halberstam, Judith and Ira Livingston (1995). "Introduction: Posthuman Bodies." *Posthuman Bodies*. Ed. Judith Halberstam and Ira Livingston. Bloomington, IN: Indiana University Press, 1-19.

Ishiguro, Kazuo (2005). *Never Let Me Go*. London: Faber and Faber.

Jennings, Bruce (2010). "Biopower and the Liberationist Romance." *The Hastings Center Report* 40.4, 16-20.

Lough, Richard (2014). "Captive Orangutan Has Human Right to Freedom, Argentine Court Rules." *Reuters* 21 December 2014: n. pag. Web. 11 February 2018.

Nussbaum, Martha (2008). "Human Dignity and Political Entitlements." *Human Dignity and Bioethics: Essays Commissioned by the President's Council on Bioethics*. Ed. Edmund D. Pellegrino, Adam Schulman and Thomas W. Merrill. Washington, D.C.: The President's Council on Bioethics, 351-380. Web. 11 December 2015. <https://bioethicsarchive.georgetown.edu/pcbe/reports/human_dignity/chapter14.html>.

Nussbaum, Martha C., and Cass R. Sunstein (1998). *Clones and Clones: Facts and Fantasies about Human Cloning*. New York: Norton.

Powell, Anna (2015). "Growing Your Own: Monsters from the Lab and Molecular Ethics in Posthumanist Film." *The Palgrave Handbook of Posthumanism in Film and Television*. Eds. Michael Hauskeller, Thomas D. Philbeck and Curtis D. Carbonell. New York: Palgrave Macmillan, 77-87.

Probst, Maximilian (2017). "Umdenken oder Untergehen!" *Die Zeit* 25 October n. pag. Web. 2 April 2018.

Rachels, James, and Stuart Rachels (2011). *The Elements of Moral Philosophy*. 7th ed. New York: McGraw-Hill Education.

Salzani, Carlo (2017). "From Post-Human to Post-Animal: Posthumanism and the 'Animal Turn.'" *Limits and Boundaries of the Posthuman*. Spec. issue of *Lo Sguardo: Rivista di Filosofia* 24, 97-109.

Shelley, Mary (1971). *Frankenstein or the Modern Prometheus*. 1818. Ed. M.K. Joseph. London: Oxford University Press.

Simon, Bart (2003). "Introduction: Toward a Critique of Posthuman Futures." *Posthumanism*. Spec. issue of *Cultural Critique* 53, 1-9.

Toker, Leona, and Daniel Chertoff (2008). "Reader-Response and the Recycling of Topoi in Kazuo Ishiguro's *Never Let Me Go*." *Partial Answers: Journal of Literature and the History of Ideas* 6.1, 163-180.

Vint, Sherryl (2007). *Bodies of Tomorrow: Technology, Subjectivity, Science Fiction*. Toronto: University of Toronto Press.

--- (2010). "Animal Studies in the Era of Biopower." *Science Fiction Studies* 37.3, 444-455.

Vermeulen, Pieter (2017). "Creaturely Memory: Shakespeare, the Anthropocene and the New *Nomos* of the Earth." *Parallax* 23.4, 384-397.

Wallace, Jeff (2010). "Literature and Posthumanism." *Literature Compass* 7.8, 692-701.

Wilkinson, Nils (2013). "Programmable Bodies: Ayckbourn's Robots and Churchill's Clones." *Journal of Contemporary Drama in English* 1.1, 34-42.

Wolfe, Cary (2003). "Introduction." *Zoontologies: The Question of the Animal.* Ed. Cary Wolfe. Minneapolis, MN: University of Minnesota Press, ix-xxiii.

Julia Hoydis

Posthuman Lessons from the Past and the Future: Narrating Selves and Otherness between History, Folklore, and Technology

Introduction

The endeavour of teaching 'the posthuman' at tertiary level and seeking to engage a student audience, of which a majority are future teachers of English in secondary schools, allows – and forces – one to confront a number of old questions in new guises. In my experience, students tend to show an intuitive, immediate interest in topics such as human cloning, and the impact and boundaries of scientific and technological experimentation and developments. And there is a great number of fascinating and suitable texts across different genres and media on offer which can be used to discuss and illustrate the theoretical accounts of posthumanism and the numerous debates shaping this field of study. We are also already starting to see the emergence of an academic core 'canon' of posthuman fictions on which a steadily growing, useful body of criticism is available (including, for instance, texts such as Atwood's *Oryx and Crake*, Ishiguro's *Never Let Go* and Churchill's *A Number*; the latter two examples are discussed in Boller and Voigt's contribution to this volume).

But there are also inevitable challenges: trying to do justice to the complexity and heterogeneity of the subject matter in an undergraduate classroom, one runs the risk of overburdening the curriculum with just one too many '-isms,' 'post-,' and 'trans-,' each of which, of course, easily warrants instructional consideration and a class (or several) on its own, for example, when tracing the intersections and historical lineages between (post)humanism and (post)feminism, (post)colonialism, or (post)modernism. In addition, there are genre- and media-specific aspects to consider. Dealing with the posthuman as an encounter with alterity on various levels presupposes and requires quite a lot of theoretical knowledge, textual-analytical skills and understanding which are both aided and complicated by the strong imaginative appeal posthumanist fictions – mostly classifiable as speculative, SF, Gothic, and dystopian fictions – undoubtedly possess. In particular, current award-winning, and so-called 'binge-worthy,' TV-series such as *Westworld* (HBO), *Black Mirror* (Netflix) and *Orphan Black* (Netflix), which capture global audiences, also rouse students' interests. While they offer grounds for new and fruitful investigations of narrations of the posthuman, supervising student BA-theses[1] on them requires support in the careful navigation of territories that are at the same time unchartered (i.e. with regard to the relative lack of secondary sources (to date) on these series), and well-trodden (e.g., with regard to intertextual and aesthetic references, plots and motifs, serial narration).

My reflections in this chapter are based on classes I have taught over the last few years (at BA and MA level at the University of Cologne), including the seminars "Postcolonial Science Fiction," "Science Plays," and "(Post)humanism?: Narrating Fictions of Women and Other Animals," as well as other seminars on literary genre theory, Gothic fiction, and literature and science studies. A main point I want to stress is that rather than teaching posthumanism as yet another, separate branch of (relatively new) theory, it can be integrated and stipulate interesting discussions in literature, media and cultural studies classes on a variety of subjects and theoretical approaches. For example, primary texts discussed in "Postcolonial Science Fiction," a class which tackles the posthuman in the context of imperialism and science fiction, with a focus on conceptions of race and cyberspace, Afrofuturism, and feminism,[2] are contemporary speculative novels, short stories, and films by Canadian, South-African, Indian, and Canadian-Caribbean writers (Atwood's *Oryx and Crake,* Beukes's *Moxyland,* Ghosh's *The Calcutta Chromosome,* Hopkinson's *Midnight Robber,* Singh's "The Woman Who Thought She Was a Planet," Neil Blomkamp's *District 9*). The text selection, above all, displaces the imaginative dominance of US/Europe, masculinity and whiteness in the genre of speculative fiction as well as in posthumanism (see Hoydis 2015; also Adair's contribution to this volume).

The seminar "Science Plays" deals with the tradition of staging science and the unbroken prominence of this topic in (British) drama. Primary texts here include, for example, Michael Frayn's famous play about the principle of uncertainty, the atomic bomb, and the 1941 meeting between Nils Bohr and Werner Heisenberg in *Copenhagen* and the film version directed by Howard Davies, Shelagh Stephenson's *An Experiment with an Air Pump* presents a dramatic text which thematises the old "two-culture debate" by juxtaposing art/literature/humanity and science/inhumanity on two time levels (1799 and 1999); the practices of radical Enlightenment scientist Joseph Fenwick, and the anatomist Thomas Armstrong are set against the modern life of geneticist Ellen and the ethical debate surrounding stem-cell research. The play thus raises questions about the hubris, power and responsibility of scientists and the limits in the pursuits of knowledge, as well as inviting critical debate of the depicted gender roles in their historical dimension. Tom Stoppard's 2015 play *The Hard Problem* stages questions of human consciousness, compassion and the (un)predictability of behaviour; reading it alongside the other texts highlights the inherent issues of (family, romantic) relationships, gender, and the responsibilities of science/scientists. Carly Churchill's 'father-and-son'-play *A Number*, the only text in this selection which features actual 'posthuman,' i.e. clone characters, ties in well with the ethical debates of scientific practices past and present; the (in)humanity of relationships, and the question of how science can and should be staged with regard to its effect on the audience.

In the seminar "(Post)humanism?: Narrating Fictions of Women and Other Animals", the focus is clearly put on posthumanism but the aspect of science and technology does not take centre stage. J.M. Coetzee's philosophical novel *The Lives of Animals* makes for an excellent, accessible introduction to the discussion of human-animal relations, species boundaries and conceptions of the in/human, all the while also drawing attention to the nature and distinctions between fiction and 'objective' academic discourse. This is continued by reading Carol Emshwiller's much less known feminist SF novel *Carmen Dog*, admittedly a challenging text for students due to the style of writing, which tells a weird tale in which all the women in New York are transformed into dogs and vice versa, causing only mild disturbance and change in treatment of each group from the side of the city's human males. H.G. Wells' *The Island of Dr Moreau*, one of the classic British dystopian SF texts for good reason, opens yet another angle on the discussion of the boundaries between human and 'beast' and questions the direction of human (d)evolution and civilization. Followed by Kazuo

Ishiguro speculative memoir *Never Let Me Go,* the discussion returns to the issue of value of life, creating a parallel between the novel's exploited clone children, who are confined to a less-than-human existence, and other human 'Others' (in and outside of fiction), marginalized due to race or gender, or being animals.

Dealing with narrations of the posthuman across different media and genres, I find that it is generally important and fruitful to open multiple, and in particular also historical, trajectories. With regard to the latter, Mary Shelley's *Frankenstein* is a – if not *the* – go-to text and point of reference, as is Wells's *The Island of Dr Moreau*, both work well in class and, in addition, serve as good introductions of the characteristics of the Gothic and science fiction genres. Mixing readings of canonical and non-canonical, historical and contemporary fictions underlines the impression that the debate of 'what makes us human,' of race and species boundaries, of the progress and limits of science and, above all, of the fears of and the behaviour towards Otherness, are not a new subject matter at all. This truism is worth stressing with regard to (proposing) the inclusion of 'the posthuman' into a range of literary and cultural studies classes. And while my teaching suggestions are surely modelled on 'old-fashioned,', human(ist) ways and bracket the use of 'innovative' digital media teaching technologies (which potentially confront students, with a largely *posthuman* environment)[3], it is the choice of texts and the joint analyses of students, not technological affordances, that enable critical debate.

In the following, rather than detailing a full course syllabus, I will discuss three representative examples which illustrate different aspects and prominent themes and characteristics of posthuman narratives in drama, film/TV-series, and prose fiction, but are not (yet) part of the emerging academic class-room canon: Linda Marshall-Griffith's *Charlotte Brontë's Villette Re-imagined* (2016), Jonathan Nolan and Lisa Joy's *Westworld* (season 1; 2016) and Nalo Hopkinson's *Midnight Robber* (2000). The readings are linked by the question about the depicted demarcations between self/other and human/non/post/inhuman which are central in all three texts. They illustrate in different ways how the importance of engaging (with) the posthuman

> does not necessitate the obsolescence of the human; it does not represent an evolution or devolution of the human. Rather it participates in *re-distributions of difference and identity*. The human functions to

> domesticate and hierarchize difference within the human (whether according to race, class, gender) and absolutize difference between the human and the nonhuman. The posthuman does not reduce difference-from-others to difference-from-self, but rather emerges in the pattern of resonance and interference between the two. (Halberstam and Livingston 1995, 10; my emphasis)

Case Study (I): *Charlotte Brontë's Villette Re-imagined*

Aside from cyborgs and robots, clones appear as the kind of posthuman characters that populate with increasing frequency speculative science fictions and capture the interest of students. In comparison to novels and films, in dramatic texts written for and on stage clone characters are much rarer in occurrence. Yet Linda Marshall-Griffiths' *Charlotte Brontë's Villette Re-imagined*, a much less known drama than Churchill's *A Numb*er, which is written by one of Britain's most famous contemporary playwrights, warrants attention. Both plays utilize the figure of the clone to raise questions about identity, suffering, love, and nature vs. nurture debates. They can be taught and analysed in relation to theories of posthumanism, the tradition of British 'science plays,' and characteristics of contemporary clone narratives, which are shaped by popular imaginations and fears, such as the negative perception of clones as inferior copies, monstrous creatures, and threats to human individuality and society.

The tradition of the 'science play' is commonly traced back as far as Ben Johnson's *The Alchemist* and Christopher Marlowe's *Doctor Faustus*. Influential and successful twentieth-century plays include Michael Frayn's *Copenhagen,* Tom Stoppard's *Arcadia,* and Shelagh Stephenson's *An Experiment with an Air Pump*; at the beginning of the new millennium, science plays (fully) emerge as a distinct dramatic subgenre in theory and practice. Important studies of the field are Kirsten Shepherd-Barr's *Science on Stage: From 'Doctor Faustus' to 'Copenhagen'* (2006), Eva Zehelein's *Science Dramatic* (2009) and Martin Willis's *Staging Science* (2016). Although "theatre scholars and practitioners have been investigating the interconnections between science and performance for decades" (Shepherd-Barr 2016, 106), science has been called "the hottest topic in theatre today, so much so that it's identifiable as a millennial phenomenon on the English-speaking stage" (Rocamora 2000, 50). Similarly, in their recent survey of twenty-first-century British drama, editors Kerstin Frank and Caroline Lusin identify "science and technology" as an important realm of dramatic debate, clustering around the impact of science on issues of identity and selfhood and freedom vs. determinism (Frank and Lusin 2017, 14). Playwrights continue to respond to ethical, cognitive, and aesthetic challenges posed by scientific advances in the fields of medicine (genetic engineering, cloning, IVF, neuropsychology), nuclear and information technology, and mass media (see Higgins 2008). Interestingly, contemporary science plays are mostly 'realist' with regards to setting and characters (in opposition to 'science fiction' proper) and rely heavily on dialogue, i.e. they are "text theatre" rather than "director's theatre," as Eva Zehelein points out (2009, 97, 84). There are various subcategories of science drama one can distinguish between: biotechnology or DNA-plays, "information-age-plays" such as Jules Horne's *Gorgeous Avatar* (see Schwanecke 2017), or "age-of-the-brain-plays" like Nick Payne's *Incognito* (see Glomb 2017), which reflect on cognition and neuroscience. Then there is the unbroken trend of plays dealing with the (after)lives of famous scientists (most notably Einstein and Darwin). With the moral permissibility or the perceived 'sinfulness' or dangers, etc. of scientific practices often taking centre stage, one can differentiate between two fictional modes (across dramatic and prose genres): one, Sabine Sielke explains, explores questions and themes of science in order to critique its methods and goals, the other "takes the sciences on their own shifting terms and aims at adopting and adapting its principles, models, and metaphors into the spaces of literary narrative" (Sielke 2015, 17). Thus there is a difference, though often also an overlap, between science used as a metaphor and/or stagings of science and science history. In particular with regard to cloning or DNA plays, this metaphorical overlap, analysed in Zehelein's survey of science plays (see 2009, 87), concerns one of the most pervasive topics in British drama at the beginning of the twenty-first century: the crisis and collapse of the traditional family unit, and issues of psychology and gender (see Middeke 2011, xvii; Sierz 2010, xvii).

Villette Re-imagined uses more technology on stage (i.e. huge TV screens) than *A Number*, but still the posthuman is staged on the level of text and content rather than primarily through the use of multi-media technology. Whereas Alan Read has referred to the theatrical space as the "last human venue" (Read 2008), new areas of research in theatre and performance studies address digital culture, changing ontologies of performance, the potential for exploring alternative models of identity, the impact of cyber theory, experiments with multi-media or robotics technology on stage, the participation in virtual communities and performance in virtual spaces (see Causey 2016, 428). Against this background, 'posthuman,' 'postorganic' or (post)digital theatre (see Causey 1999; 2009) can be understood as "performance works where computer technologies play a *key* role rather than a subsidiary one in content, techniques, aesthetics, or delivery forms" (Dixon 2007, 3; original emphasis), or as a dramatic practice which refuses "humankind its taken-for-granted position at the centre of the theatrical and world stages" (Lepage 2008, 145), for example, by replacing subjects on stage by robots. Whereas Matthew Causey first argued that due to the developments in technology and the rise of the Internet theatre has entered "a posthuman phase" (1999, 185f), there has since been an upsurge of studies and conceptions such as Steve Dixon's "digital performance" (2002), Gabriella Giannachi's "virtual theatre" (2004), Jennifer Parker-Starbuck's "cyborg theatre" (2014), Rosemary Klich and Edward Scheer's "multimedia performance" (2012). But, as Richard Jordan sums up, performance theorists mostly focus on techniques rather than thematic concerns; "for all of these authors, the posthuman subject on stage is defined in the first instance not by content, but by spectacle" (Jordan 2015, 27). Jordan himself, however, suggests another angle on what he defines as posthuman drama, which applies to plays such as *A Number* and *Villette Re-imagined*, as a new "genre of playwright-driven performance that asks what it means to be 'human' in the digital age" (Jordan 2014, 40). The focus is not placed on the play's production potential, but on how posthuman subjectivity is constructed in the dramatic text itself or on how a fictional world is created in which the boundaries between human and nonhuman agents are dissolved or questioned (ibid). This is then more truly a posthuman perspective rather than a transhumant interest in replacing traditional forms with new technology. And while it would certainly also be worthwhile to consider the rapidly emerging field of 'posthuman drama' in more detail, I will look at how a particular figure of the posthuman is employed *in* the play and furthermore link it to adaptation studies. For *Villette Re-imagined* is based on Charlotte Brontë's final, autobiographical novel and reimagines the protagonist Lucy Snowe – arguably a stand-in for the author herself – as a clone who has survived a deadly viral epidemic.

Clone characters, to give but a few examples, feature in novels such as Fay Weldon's *The Cloning of Joanna May*, Kazuo Ishiguro's *Never Let Me Go,* in films like *Island*, *The Boys from Brazil* and *Star Wars II: Attack of the Clones*, and in TV-series like *Orphan Black* and *Humans.* As a result, the depiction of clones in fiction has received critical attention and led to the identification of recurring figurations and narrative patterns.[4] Generally, these fictions negotiate and successfully exploit, as Mary Luckhurst argues, "widespread cultural anxiety about human cloning, as well as its attendant popular myths" (2015, 158), which are also aired in the *Villette*-play.

A useful starting point for class discussions of clone fictions is the distinction between therapeutic and reproductive cloning, i.e. between the creation of body parts or cell material and full human beings. The first is usually seen as beneficial, the second as a dangerous, if yet unreal, scenario. From a narratological point of view, there is a good reason why therapeutic cloning, in contrast to reproductive cloning, hardly features in fictions because, as Amit Marcus underlines, "these uses of cloning are not narratively appealing" (2012, 406). In other words, one is then robbed of the opportunity of having clones feature as characters. Typically, clone fictions – and this applies across genres and media – "provide only perfunctory remarks on the technique of cloning or even utterly avoid this topic" (2012, 406). Rather than give exact descriptions of the scientific 'how,' the focus is placed on the psychology of the clones, the sociology of a community of clones, or on the relationship between clones and 'real' humans.

Nerlich, Clarke and Dingwall explain how, as characters (in mostly dystopian speculative fictions) clones "nourish and reflect the general public's fears about an increasing process of biological hybridization which blurs the boundaries between humans, plants, animals, and machines" (Nerlich, Clarke, Dingwall 2001, 37); this "threatens not only our perception of what humanity is but of what personal identity and personal dignity are" (2001, 50). Challenging the boundaries between self and other, and threatening the subjectivity of the individual, founding pillars in Western culture and social organization, cloning narratives epitomize the ethical and cognitive negotiation of otherness and sameness. While clone characters are often shown to "tackle similar problems of those of 'normal' human beings (e.g., constituting an autonomous self, developing a loving relationship with a significant other [...])" (Marcus 2012, 430), they expand a biotechnological ethical controversy into the realm of the social, for example, questions of how humans/clones are or must be treated and raised are central. They raise urgent questions not just about the reach, dangers, and permissibility of science, but also "the status of the family in modern society" (2012, 406). As such the (narrative) use of the clone (as metaphor) "is neither purely poetic nor purely cognitive, but it provides a framework for the expression of social concerns" (Nerlich, Clarke, Dingwall 2001, 50). This, of course, suggests links to the agenda and discussions in animal studies, disability studies, and postcolonial studies.

It is also interesting to consider what Buchanan et al. refer to as the current "gene-mania" (Buchanan et al. 2009, 23), the extensive media coverage and presence of genetics in popular scientific discourse. They emphasize the risk of a general sense of genetic determinism being reinforced by overestimating "the developing powers of genetic intervention and the impact of genes on individual and social life" (ibid.). The admiration for achievements of genetic science leads to a false worship of genes as the source and solution to all problems: "We thereby conveniently blind ourselves to the uncomfortable possibility that many of our most serious problems result from our social practices and institutions" (2009, 24). This tension between genetic determinism, and the impact of society and the environment is at the heart of many clone fictions. Other recurring issues and motifs, which are present in Marshall-Griffith's play, are cloning without knowledge and consent, the status of clones as commodity and property, the rebellion against a system which treats the clones as 'slaves,' exploiting them for work, their body parts, or personal egotism. Often narratives also focus on the cure for disease, the search for immortality, while a typical figure (even if often only in absentia) is the cloner as the 'evil scientist'. A typical point of departure for clone as well as other cyborg narratives is the question what happens if technology or 'the creation' begins to develop its own agency, usually told as a cautionary tale in which order is restored with the human regaining control over the 'unnatural' others, a well-established narrative pattern since *Frankenstein*. And even if the cloning is done out of benevolent motives (i.e. other than scientific curiousity or capitalist interests), the results and the implication for the familial and other relationships are usually devastating.

Professor of Law Kerry Macintosh's study *Human Cloning: Four Fallacies and Their Legal Consequences* (2013) is a critical account of or, in fact, even a 'writing against' contemporary clone fictions which she sees as increasing people's "confusion by promoting nightmare visions that are more consistent with essentialism than biological fact" (Macintosh 2013, 230). She argues that the way 'clone/cloning' has come to be publically perceived "reinforces essentialist intuitions that are scientifically inaccurate" (2013, xvi, footnote 1). To be clear, the underlying aim of her study is to debunk myths and defuse public opposition against human cloning and thus offer an argument for scientific freedom against laws and policies which impede research (see ibid., 225). But her argument, in fact, gives a lot of power to fictional narratives and, I think, shows why it is necessary to engage with and teach these narratives, and to ask what they reveal about common perceptions of human nature and scientific facts. Macintosh identifies four fallacies that are pervasive in pop culture, media and government reports, and reflected in many fictional representations of clones – though the latter can also be understood to help to deconstruct the following (mis)consceptions: the identity fallacy, i.e. the view of a series of clones, all identical and lacking individuality; the artefact fallacy, i.e. the perception of clones as unnatural, inhuman 'things' and 'products,' as bodies devoid of autonomy, agency, and political identity, and which, as a consequence, can be killed legally;[5] the resurrection fallacy, i.e. that it is possible to replace lost children or other loved ones through human reproductive cloning (HRC); and the impostor fallacy, i.e. the fear of a clone stealing a human's identity.

All of these fearful (fictional) imaginations are, according to Macintosh, contradicted by scientific facts (derived from the case of animals born through cloning). For example, clones are unique individuals because genetic factors and environmental influences give each its own psychological and behavioural traits; thus they are neither flawed products nor copies (see 2013, 61). As they are always born as babies, not adults, one cannot inherit or take over the life of a genetic predecessor; clones thus are no means of extending life or resurrecting the dead. They have their own lifespans, which also contradicts the fear of 'evil' clones as interlopers, capable of stealing the identity of loved ones of their DNA donors. What Macintosh misses, of course, is that clone narratives are often a lot more nuanced; plays such as *Villette Reimagined* negotiate several of these fears, but do not subscribe to them and employ the clone in a metaphorical, rather than a literal, way. The clone Lucy Snowe, evoking the social isolation and discrimination of her fictional predecessor in Brontë's novel, embodies a sense of alterity and a cluster of fears beyond scientific advancement.

Charlotte Brontë's final novel (1853) is usually read as being only thinly disguised autobiography of the author's grief following the TB deaths of her sisters Emily and Anne, her own experiences as a girls' school teacher in Brussels, and her painful unrequited passion for an older professor and married man (Mr. Heger). In the novel, poor, plain, single Lucy Snowe travels to the fictional Belgian town of Villette, after the death of her family, and obtains a job at a girls' school; the text is suffused with loneliness and melancholy but tells the story of a single working woman's striving for radical independence. The main subject and focus is the narrator's inner life, her extreme emotional states and dream-like reflections, and the eventual love story between Lucy and Paul (the professor). There are also three encounters between Lucy and a ghostly nun. While there are, curiously, no film adaptations of *Villette*,[6] this gives greater freedom to playwrights to capitalize on *Villette*'s status as an enigmatic, ambiguous novel, but still a famous Brontë text (see Poore 2017, 32).[7] There have been four stage adaptations of *Villette* since the 1990s, with Linda Marshall-Griffiths' version for the West Yorkshire playhouse being the latest example to date. However, Marshall-Griffiths' re-telling, as one reviewer observes, is "probably not one for Brontë devotees" (Simpson 2016). It relocates the plot to an archaeological excavation site 100 years in the future; Lucy Snowe is a clone and geneticist exploited to work on the site to search for the bones of a nun (the Lady of Villette) who has survived a deadly virus a century earlier, and which the scientists hope may hold the secret of an antidote (a currently raging Ebola-like virus is killing millions of people). The pain, isolation, and otherness Brontë's original Lucy struggles with, are captured by her being a clone, and thus supposedly essentially different from the human characters that surround her. Lucy is apparently created solely for the purpose of difficult, dangerous work; tagged with a metal wrist band, she is under constant surveillance by the archaeological dig leader Beck – modelled on the novel's school director Mme Beck – who views her as less than human. The play's stage version uses a screen suspended over the stage, translating Mme Beck's original spying-through-keyholes-surveillance into hi-tech; she is literally looking down on the characters, seeing everything like a panoptic eye. Lucy's in-experience, acted on stage with broken speech and mechanical, jerky movement but also reflected in the text, inspires pity and ridicule in the other characters. While she constantly has to answer questions about what she is 'like,' she is simultaneously part of society and perceived to be outside of humanity. Like Frankenstein's creature, she longs for and discovers love, first falling for Doctor John Bretton and then the strange scientist Paul. Between the two, a moving, comically awkward courtship ensues, culminating in Paul setting Lucy free by cutting her wrist band off and helping her escape from the site. She ends up standing near the ocean alone, waiting for him to return.

Reading the play alongside Brontë's novel, one has a similar feeling of engaging with a limited, unreliable narrator (the clone Lucy also evokes parallels to Kathy in *Never Let Me Go*); there is a strong sense that Lucy misunderstands or misrepresents events or withholds crucial information (cf. Poore 2017, 190). In the play, her inner monologues[8] suddenly reveal her mourning of the loss of her clone siblings Esme and Ashe (Emily and Anne Brontë), all created from the DNA of their mother, renowned Professor Snowe. Mostly Lucy's rebellion and suffering is silent and takes place on the inside; she has fully internalized society's discriminatory, exploitative view of her. But occasionally she erupts into defiant statements: 'Do not/presume/to know me/you do not'" (VR, 43). She contemplates writing a letter to Dr John, to convince him that "I work in all the same ways as a woman. […] My blood is red like yours. My heart fires/Like yours" (VR, 73); but he betrays her and starts instead an affair with a 'real' woman, Gin. Paul, on the other hand, cannot be dissuaded from his interest in Lucy, although Beck warns him repeatedly: "They have no capacity to love. […] She's so cold, so odd. […] You can't Paul, it's not…." (VR, 104); "they're not even properly formed…"; but Paul is determined to choose Lucy: "Beck – if you cannot stand it don't watch" (VR, 105).

Lucy finally identifies the bones of the Lady of Villette, but she has no virus antibodies; the discovery is that the nun still somehow survived the epidemic, only to be brutally killed by being thrown onto a sharp stone which punctured her heart, punishment for breaking the rule of chastity. Thus they excavate a case of female sexual transgression being punished by the authorities instead of a cure and scientific breakthrough. Paul says: "Check again for the virus./Then look at her genome – there must have been/something that made her resistant." Lucy replies: "Not to brutality" (VR, 108). Throughout, the play's emphasis is on likeness and posthuman kinship instead of difference, as well as on the historical continuity of discrimination and isolation of women who are perceived as different: Lucy tells Beck: "I'm exactly like you that's the point" (VR, 80). And the ending, when Lucy is being 'recalled' after the nun's skeleton has been found, makes a clear statement against a biological determinant of identity in favour of professional identity. Lucy says: "I applied for a permit to travel and I got it." "As a descendant?" [the official terminology for clones employed in the play] "As a scientist" (VR, 109). One can read the ending as cautiously optimistic; it echoes Brontë's final lines which also serve as an epigraph to the play: "Trouble no quiet, kind heart, leave sunny imaginations hope. [...] Let them picture union and a happy succeeding life" (Brontë, 1999, 462). Lucy's final words are: "You will come back./I will.../We will.../Find a way to be happy./We will... Love" (VR, 117).

While there is a strong shared emphasis on suffering and a confrontation with essentialist categories of difference in both texts, *Villette Re-imagined* adapts the feminist issues at the heart of Brontë's novel (the championing of female passion outside of marriage, of women's right to independence and a professional identity; see Liggins 2017, 166) as well as the key themes of surveillance and education into a twenty-first-century, futuristic context. The clone Lucy Snowe appears as an apt posthuman re-imagination of Brontë's suffering Victorian heroine, all the while her hope of romantic fulfilment remains just as ambiguous. Aside from illustrating aspects of the morally charged scientific debates of human cloning, and the terrors and hopes connected to imaginations of "the new genetics" (Luckhurst 2016, 254), a comparative reading of both Brontë's novel and Marshall-Griffith's play highlights historical continuities in the negotiation of gender matters and the fragility of concepts such as authenticity and autonomy. Drawing on debates within adaptation studies extends the critical discussion to reveal an "'intertextual dialogism'" between these texts but one that aids the transcendence of what Robert Stam and other scholars have long identified as "the aporias of 'fidelity'" (2005, 4). *Villette Re-imagined*, far from being a traditional ('faithful') page-to-stage adaptation, is "a standalone play inspired by source material" (Gardner 2016, n.p.), with the depiction and experience of otherness at its core.

Case Study (II): *Westworld*

Taking its name from and based on a 1973 SF film by Michael Crichton, which is often seen as a technical precursor of the director's later mega success *Jurassic Park*, the TV series *Westworld*, written by Jonathan Nolan and Lisa Joy, premiered its first ten-episode season on HBO in 2016 and has just been renewed for season three, due to be released in 2020. With each episode being roughly one hour in duration, season one alone far exceeds the running time of Crichton's movie, let alone the typical ninety-minutes-slot of a university seminar.[9] Using this example for class discussion, though a worthwhile undertaking, thus requires a strategic selection of scenes, in particular if it is taught in comparison with the older film version or in a class dealing with serialized narration formats. The pilot (episode 101, "The Original") offers a good starting point and material for discussing the depicted differences between human 'guests' and the nonhuman android 'hosts' in the theme park microcosm of Westworld, run by the tech-company Delos, basically an expensive vacation from the limitations of reality – or rather from the moral constraints of human society. However, the intricacies of plot and character development only become apparent when considering the whole first season, which contains many classic tropes of narrations of the posthuman.

The series, as becomes obvious just from watching the first episode, suggests discussion and application of concepts such as hyperreality, simulation and authenticity,[10] nostalgia and popular imagination, gaming, or the uncanny. One might further consider the question how the series updates the film and the 'prophetic' aspect of science fiction. For in contrast to the *Westworld* series, Crichton's film, as Larry Alan Busk argues, "is a prophetic cultural document evocative of tendencies that were only nascent at the time of its production, something of an omen for political-cultural phenomena that would only later be fully articulated in theory" (Busk 2016, 2). Central issues are the relations and likeness/difference between human and android characters, and the question of the (long-term) effects of a particular engagement with technology, here entering and immersing oneself in a hyperreal, high-tech world of violent, sexualized gaming supposedly permissible due to the 'victims' nonhuman status.

The Westworld experience aims to mimic the real as closely as possible, featuring "a colourful cast of predictable old west characters" (Busk 2016, 2), though the series updates them to be (slightly) more diverse, and women feature much more prominently than in the original film. The stories, written by Delos employees and staged by the Frankenstein-type creator and director of the park and its posthuman inhabitants, Dr Robert Ford (memorably played by Anthony Hopkins), allows for a 'realist' living out of cowboy-and-Indian games, including barroom fights, robberies, sex with the Mariposa saloon prostitutes, all set in the small town of Sweetwater. A key aspect, taken from the film version, is the function of the park as a guarded, sealed off microcosm, offering "a safe and controlled version of dangerous and unforgiving situations" (2016, 4). These are beautified and whitewashed. Because no one, Busk explains

> would visit Westworld if it meant being a malnourished prostitute; […] the advertised 'immersion' into another world is not so much an immersion into the world alleged as an immersion into the glossy caricatures […] seen in Hollywood films and Arthurian legend (only with more explicit sex and violence). (2016, 4)

The park, which can thus also be described as "an X-rated Disneyland" (Alkhen 2017, 8) presents a nostalgic simulation of the (White western) fantasy of a law-free Wild West and the 1880s American frontier myth; in this setting the human guests get to enjoy living out every violent fantasy they might harbour. They can fight, rape and kill the hosts, which are in turn programmed to be incapable of (fatally) hurting the guests but made to react, look (and bleed) as human-like as possible. The attraction for the visitors of Westworld – and by extension for the viewers of the series, as many reviewers argue[11] – consist in the opportunity to: "Live without limits in a world where every human appetite can be indulged. [...] [T]his dark odyssey follows the dawn of artificial consciousness and the evolution of sin" ('Westworld', n.d.). This is also the park's official commercial slogan, for example, quoted in the series in episode 106: "Welcome to Westworld. Live without limits" (TC: 00:21:13). It calls for historical comparison between the behaviour of the guests towards the posthuman inhabitants of the park and the settler colonialist towards the American natives, and the ongoing apparently 'lawless' exploitative and cruel behaviour of those who can afford it (as the *Westworld* is a highly exclusive vacation) towards less privileged members of another class, sex, or race, or towards animals. An explicit, highly critical reference which links the whole evolutionary of project of human civilization to imperialism and cannibalism is made in episode 109, where Dr Ford says:

> 'We humans are in this world for a reason. We murdered and butchered anything that challenged our primacy. Do you know what happened to the Neanderthals, Bernard? We are them. We destroyed and subjugated our world and when we eventually ran out of creatures to dominate, we built this beautiful place.' (TC: 00:54:15)

For the guests, the thrill comes from living out limited agency in these narratives controlled by others; for Ford, a complex god-like scientist/ artist/creator/father figure, and the other Delos story-writers it comes from seeing their imagined stories come to life. From the first episode onwards there are signs of disturbance. There are sudden changes in the behaviour and programming of the hosts, which increase to hallucinations, violent behaviour and the return of memories. These include not only the treatment by the guests but also their often traumatic "back stories," for example, in Maeve's case the loss of a daughter and husband, which are usually erased regularly. Each host's backstory is written and programmed to fit the current story the guests can enter and play out in the park. The stories become more and elaborate but also harder to control. While the 'plot' usually starts with a fight outside the Mariposa saloon, the more violent the stories get, the further away from Sweetwater are they, and they acquire a labyrinthine quality.

Westworld lends itself to psychoanalytical interpretation. In Freudian terms, part of the series' success arguably derives from the imaginative delve into the intriguing idea of living out the *id* without the *super ego* and without consequences (see Alkhen 2017, 36). Interestingly, once Dr Ford decides to program a so-called 'Reveries-code' into an update of the hosts, they acquire something like a subconscious, a change which further narrows the difference between humans and androids and leads them to feel destructive urges and a death drive (see 2017, 18).

Before the viewer is familiar with all the different characters, but also afterwards, one struggles, like the fictional human characters, to tell humans and posthuman 'others' apart. This is one of the most important points of the series, which continually seeks to blur these boundaries. It is a strange sensation to watch one of the many violent shooting scenes wondering (with dread or anticipated relief) who might be dead or not, though realizing eventually that nobody is killed and the 'dead' hosts are routinely taken back for maintenance by the Delos technicians and returned 'alive' to the game as soon as possible. Although the guests are supposed to enjoy the safety of the environment which allows for the thrill of violence without regrets and punishments, for several of them, this is not enough. They desire and start searching for the 'real' thing, at least those that get hooked and return to the park again and again, like the mysterious Man in Black, who, as is revealed over the course of season one, has been a guest for over thirty years. They also – as the love story between guest William and Dolores (the blond damsel-in-distress-type host who also undergoes a significant change) shows – want 'real' emotional attachments. Meanwhile the erasure of the hosts' memories is supposed to stop trauma and the build-up of emotions such as love, mourning, feelings of loss and revenge, etc. But this is, of course, exactly what starts to fail.

At the heart of the series is the breakdown of (narrative, social, moral) order, and corruption of good and evil. One obvious signifier are the black and white cowboy hats the guests can choose to wear, which corresponds to the boundaries they are willing to cross, and the turn of originally white-hatted William into the Man in Black, one of the central plot strands slowly revealed through the narration on two time levels, thirty years apart.[12] More and more, the hosts start to "go berserk – or, rather, they begin acting *as they would in real life*" (Busk 2016, 7; original emphasis). This includes rebellion against their makers and their human torturers. Thus the park turns from utopia into threat once the promise of authenticity is (at least partially) fulfilled – once the experience becomes real for both guests and hosts (cf. 2016, 8). While the motif of the posthuman creature seeking revenge against their creators is an old one, as are questions about what is permissible in the treatment of supposedly inferior Others, *Westworld* highlights the perversity of pleasure as well how the assumptions humans might have about an Other's abilities might turn out to be altogether faulty or at least subject to change, which opens all sorts of narrative parallels.

Perception of boundaries becomes more and more blurred. The host Maeve, forced to act the story of a Black woman working as a prostitute, tricks the Delos technician Felix into modifying her programming to give her more agency and control over her memories; this is another instance of crossover into 'real' feelings between a human male and a female android; while Maeve fakes her sympathy to get what she wants, Felix is attracted to her, as William is to Dolores. Bernard, in charge of running the behavioural unit of the hosts at Delos, later turns out to be a replicant himself, created by Ford in the image of the diseased co-founder Arnold Weber.

It is revealed how there was a disagreement between Weber and Ford before the first opening of the park about the ability of the hosts to gain consciousness, a possibility which would mean submitting them to inhuman cruelty and suffering. The season finale culminates in a bloody rebellion of the hosts during which Ford is killed, while Maeve does not board the train to the 'freedom' of the human world. She does, however, sum up the inhuman treatment of the hosts by the Delos company in a final accusation: "[You] just wipe us clean and toss us out to get fucked and murdered over and over again" (TC: 00:46:49). *Westworld* shatters many illusions, one being that cruelty against whatever kind of (post)human in whatever kind of 'reality' comes without eventual consequences, another is that any kind of (post)human interaction can exist without affect, consciousness and with leaving perceived boundaries intact. To supplement the discussion of the series and theoretical debates of posthumanism today, students might by invited to visit the (fan) website <https://discoverwestworld.com> that simulates the possibility of booking such a vacation in 'real' life. If one tries to fill out the online booking form to reserve specific dates, one is told: "There is no entering the park. There is no leaving the park." This message, at once relieving and threatening, needs no further explanation.

Case Study (III): *Midnight Robber*

The early twenty-first century has seen an upsurge of writing in the field of black female science/speculative fiction (see Hoydis 2015). Re-appropriations of the genre by Black women are so important because mainstream SF is considered to be a stereotypically "white male genre" (Hoagland and Sarwal 2010, 6), or as Donna Bailey Nurse puts it, "a literature in which humans are traditionally white, and aliens, by definition are the other" (Nurse 2003, 14). Continuing a line of tradition starting with Octavia Butler, authors like Nalo Hopkinson or Nnedi

Okorafor; continue to produce a hybridization of SF and fantasy that has been the subject of much debate.[13] Works of fiction like *Midnight Robber* by Caribbean-Canadian writer Nalo Hopkinson pose critical challenges on many levels, not just due to the linguistic aspect, as it is largely written in a mix of English and Creole, and which, it needs saying, is challenging to students who might already struggle with reading standard English. While one can discuss questions of genre affiliation, or linguistic hybridity, the depiction of species, of the 'human,' and humanity is what is most interesting. Published in 2000, *Midnight Robber* confronts readers with complex ethical questions in a postcolonial, feminist context, and an Afrofuturist aesthetic, which mixes science fiction, fantasy, and Caribbean folklore. It takes up difficult subjects including colonization and sexual violence. (Concerning the latter, though not described explicitly, a 'trigger warning' might be advisable before giving this text to students because it deals with incestuous rape). Beyond the engagement with matters of (self)justice, victimization and liberation, the exploration of various forms of 'personhood' (including animals, cyborgs, machines, or supernatural-mythological creatures) and the intra-species relationships deserve attention.

The story opens in the far future on the technologically advanced planet Toussaint, whose all-Caribbean population is controlled by a benevolent, feminine, and sentient Artificial Intelligence, called the Grande Anansi Web, "Granny Nanny" for short. The re-gendering and allusions to Orwell's 'Big Brother' are obvious. Technically, the Toussaint citizens are part-cyborgs, humans with a nanomite ear-bug, which permanently links them to the AI system and supplies information and surveillance. The young protagonist Tan-Tan, daughter of the town's mayor, Antonio, is brought up in this somewhat utopian, comfortable environment, looked after by an Eshu, a house-computer/virtual-guardian figure and a robotic nurse. After the tumultuous marriage of Tan-Tan's parents erupts in a fatal climax (Antonio kills his wife's lover), Antonio is forced into exile, taking Tan-Tan with him. They are deported, via a dimensional shift, onto the planet New Half-Way Tree, a prison-colony for outlaws, devoid of all technology, and populated by flora and fauna extinct on Toussaint. Thus New Half-Way Tree functions as a mirror of the past: "it look a little bit like this Toussaint planet [...] same clouds in the high, [...] same green rich valleys. But where Toussaint civilized, New Halfway Tree does be rough" (MR, 2). Tan-Tan lives through years of sexual abuse by Antonio and hatred from her step-mother Janisette; on her sixteenth birthday, she finally kills Antonio with a knife when he tries to rape her again. Forced into hiding, Tan-Tan finds shelter in the bush with the Douen, the planet's indigenous creatures and an intelligent, bird-like species. The novel's title refers to a figure of Caribbean carnival, the Robber Queen, a female 'Robin Hood-type' alter-ego the traumatized Tan-Tan assumes after killing her father. She uses the persona of the Midnight Robber to avenge human cruelty, and aid the weak and suffering. In the end, she finds safety and peace only outside of human community, after giving birth to a cyborg baby, Antonio's son.

The novels offers a myriad of interesting aspects for analysis, including the Midnight Robber persona, Tan-Tan's trauma, questions of justice, and the embedded folktales and historical-cultural references. I concentrate here first on the depiction of the Douen and their ethical function, secondly, on the ending and the question what the cyborg baby signifies. This is tied to a brief assessment of feminist/cyborg theory and the potential of Hopkinson's Afrofuturist narrative.

The novel is for the most part narrated by an omniscient third-person narrator whose identity is only revealed at the very end: it is the voice of the Eshu, telling Tan-Tan's story in the tradition of Anansi-tales (Anansi being a trickster figure of Caribbean and West-African folklore). So the novel features a non-human, unreliable narrator. Throughout, Hopkinson's text shows machines and animals as more humane than humans. Also, what makes humans 'human' is not factors like language or cognitive skills, but the capacity for emotions like anger, jealousy, and violence. Monstrosity and bestiality are attributed to humans, especially human males, underlining the narrative's feminist stance. For instance, Antonio gives the following explanation for human crime and his own deportation: "Is just so. Most of we get send here because anger get the better of we too often" (MR, 126). In the novel, the relationship between women and men is the worst; by comparison, the interactions between women, animals, machines, and any other 'others' are evaluated more favourably – and shown to be less dangerous (cf. Georgi 2011, 369). In this futurist text, we find no human evolution, but a repetition of colonization, exclusion, violence. Also, as frequently found in female Afrofuturist/speculative writing, gender is inescapable and a determining factor of identity, despite the blurring of many other boundaries. Masculinity is not the only negative; we also find negative human mother figures, including Tan-Tan's biological mother, who neglects her, while her stepmother accepts the abuse she suffers. Significantly, the text's positive mother figures are all non-human: Granny Nanny, the house Eshu, the robotic nurse, and Benta, the female Douen (cf. Anatol 2006, 117).

First arriving on New Half-Way Tree, Tan-Tan and Antonio meet Chichibud, one of the tree-dwelling aliens, the Douen. In Caribbean folklore, Douen are the spirits of children who died before being baptized and live in the forest. Here, the Douen males appear like crossovers between lizards and goats, the much larger females resemble strong pack birds. Ironically, in this first encounter, Douen and human mutually refer to one another as "beast." Antonio warns his daughter: "We don't know nothing about this beast," to which Chichibud replies: "Beast that could talk and know it own mind. Oonuh tallpeople quick to name what is people and what is beast" (MR, 93). By the way, 'tallpeople' is also a term for White people applied by Black people.

The novel shows the Douen being threatened by the 'tallpeople', who treat them as slave-, child-like, or "subhuman" (cf. Georgi 2011, 348; Dillon 2008, 30; Clemente 2004, 16). The narrative plays with a racist, colonialist rhetoric on multiple levels, as the discrimination functions equally within animal/human, indigenous people/colonizers, black people/white people relationships. The humans consider the Douen as "ugly," as well as immature: "You have to watch them all the time," "Them like children" (MR, 128). Tan-Tan notices how the human men "spoke to Chichibud the way adults spoke to her" (MR, 120). Meanwhile Chichibud addresses them in return as "Master," which causes Tan-Tan to wonder: "Master? Only machines were supposed to give anybody rank like that" (MR, 121). The hierarchies of Toussaint are modified here, animal substituting machine in the master-slave relationship with the human colonizers. The Douen are seen as backwards because of their apparent lack and knowledge of technology: "They did everything with their hands and never thought to advance themselves any further" (MR, 139). But in fact, the Douen conceal their abilities from the humans and use their 'animal status' as a safeguard. They educate themselves about fire and gun-making in order to be ready for the inevitable fight against the humans: "We see how allyou does act, even towards your own, and we preparing weself" (MR, 231). From the Douen's perspective, what makes the humans 'human,' is again their capacity for violence and unpredictable emotions, as well as ignorance about how to maintain a reciprocal relationship with the environment. In marked contrast, the Douen are compassionate, generous beings, and display a strong sense of environmental responsibility. The importance of reciprocity in the relationship with nature is captured in the central lesson Chichibud teaches Tan-Tan: "When you take one, you must give back two" (MR, 248). This mantra draws attention to a notion of nature in danger of extermination, the necessity of exchange and the replenishing of resources (cf. Dillon 2008, 35), but also that everything comes at a cost. We find here a criticism of the Western attitudes toward nature, largely shaped by "an epistemology of domination" (Cheney 2005, 117); this is contrasted with indigenous concepts of respect, survival, and reciprocity, as also Grace Dillon (2008) argues. The narrative alludes to indigenous scientific knowledge as a prerequisite for "adaptive fit, the notion that we survive not by conquering the world but by recognizing ourselves as part of it" (Cheney 2005, 118). The relationship between Tan-Tan and the Douen develops from initial distrust to friendship. She continues, however, to threaten their habitat. In the end, Tan-Tan's contact with human society tragically forces the Douen to give up their home and flee; Tan-Tan's ends up living alone with Abitefa, Chichibud's daughter in the bush.

In the novel, technology is not presented as either good or bad, the focus is placed on how humans deal with it, as well as with nature and other species. While Hopkinson herself argues for a depiction of technology as neutral in her novel, in various interviews she stresses her interest in finding non-Western metaphors for how people (might) think about technology as an important point of departure. For example, she says, "a diasporic Caribbean culture might name its computer operating systems after a West African deity with the power to go anywhere, see anything" (Hopkinson, n.d.). She refers to the figure of the Eshu, an omniscient deity in Yoruba mythology but in the novel a personal computer/'virtual' presence. It is a good example for Hopkinson's fusion of folklore and technology, and its ambivalence also makes the question about humanity interesting. The virtual Eshu functions as a sort of guardian angel, providing protection and education first for Tan-Tan, and later the child in her womb. Yet the folklore associations of the

Eshu are also with a mischievous trickster figure, as several critics (see e.g. Clemente 2004, Georgi 2011, Enteen 2007) have noted. Technology is personalized, given a voice, responsibility, and a distinct, gendered persona; it is also humanly unreliable. Similarly, Granny Nanny, the reigning AI, assumes a sort of nurturing role, and is not projected as an outright threat to humans. However, it does allude to nightmares of "the 24/7 surveillance state" (Thaler 2010, 110) and, like the Eshu, is imperfect and somewhat devious (cf. Georgi 2011, 341).

One of the central questions in theoretical debates of the posthuman concerns the agency, the body-mind relation and the subject position of the individual posthuman self. Hopkinson's text, which assigns a strong personality and humanity to all in its varied cast of characters, illustrates N. Katherine Hayles' argument that what is at stake is the humanity of posthumanity, in an ethical sense, rather than in an ontological one: "Increasingly the question is not whether we will become posthuman, [...]. Rather, the question is what kind of posthumans we will be" (Hayles 1999, 246). Especially the ending of the novel also corresponds to Hayles' argument that conceptualizing the posthuman does not necessarily mean the end of humanity: "Just as the posthuman need not be antihuman, so it also need not be apocalyptic" (ibid., 288). It is furthermore a clear illustration of the arguments of theorists like Anne Balsamo who have emphasized – as a reaction to and seeking to modify Donna Haraway's ground-breaking celebration of the posthuman as a possibility for post-gender identity – that "bodies are always gendered and always marked by race" and thus constitute "defining elements of post-human identity" (Balsamo 1999, 144). Race and gender do not disappear in the futurist setting of Hopkinson's narrative, neither do species boundaries, but they are blurred and everybody/thing is (for lack of a better term) 'humanized', at the same, the very category is thoroughly questioned.

Furthermore, in *Midnight Robber*, we find cyborgs losing their cyborg status, like Tan-Tan and Antonio who reverse to 'pure' human state on New Half-Way Tree, as the dimensional shift destroys their earplugs. The depicted 'fusion of bodies,' bearing in mind that the central incident is a case of incestuous rape, is presented as violation, not joyful transgression. It is a marked difference to Haraway's celebration of boundary crossing (cf. Dubey 2008, 48). The result is baby Tubman, born from a human mother but also a human-machine fusion in utero. In the final twist of the narrative, the Eshu voice tells Tubman about his special abilities and Granny Nanny's protective reach which they managed to restore after having lost connection with Tan-Tan:

> 'By the time she get pregnant with you, Nanny had figure out the calibration. [...] You could hear me because your whole body is one living connection with the Grande Anansi Nanotech Interface. Your little bodystring will sing to Nanny tune, doux-doux. You will be a weave of she web. [...] you really have that extra limb.' (MR, 327f)

Baby Tubman is surely an "odd boundary creature" in Haraway's sense (1991, 2, 180), and the myth of innocence is undermined even before he is born. But is he a posthuman monster, or does he signal hope and unification? Granny Nanny web claims Tubman through pre-natal manipulation of DNA. Even if it is a benevolent, organic connection, he is in some way colonized by the network. Meanwhile his mother fears that another part of his DNA, namely his father's genes, might make him grow into a monster. Yet he is still somehow invested with hopes for the future, born as a true hybrid, linking generations, planets, and species. Opinions in the criticism of Hopkinson's novel are divided on this matter. Some read the ending as idyllic and the child (through his extra limb) embodying new possibilities, and if not utopian hope, then at the very least an "emancipatory promise" (Smith 2009, 159) and a symbiosis between humans and technology (cf. Thaler 2010, 128; Georgi 2011, 362). Clemente takes the ending in this way as a signal of "hope in the new world for the melding of the Douen empathy and environmental sensitivity with the technical achievement Granny Nanny represents" (Clemente 2004, 23). Indeed, the closing 'family' image consists of two humans, Tan-Tan, and her childhood friend Charlie, and an animal, Abitefa, gathered around a cyborg baby. It is a temporary happy union. However, Tan-Tan is still an exile who avoids human community and returns to the bush: "She didn't belong here, amongst people like this" (MR, 313). Meanwhile the baby is connected to all three species and to the tech-culture of Toussaint as well as to the native culture on New Half-Way Tree. Besides the baby's positive connective symbolism, and typically for Hopkinson's narrative, Tubman's name is also charged with historical-political significance. The narrator call him "Tubman: the human bridge from slavery to freedom" (MR, 329). His name is an obvious reference to Harriet Tubman, the nineteenth-century

Afro-American woman who led slaves to freedom on the Underground Railroad in the South (for protection dressed in male clothes). The narrative ends with a self-reflexive acknowledgement of its own fictional status. The last paragraph consists of the traditional disclaimer at the end of Jamaican folktales: "Call that George, the story done. Jack Mandora, me nah choose none!" (MR, 329). There is no final closure; the reader is left guessing what kind of posthuman baby Tubman will grow up to be. While *Midnight Robber* is not overly optimistic about different species, let alone human family members, living peacefully together, it illustrates the ways in which contemporary speculative fiction can displace "our worldview away from the human epicentre" and point "to a posthumanist, biocentered egalitarianism" (Braidotti 2003, 150). Most of all, I think, the ending of *Midnight Robber* echoes what Donna Haraway said about the future of humanity: "It's not a 'happy ending' we need, but a non-ending" (1992, 327).

The Haraway quote above might serve as a good conclusion to one of the central lessons to be derived from teaching the posthuman. While science and technology remain crucial factors, the focus on them needs to be broadened to encompass renegotiations of difference and identity, and the place of humankind in the natural world beyond cybernetics, genetic engineering and virtual realities. Fictional narratives suggest complex engagements with history, culture and technologies, but above all they call for the recognition of alterity and various kinds of violence done to others. In a twenty-first-century teaching context, the posthuman should be added to the triad of identity politics and difference, 'race, class, gender', commonly evoked in literary and cultural studies classes – or may be even substitute it altogether, depending on where the emphasis is placed. Beyond the examples of the posthuman as characters in different genres discussed here, much is to gain by also shifting the focus on to nonhuman agency in the attempt to challenge anthropocentric positionality.

Notes

1 Examples I draw on here include the BA-theses by my students Muhammad Sari Alkhen. '*Playground of Aggression': A Psychoanalytical Perspective on Jonathan Nolan and Lisa Joy's 'Westworld'* (2017) and Kaya Verhoeven.

Posthumanism, Technology and Relationships in Three Selected Episodes of 'Black Mirror' (2018).

2 On postcolonialism, race and science fiction see, e.g. Langer (2011); Womack (2013) on Afrofuturism, and Kola, Nakamura, and Rodman (2000) on race and cyberspace.

3 Though worthy of further study, this aspect is undoubtedly beyond the scope of the present volume.

4 See Nerlich, Clarke, and Dingwall (2001); Marcus (2012); Escudero Pérez (2014); also Wasson (2011).

5 Clones are comparable to animals in the way they are often excluded from the concept of the fully human and considered biological substance akin to Giorgio Agamben's concept of bare life; it is therefore interesting to read Coetzee's *Lives of Animals* alongside clone fictions.

6 There is only a lost TV-series from the 1970s, and various stage and radio adaptations; possible explanations are the novel's lacks of cinematic presence and the complicated unreliable narrative perspective (see Regis and Wynne 2017, 31; also Poore 2017).

7 On the ongoing interest in Victorian afterlives and the impact of the Brontë sisters, see Regis and Wynne (2017, 3).

8 In the script of the play, Lucy's thoughts ("words inside her head") are printed in bold type to set them apart from dialogue; in the stage version they are projected onto screens.

9 Highly recommendable and also suitable for teaching purposes is the Netflix series *Black Mirror*, full of speculative dread and dark humour. Each episode, forty-five minutes in duration, tells a self-contained, different story. Themes addressed include the impact of technologies on our already posthuman lives in many forms, e.g. the use of social media, YouTube, twitter, etc., all sorts of enhancement (manipulation of memories via implanted microchips or the escape from reality and death via a fantasies stored in the cloud). I recommend the episodes "Nose Dive" (Season 3.1), "San Junipero" (season 3.4) and "The Entire History of You" (Season 1.3).

10 See Busk's reading of Crichton's *Westworld* which draws on Baudrillard's theory of the hyperreal and Žižek's "spectacular reality" (Busk 2016).

11 See, e.g., Sokolove who writes: "We, the audience, are as guilty as the fictional park guest characters on the screen" (Sokolove 2013, n.p.).

12 There are various colour metaphors running through the film; regarding aesthetics, the elaborate opening trailer of the series alone offers plenty of material for analysis.

13 Recently, US-Nigerian writer Tomi Adeyemi has been celebrated for *Children of Blood and Bone*, the debut of the fantasy trilogy *The Legacy of Orïsha*, which has been called the long-awaited 'black Harry-Potter' by many online reviews.

Works Cited

Adeyemi, Tomi (2018). *Children of Blood and Bone*. London: Palgrave Macmillan.

Alkhen, Muhammad Sari (2017). *'Playground of Aggression': A Psychoanalytical Perspective on Jonathan Nolan and Lisa Joy's 'Westworld'*. BA Thesis. Unpublished. University of Cologne. 1-38.

Anatol, Giselle Liza (2006). "Maternal Discourses in Nalo Hopkinson's "Midnight Robber." *African American Review* 40.1, 111-124.

Atwood, Margaret (2009) [2003]. *Oryx and Crake*. London: Virago.

Balsamo, Anne (1999). *Technologies of the Gendered Body. Reading Cyborg Women*. 3rd ed. Durham and London: Duke University Press.

Beukes, Lauren (2009) [2008]. *Moxyland,* London: Angry Robot.

Black Mirror (2011-). Creat. Charlie Brooker. Channel 4/Netflix Originals.

Braidotti, Rosi (2003). "Cyberatologies: Female Monsters Negotiate the Other's Participation in Humanity's Far Future." *Envisioning the Future. Science Fiction and the Next Millennium*. Ed. Marleen S. Barr. Middletown, CT: Wesleyan University Press, 146-169.

Brontë, Charlotte (1999) [1853]. *Villette*. Ware, Hertfordshire: Wordsworth.

Buchanan, Allen, et al. (2009) [2002]. *From Chance to Choice. Genetics and Justice*. 2002. Cambridge: Cambridge University.

Busk, Larry Alan (2016). "*Westworld*: Ideology, Simulation, Spectacle." *Mediations* 30.1, 1-11..

Causey, Matthew (1999). "Postorganic Performance: The Appearance of Theater in Virtual Spaces." *Cyberspace Textuality: Computer Technology and Literary Theory*. Ed. Marie-Laure Ryan. Bloomington, IN: Indiana University Press, 182-202.

--- (2006). *Theatre and Performance in Digital Culture*. London and New York: Routledge.

--- (2016). "Postdigital Performance." *Theatre Journal* 68.3, 427-441.

Cheney, Jim (2005). "Truth, Knowledge, and the Wild World." *Ethics and Environment* 10.2, 101-135.

Churchill, Caryl (2002). *A Number*. Theatre Communications Group New York.

Clemente, Bill (2004). "Tan-Tan's Exile and Odyssey in Nalo Hopkinson's *Midnight Robber*." *Foundation* 33.91, 10-24.

Coetzee, John Maxwell. (1999). *The Lives of Animals*. Princeton, NJ: Princeton University Press.

Copenhagen (1996). Dir. Howard Davies. Written by Michael Frayn, Howard Davies. Starr. Daniel Craig, Stephen Rea. BBC, UK.

Dillon, Grace L. (2008). "Indigenous Scientific Literacies in Nalo Hopkinson's Ceremonial Worlds." *Journal of the Fantastic in the Arts* 18.1, 23-41.

District 9 (2009). Dir. Neil Blomkamp. Starr. Sharlto Copley, Jason Cope. USA.
Dixon, Steve (2007). *Digital Performance. A History of New Media in Theatre, Dance, Performance Art, and Installation*. Cambridge, MA: MIT Press.
Dubey, Madhu (2008). "Becoming Animal in Black Women's Science Fiction." *Afro-future Females: Black Writers Chart Science Fiction's Newest New-wave Trajectory.* Ed. Marleen S. Barr. Columbus, OH: Ohio State University Press, 31-51.
Emshwiller, Carol (1990). *Carmen Dog*. Northampton, MA: Peapod Classics.
Enteen, Jillana (2007). "On the Receiving End of the Colonization: Nalo Hopkinson's 'Nansi Web." *Science Fiction Studies* 34.2, 262-282.
Escudero Pérez, Jimena (2014). "Sympathy for the Clone: (Post)Human Identities Enhanced by the 'Evil Science' Construct and Its Commodifying Practices in Contemporary Clone Fiction." *Between* IV.8, 1-24.
Frank, Kerstin, and Caroline Lusin (2017). "Introduction: Current Debates and British Drama since 2000." *Finance, Terror, and Science on Stage: Current Public Concerns in 21st Century British Drama.* Eds. K.F. and C.L. Tübingen: Narr Francke Attempo, 9-18.
Frayn, Michael (1998). *Copenhagen.* London: Anchor Books.
Gardner, Lyn (2016). "From Sci-fi Brontë to Hamlet on the Savanna: When Classics are Relocated." *The Guardian* 4 October Web. 10 Aug 2018.
Georgi, Donja (2011). *Bodies and/as Technology. Counter-Discourses on Ethnicity and Globalization in the Works of Alejandro Morales, Larissa Lai and Nalo Hopkinson*. Heidelberg: Winter.
Ghosh, Amitav (1995). *The Calcutta Chromosome,* New York: Avon Books.
Giannachi, Gabriella (2004). *Virtual Theatres: An Introduction*. New York and London: Routledge.
Glomb, Stefan (2017). "A View from Nowhere: Science, Freedom and Determinism in Nick Payne's *Incognito* (2014)." *Finance, Terror, and Science on Stage.* Eds. Kerstin Frank and Caroline Lusin. Tübingen: Narr Francke Attempo, 185-210.
Halberstam, Judith, and Ira Livingston (1995). "Introduction: Posthuman Bodies." *Posthuman Bodies*. Eds. J.H. and I.L. Bloomington and Indianapolis, IN: Indiana University Press, 1-22.
Haraway, Donna J. (1991). *Simians, Cyborgs, and Women. The Reinvention of Nature*. London: Free Association Books.
--- (1992). "The Promises of Monsters: A Regenerative Politics for Inappropriate/d Others." *Cultural Studies*. Eds. Lawrence Grossberg, Cary Nelson and Paula A. Treichler. New York; Routledge, 295-337.
Hayles, N. Katherine (1999). *How We Became Posthuman: Virtual Bodies in Cybernetics, Literature and Informatics.* Chicago and London: University of Chicago Press.

Higgins, David (2008). "Theatre and Science." *A Concise Companion to Contemporary British and Irish Drama*. Eds. Nadine Holdsworth and Mary Luckhurst. Oxford: Blackwell, 225-244.

Hoagland, Ericka, and Reema Sarwal (2010). "Introduction: Imperialism, the Third World and Postcolonial Science Fiction." *Science Fiction, Imperialism and the Third World*. Eds. E.H. and R.S. Jefferson, NC: McFarland, 5-19.

Hopkinson, Nalo. (2000). *Midnight Robber*. New York: Warner Books.

--- "Code Sliding." *Black Net Art*. n.d. Web. 10 August 2018. <http://blacknetart.com/Hopkinson.html>.

Hoydis, Julia (2015). "Fantastically Hybrid: Race, Gender, and Genre in Black Female Speculative Fiction." *Anglistik* 26.2, 71-88.

Ishiguro, Kazuo (2005). *Never Let Me Go*. London: Faber and Faber.

Jordan, Richard (2014). "Digital Alchemy: The Posthuman Drama of Adam J.A. Cass I Love You, Bro." *Australasian Drama Studies* 65, 37-52.

--- (2015). *Posthuman Drama: Identity and the Machine in Twenty-First-Century Playwriting*. PhD Thesis. University of Queensland. Open Access. Web. 10 August 2018. <https://doi.org/10.14264/uql.2015.1010>.

Klich, Rosemary, and Edward Scheer (2012). *Multimedia Performance*. Basingstoke and New York: Palgrave Macmillan.

Kolko, Beth, Lisa Nakamura, and Gilbert Rodman (eds.) (2000). *Race in Cyberspace*. London and New York: Routledge.

Langer, Jessica (2011). *Postcolonialism and Science Fiction*. New York: Palgrave Macmillan.

Lepage, Louise (2008). "Posthuman Perspectives and Postdramatic Theatre: the Theory and Practice of Hybrid Ontology in Katie Mitchell's The Waves." *Culture, Language and Representation* VI, 137-149.

Liggins, Emma (2017). "The Legacy of Lucy Snowe: Reconfiguring Spinsterhood and the Victorian Family in Inter-war Women's Writing." *Charlotte Brontë: Legacies and Afterlives*. Eds. Amber K. Regis and Deborah Wynne. Manchester: Manchester University Press, 164-181.

Luckhurst, Mary (2015). "Churchill in the Twenty-First Century." *Caryl Churchill*. London: Routledge, 155-182.

--- (2016). "The New Genetics, Genocide and Caryl Churchill." *Twenty-First Century Drama. What Happens Now*. Eds. Siân Adiseshiah and Louise LePage. London: Palgrave Macmillan, 239-256.

Macintosh, Kerry Lynn (2012). *Human Cloning: Four Fallacies and Their Legal Consequences*. Cambridge: Cambridge University Press.

Marcus, Amit (2012). "The Ethics of Human Cloning in Narrative Fiction." *Comparative Literary Studies* 49.3, 405-433.

Marshall-Griffith, Linda (2016). *Charlotte Brontë's Villette. Re-imagined by Linda Marshall-Griffiths*. A West Yorkshire Playhouse Production. London: Oberon Books.

Middeke, Martin (2011). "Introduction." *The Methuen Drama Guide to Contemporary British Playwrights*. Eds. M.M., Peter Paul Schnierer and Aleks Sierz. London: Methuen Drama, vii-xxiv.

Nerlich, Brigitte, David D. Clarke, and Robert Dingwall (2001). "Fictions, Fantasies, and Fears: The Literary Foundations of the Cloning Debate." *Journal of Literary Studies* 30, 37-52.

Nurse, Donna Bailey (2003). "Brown Girl in the Ring: How a Caribbean-born Writer Reinvented a Genre." *Quill & Quire* (Nov), 14-15..

Orphan Black (2013-). Creat. John Fawcett and Graeme Manson. Starr. Tatiana Maslany. BBC America/Canada.

Poore, Benjamin (2017). "Hunger, Rebellion, and Rage: Adapting *Villette*." *Charlotte Brontë: Legacies and Afterlives*. Eds. Amber K. Regis and Deborah Wynne. Manchester: Manchester University Press, 182-195.

Read, Alan (2008). *Theatre, Intimacy and Engagement: The Last Human Venue*. Basingstoke and New York: Palgrave Macmillan.

Regis, Amber K., and Deborah Wynne (eds.) (2017). *Charlotte Brontë: Legacies and Afterlives*. Manchester: Manchester University Press.

Rocamora, Carol (2000). "Scientific Dramaturgy." *The Nation* 5 June, 49-51.

Schwanecke, Christine (2017). "Data Streams, Post-Human Lives, and (Virtual) Realities: Jules Horne's Gorgeous Avatar (2006)." *Finance, Terror, and Science on Stage.* Eds. Kerstin Frank and Caroline Lusin. Tübingen: Narr Francke Attempo, 145-166.

Shelley, Mary (1999) [1818]. *Frankenstein, or, The Modern Prometheus*. Ware, Hertfordshire: Wordsworth.

Shepherd-Barr, Kirsten (2006). *Science on Stage: From Doctor Faustus to Copenhagen.* Princeton, NJ, and Oxford: Princeton University Press.

Sielke, Sabine (2015). "Science Studies and Literature." *Anglia* 133.1, 9-2.

Sierz, Aleks (2010). "Introduction." *The Methuen Drama Book of Twenty-First Century British Plays*. Eds. A.S. London et al.: Bloomsbury, vii-xviii.

Simpson, Ron (2016). "Review: *Villette* (West Yorkshire Playhouse) West Yorkshire Playhouse Adapt Charlotte Bronte's Novel as Part of Their Bronte Season." 29 September Web. 10 Aug 2018. <https://www.whatsonstage.com/leeds-theatre/reviews/villette-west-yorkshire-playhouse_41893.html>.

Singh, Vandana (2009). "The Woman Who Thought She Was a Planet." *The Woman Who Thought She Was a Planet and Other Stories.* New Delhi: Zubaan/Penguin Books, 39-54.

Smith, Eric D. (2009). "The Only Way Out is Through: Space, Narrative, and

Utopia in Nalo Hopkinson's *Midnight Robber*." *Genre* 42.1/2, 135-163.

Sokolove, Todd (2013). "Why Westworld Matters." *Forces of Geek*. 11 June 2013. Web. 10 August 2018. <http://www.forcesofgeek.com/2013/06/why-westworld-matters.html>.

Stam, Robert (2005). "Introduction: The Theory and Practice of Adaptation." *Literature and Film*. Eds. Robert Stam and Alessandra Raengo. Oxford: Blackwell, 1-52.

Starbuck-Parker, Jennifer (2014). *Cyborg Theatre. Corporeal/Technological Intersections in Multimedia Performance*. Houndsmills, Basingstoke: Palgrave Macmillan.

Stephenson, Shelagh (1998). *An Experiment with an Air Pump*. London: Methuen Drama.

Stoppard, Tom (2015). *The Hard Problem*. London: Faber and Faber.

Thaler, Ingrid (2010). *Black Atlantic Speculative Fictions. Octavia E. Butler, Jewelle Gomez, and Nalo Hopkinson*. New York and London: Routledge.

Verhoeven, Kaya (2018). *Posthumanism, Technology and Relationships in Three Selected Episodes of 'Black Mirror'*. BA Thesis. Unpublished. University of Cologne, 1-38.

Wasson, Sara (2011). "'A Butcher's Shop Where the Meat Still Moved': Gothic Doubles, Organ Harvesting and Human Cloning." *Gothic Science Fiction, 1980-2010*. Eds. Sara Wasson and Emily Alder. Liverpool: Liverpool University Press, 73-86.

Weldon, Fay (1989). *The Cloning of Joanna May*. Glasgow: Fontana/Collins.

Wells, Herbert George (1994) [1894]. *The Island of Dr Moreau*. New York: Bantham Classics.

Westworld (2016-). Creat. Jonathan Nolan, Lisa Joy. Starr. Evan Rachel Wood, Thandie Newton, Jeffery Wright. Warner Bros. USA.

Westworld (1973). Dir. Michael Crichton. Starr. Yul Brynner, Richard Benjamin, James Brolin. Warner Bros. USA.

Westworld. Official Website. 10 August 2018. <https://www.hbo.com/westworld>.

Willis, Martin (ed.) (2016). *Staging Science. Scientific Performance on Street, Stage and Screen*. London: Palgrave Macmillan.

Womack, Ytasha (2013). *Afrofuturism: The World of Black Sci-fi and Fantasy Culture*. Chicago: Lawrence Hill Books.

Zehelein, Eva-Sabine (2009). *Science Dramatic. Science Plays in America and Great Britain 1990-2007*. Heidelberg: Winter.

Contributors' Addresses

Dr. Gigi Adair, Universität Potsdam, Philosophische Fakultät, Institut für Anglistik und Amerikanistik, Am Neuen Palais 10, 14469 Potsdam, Germany.

Jun.-Prof. Dr. Roman Bartosch, Universität zu Köln, Philosophische Fakultät, Englisches Seminar II, Gronewaldstraße 2, 50931 Köln, Germany.

Dr. Alessandra Boller, Universität Marburg, Fachbereich Fremdsprachliche Philologien, Institut für Anglistik und Amerikanistik, Wilhelm-Röpke-Straße 6, 35032 Marburg, Germany.

PD Dr. Stefan Herbrechter, Universität Heidelberg, Neuphilologische Fakultät, Anglistisches Seminar, Kettengasse 12, 69117 Heidelberg, Germany.

PD Dr. Julia Hoydis, Universität zu Köln, Philosophische Fakultät, Englisches Seminar I, Albertus-Magnus-Platz, 50923 Köln, Germany.

Vertr.-Prof. Dr. Christian Ludwig, Pädagogische Hochschule Karlsruhe, Institut für Mehrsprachigkeit/Englisch, Bismarckstr. 10, 76133 Karlsruhe, Germany.

Prof. Dr. Christian Schmitt-Kilb, Universität Rostock, Philosophische Fakultät, Institut für Anglistik/Amerikanistik, August-Bebel-Straße 28, 18055 Rostock, Germany.

Dr. Elizabeth Shipley, Pädagogische Hochschule Karlsruhe, Institut für Mehrsprachigkeit/Englisch, Bismarckstr. 10, 76133 Karlsruhe, Germany.

Prof. Dr. Eckart Voigts, Technische Universität Braunschweig, Fakultät für Geistes- und Erziehungswissenschaften, Institut für Anglistik und Amerikanistik, Bienroder Weg 80, 38106 Braunschweig, Germany.

Prof. Dr. Berbeli Wanning, Universität Siegen, Philosophische Fakultät, Germanistisches Seminar, Hölderlinstr. 3, 57068 Siegen, Germany.